00472301

KU-490-211

822.3304 SAN
SANDERS
78/4983

B.C.H.E. – LIBRARY

00131629

SHAKESPEARE'S MAGNANIMITY

SHAKESPEARE'S MAGNANIMITY
Four Tragic Heroes, Their Friends and Families

By

WILBUR SANDERS

and

HOWARD JACOBSON

1978

CHATTO & WINDUS

LONDON

Published by
Chatto & Windus Ltd
40 William IV Street
London WC2N 4DF

*

Clarke, Irwin & Co Ltd
Toronto

All rights reserved. No part of this publication may be reproduced, stored in a
retrieval system, or transmitted in any
form, or by any means electronic,
mechanical, photocopying, recording or
otherwise, without the prior permission of
Chatto & Windus Ltd.

British Library Cataloguing in Publication Data

Sanders, Wilbur
Shakespeare's magnanimity.
1. Shakespeare, William — Tragedies
2. Shakespeare, William — Characters — Heroes
I. Title II. Jacobson, Howard
822.3'3   PR299.2H4

ISBN 0-7011-2281-1

© Wilbur Sanders and Howard Jacobson 1978

Printed in Great Britain by
Redwood Burn Limited
Trowbridge and Esher

NEWTON PARK
COLLEGE
BATH
LIBRARY
DISCARD

CLASS
NO. 822.3304
SAN

ACC.
NO. 78/4983

CONTENTS

I

The Induction
Please, No More Cakes and Ale

DRAMATIS PERSONAE

Mulligrub, *a Vintner, Host of the Ordinary*
Mistress Mulligrub, *his wife*
Sir Affable Ponder, *a learned Country Gentleman*
Sophonisba, *his Lady*
Bullfinch, *a Roaring Boy*
Whipstalk, *a Clerk of Oxenbrigge*
Snipe, *a shrewd Gallant*
Sottopassagio, *a Fantastic*

Our party, by now well-fed and contented, had reached the expansive stage of toying with its dessert, and contemplating nostalgically the ruins of its satiation. Nobody seemed disposed to clear away, and our host's refusal, despite his wife's pressure, to go and make coffee, didn't seem to distress anybody unduly. Two or three desultory though amiable conversations were progressing — lightly pursued, as if in readiness to be lightly relinquished. There was an implicit request in the air for someone to say something which would involve the whole table, and Bullfinch, who normally conceived it as his role to meet any corporate request, especially when it came late in the evening, did not let us down:

'Right everybody? I think it's time for the singing game.'

'Oh no, not the singing game!' exclaimed Mistress Mulligrub, in involuntary woe.

'I'm not altogether sure what the singing game is,' muttered Sir Affable, more to himself than to anyone else. He was as accustomed to being not altogether sure what things were, as his wife, Sophonisba, was accustomed to telling him.

'I should imagine, dearest love,' she said, 'that it's yet another of those splendid contests of wit and lung which our Bullfinch delights in promoting.'

'I thought he mentioned singing,' remarked her husband, before subsiding again.

'Not the *old* singing game,' cried Bullfinch, with a pitying emphasis. 'This is a new one. The idea is to sing the most

mawkish song you can think of. I'll begin.'
He gave it his richest bass barreltone:
'I believe
For every drop of rain that falls,
A flower grows.
I believe
That somewhere in the darkest night,
A candle glows.
Every time . . . .'
'Stop it! Stop it! You've won,' pleaded Mulligrub, our host, voicing the general feeling, the all but general feeling, that is, for Whipstalk was noticeably not groaning.
'I rather like that song,' he remarked with a defiant sincerity.
'Well, we all know about *your* taste for the mawkish,' grumbled Snipe, who would have made a thing of liking the song himself, had Whipstalk not beaten him to it.
'And we all know about your terror of sentimentality,' retorted Whipstalk. 'If there's one thing more sentimental than sentimentality, it's the fear of being thought sentimental. It's an ungenerous mind that can't enjoy — simply enjoy a song like that.'
'But it's so stupid,' protested our hostess, who was never quite at home with the rules of banter. 'And you know it.'
'Perhaps he doesn't,' put in her husband, eyeing Whipstalk suspiciously.
'Hang on,' interrupted Bullfinch. 'This isn't what is supposed to happen at all. Fortunately I have another game.'
There was a general groan:
'Oh no, not another game.'
'It's called the drinking game.'
'I think you know this one, my love,' said Sophonisba to her husband.
'Fill up, everybody,' Bullfinch ordered, before pausing in consternation. 'That is, if you can find anything to fill up with. There seems to be no more beer.'
'Who cares? We're all drinking wine.'
'I'm not. Wine constrains me. It was invented to accompany polite conversation. If a man is to relax, beer's the thing. Bring me some beer, I say.'
Mistress Mulligrub explained, without apologizing, that there was no more beer; Sophonisba opined that polite conversation had something to be said for it; Snipe wondered whether the speaker was not already adequately relaxed; and someone even suggested that Bullfinch had had enough. In short, Bullfinch's audience behaved as it was meant to.

He was therefore able to give all the rotundity of a justified indignation to his words—'Because thou art virtuous, shall there be no more cakes and ale?'—and to sit back in happy assurance of instant capitulation.

To his surprise, though, he was swiftly taken up by Snipe:

'I sometimes wish Shakespeare had never said that. It's too much of a gift to superannuated boozers who can't enjoy themselves unless they think they're making a contribution to the world's sanity. It's the bogus charter for every tired old cult of riot and anarchy.'

'But Shakespeare didn't say it,' Mulligrub nearly shouted, sniffing an argument at last. 'Sir Toby Belch did.'

'Well then, it's a pity he created Sir Toby Belch. I'm sick of all those sprightly Jacobean tipplers.'

'He's not sprightly,' replied Mulligrub. 'He's the most unappetising drunkard in literature.'

'Quoth Malvolio,' Sophonisba interpolated, arching an eyebrow. Mulligrub was unshaken:

'Flagrant miscasting. I won't take the part.'

'I will,' said Snipe.

'Oh no,' said Sophonisba, arching her other eye-brow. 'Oh no! You're Feste.'

'I would have thought,' Sir Affable ruminated, 'that he was more of a Curio.'

'Who on earth is Curio?' several voices chimed in. But the answer was lost.

'I have another game,' Bullfinch was saying excitably. 'Let's do a reading. I'll be Sir Toby.'

'Ah!' said Snipe, 'so you fancy yourself as the most unappetising drunkard in literature?'

'Oho!' Bullfinch swaggered, 'I'll *make* him appetising.'

'With or without Shakespeare's help?' Mulligrub remarked with killing dryness.

'Isn't it rather a question of whether Shakespeare needs ours?' said Whipstalk. 'From what I've heard so far, I doubt that there's enough Bacchus in any of us.'

'Well, there's enough in me,' asserted Bullfinch unapologetically. 'Bacchus is willin'.'

'Yerz, so am I,' said Sir Affable.

'No, no, my dear,' said his wife. 'Stand out for Sir Andrew or nothing.'

'Or Orsino,' he went on as if he hadn't heard. 'I've always wanted to do something with'—and he declaimed feelingly—' "Mine is all as hungry as the sea." '

'Your what?' inquired Mistress Mulligrub, really wanting to know.

'Do what with it?' corrected his wife, *not* really wanting to know.

'Werll,' Sir Affable pursued, 'I was thinking of Viola's sea-wet garments which she has to find before she can marry her elected Duke. Tempests are kind and salt waves fresh in love. The sea-change, you know, the sea-change. Into something rich and . . .'

'Are you implying,' Whipstalk interrupted eagerly, 'that *Twelfth Night* in some way looks forward to the Late Plays?'

'Or that the Late Plays in some way look back to *Twelfth Night*?' Snipe put in, with a smile.

'Or that the middle plays look backwards and forwards?' added Mulligrub.

'Because if you are,' continued Whipstalk, refusing to be side-tracked, 'I cannot agree with you. Surely those plays suffer for being without *Twelfth Night*'s authentic pagan saturnalia. Malvolio would be the hero of one of those plays.'

'He's the hero of this,' Snipe insisted, with violence.

Whereupon such pandemonium broke out, that it must hereafter be reduced to dialogue-form.

All. Oh! Oh!

Mistress Mulligrub. What can you mean?

Snipe. What I said. Malvolio is the only thing of flesh and blood in the play. Who do *you* think is the hero?

Mistress Mulligrub. I suppose there isn't one. But there is a heroine.

Snipe. I grant you Olivia.

Mistress Mulligrub. I meant Viola.

Sir Affable. I'm rather keen on Maria myself. A beagle true-bred and one that loves me. Mmm. A practical little body. No verse, though. . .no verse. . .pity!

Mulligrub. You've granted us Olivia, but who wants her? — apart from Orsino, that is. And *he* doesn't count.

Snipe. Malvolio wants her. And *he* does.

Bullfinch. What about my game? Do I have to play all the parts myself? Or are you going to make up your minds? The night is slipping away.

Snipe. Malvolio. I'll take Malvolio.

Mistress Mulligrub. Viola for me.

Snipe. Not Olivia?

Mistress Mulligrub. No, Snipe. *Not* Olivia.

Sir Affable. Orsino. Or perhaps Fabian. Yerz. I think Fabian.

Sophonisba. I *do* advise Sir Andrew.

Whipstalk. (*Warming cautiously*) Well, if this is a serious proposition—I'd quite like to do Orsino.

Mulligrub. Why Orsino? Is *that* a serious proposition?

Whipstalk. Why not?

Snipe. (*Confidentially to Mulligrub*) On the principle of re-habilitating the mawkish, you understand.

Whipstalk. A typical and, I may say, a wilful misconstruction. Why must you suppose I like Orsino? I'm sure Shakespeare detested him – the typical, languishing Renaissance prince, playing at love. It's all 'placed'. I don't like Orsino, but I do like the placing.

Mulligrub. I hate this 'placing'. It's the language of the society hostess.

Sir Affable. Mmm! Werll! Shakespeare doesn't exactly endorse him, does he?

Snipe. And *I* hate this 'endorsing'. It's the language of the bank clerk.

Sir Affable. Werll, if he's neither endorsed nor placed, what is he?

Sophonisba. Dearest love, shall we settle for saying he's just 'there'.

Mistress Mulligrub. Where?

Snipe. On the page.

Bullfinch. Why not on the stage?

Mulligrub. Why not both?

Mistress Mulligrub. Everywhere, you mean?

Whipstalk. No, *not* everywhere. Let's not forget we're dealing with the product of an artist's imagination!

Mistress Mulligrub. But is he imagining nothing? Nothing real, I mean. You just said Orsino was a typical Renaissance prince, languishing. . .

Whipstalk. Ah, I *thought* you were going to say that. But the two are not contradictory. Art creates its own parameters. Art is not reality just because it creates a symbolic refraction of reality.

Mistress Mulligrub. Oh!

Sophonisba. (*To Mistress Mulligrub*) He's forgotten the culinary art, my dear. (*To Whipstalk*) Would you say that what you have just eaten was a symbolic refraction of reality? Call yourself Bacchic!

Bullfinch. Don't listen to him. I'm the Bacchic one. I'm Bacchic. I've got a cushion up my shirt and I'm rearing to go. Who's my Maria?

Sir Affable. Isn't that you, my dear?

Sophonisba. No, it is not. I'm Olivia. Though a 'practical little body' by nature, I'd like to see if I could be a proud disdainful beauty by art.

Snipe. And I'd like to see you try – but not on Olivia. She's not disdainful.

Mistress Mulligrub. She's proud.

Snipe. And why not? She's got something to be proud about.

Mistress Mulligrub. You mean her good looks.

Sir Affable. (*To himself*) I warrant 'twill hold colour. 'Tis in grain. Mmm.

Snipe. I mean her wit.

Mulligrub. She has both.

Mistress Mulligrub. Yes, well, clearly she's a man's woman. But I don't think she's terribly nice.

Snipe. Now I understand your predilection for Viola. Niceness, eh? Mrs Jameson rides again. I'd hoped it was dead, that taste for the winsome she knight-errant. Whatever Olivia may be, Viola's the *woman's* woman all right.

Whipstalk. Precisely. That's why Olivia falls in love with her. We moderns are inclined to forget the effect upon the stage of a boy playing a girl playing a boy. It's fascinating how the androgyne. . . .

Mistress Mulligrub. Don't be dreary. I'm sure Shakespeare would have preferred real actresses if he could have got them.

Bullfinch. Right! Right! You can't tell me he enjoyed writing Cleopatra for a boy.

Sophonisba. (*Uncoiling her hair*) My pity extends to the poor boy. I've played Cleopatra in my time and I can assure you the part made demands upon even *my* womanliness.

Snipe. I don't believe it, Sophonisba.

Bullfinch. Nor do I. Anyway, I'm sure you'll stroll through Olivia. So let's begin.

Mulligrub. I'm not much interested in Whipstalk's point about boy-actors and role-playing. Certainly Shakespeare had an eye for the way people warm to their own sex — at first, anyway. How women love the woman in men, and can therefore easily fall for the woman in a woman.

Whipstalk. And vice versa — there's Antonio's infatuation with Sebastian.

Mulligrub. Yes, but it's all by-play, isn't it?

Sophonisba. (*Wriggling out of her shoes and raising both eyebrows*) Some by-play. I've never warmed to my sex in quite *that* way.

Sir Affable. Glad to hear it, my dear. But it does seem to be in the verse.

Mistress Mulligrub. I've been sidetracked. What I want to say is that Olivia is vain. Vain and silly. Viola says something or other about that.

Snipe. Oh, Viola would. Nice girls always do.

Sir Affable. 'I see you what you are, you are too proud.'

Too proud. Not very good writing though. Wonder if it's Shakespeare's?

Mistress Mulligrub. But she says it.

Mulligrub. Yes, but she's nothing like so hard on Olivia as you're being, my love. And she has other reasons — she can't help being jealous of the woman Orsino fancies, and that makes things more difficult for her. Her feelings about Olivia are tangled with her feelings for Orsino. You can't take what characters say about one another as if it were gospel.

Whipstalk. This is madness! If every speech has to be explained by the speaker's motives, and those motives explained by the speaker's relation to other people's motives. . .then everybody is speaking except Shakespeare. It's the psychologising mania run mad. You've psychologised the play out of existence. This is not a psychological novel.

Bullfinch. Correct me if I'm wrong, but I thought all novels were psychological.

Mistress Mulligrub. What's wrong with novels anyway?

Whipstalk. Nothing. Except that Shakespeare didn't write them.

Snipe. The only reason he didn't write them, is because they weren't invented. *I* call them novels anyway.

Bullfinch. Do we have to call them anything? Can't we just act them?

Mulligrub. All right, all right. It's a good idea.

Mistress Mulligrub. Let's get started then. I'll get some texts.

[Exit]

Sir Affable. Poetic drama.

Sophonisba. I beg your pardon, dearest love, did you speak?

Sir Affable. Poetic drama. That's what we have to call them.

Sophonisba. You are a little late, my own, but as usual you are felicitousness itself. Poetic drama seems to me the very phrase.

Snipe. Not just 'drama'?

Sir Affable. No. *Poetic* drama.

(*There is a pause*)

Snipe. (*Nettled*) Why this reverential hush? What magical property does this word 'poetic' have?

Sophonisba. If you don't know that, I can't imagine what can be done for you. (*Peering at Snipe through her wine glass*) But I have a shrewd little suspicion you know very well.

Mulligrub. Well, I don't know either. And I wonder whether you do.

Sophonisba. My dear Mulligrub, I know perfectly well. Poetry has the power to create meanings, instead of merely referring to them, like prose.

Sir Affable. Yerz. 'She never told her love
    But let concealment like a worm i' th'bud
    Feed on her damask'd cheek.'

Snipe. I like those lines too. Viola 'referring' with some personal feeling to what she knows about.

Mulligrub. Yes, that's right. This special intensity that is supposed to be all poetry's, the creative power and so on. . . .it's just one potentiality of ordinary speech. And you hear it as ordinary speech first, or it wouldn't have the power to move.

Mistress Mulligrub. (*Re-entering with pile of books*) You're preaching, Mulligrub.

Whipstalk. But in oh so 'ordinary speech'.

Sophonisba. It looks as if we've found our Malvolio.

Mulligrub. (*Continuing to preach*) I don't care. I want to get this straight. I've heard things said by people – we all have – things that have all the power of what you call 'poetry'. People speaking 'beyond themselves', saying more than they know they know, and saying it better than they know how. It happens. Under stress mostly.

Snipe. (*Raising a fist of solidarity*) Go, Mulligrub!

Mulligrub. (*Going*) Look. Unusually intense feelings, happy or sad, produce unusually intense speech. Not automatically, but frequently. A poet sees to the frequency. And I'm interested in the speech for the sake of the feelings—not in the feelings for the sake of the speech. If that's being philistine, I'd rather be that than literary.

Sophonisba. Well, if that's not literary!

Whipstalk. It's certainly philistine.

Bullfinch. To borrow a leaf out of your book, Mully, I think it's both.

Mulligrub. Don't take a leaf, take the book. It's all yours. I give up. I thought I was being Malvolio, but I seem to have turned out a Feste.

Sophonisba. Never believe it. You were made for the Puritan.

Snipe. (*Ripping at his beard*) Damn it! I'm past caring who plays Malvolio, but he is *not* a Puritan. No Puritan ever satisfied his Olivia so expertly.

Bullfinch. And on her *day*-bed.

Snipe. Exactly. Can you imagine what the nights would have been like!

Whipstalk. But that is the purest fantasy of the puritan mind.

Snipe. (*Brushing away hair from his shirt front*) Ah, but the language, the language! Has he not created his reality? He makes me believe he could have so satisfied her anyway. His tragedy is that he never gets the chance to prove it. If it's all in his imagination, well at least his imagination teems with vigorous and manly pleasures. Sebastian could neither do it nor think it. And the same goes for Orsino. He'd have been the one left snoozing in bed while Olivia went about her business.

Whipstalk. You've gone right outside the play. That's what comes of psychologising.

Mulligrub. Well, here goes right back into it. 'Puritan' is Maria's word—right? And she means nothing by it. It's a nonce-word—'a sort of Puritan,' she says. And when Sir Andrew thinks she refers to Malvolio's vocal register, she lets it pass. It's a chimera. Forget it.

Mistress Mulligrub. Vocal register? Chimera? What's he talking about?

Sophonisba. He's being unliterary again. (*To Mulligrub*) Well, since Malvolio isn't, by your triumphant logic, a puritan at all, you can have no objection, by my triumphant logic, to playing him.

Mulligrub. I am defeated. I'll play anything.

Bullfinch. (*To Snipe*) And if you'll settle for Feste we can begin. Please settle for Feste. Please.

Snipe. All right, settle I must. But I warn you, you're going to get the most unfunny Feste on record.

Mulligrub. Isn't he meant to be unfunny? You'd be pretty unfunny as a paid comic under constant threat of dismissal: 'And you laugh not, madam, he is gagged.' Also broke.

Snipe. Sociologist!

Bullfinch. (*In despair to himself*) He's not settling.

Whipstalk. And why not? Provided the sociology is thorough. The clown's laughter in Shakespeare is a way of dealing with social trauma—and Feste's poverty is just the visible one-tenth of that trauma.

Snipe. I like your 'trauma'. Traumas are always good for a laugh. But Feste isn't. All right, he isn't meant to be. But we *are* asked to enjoy the sourness and wryness of him, and that's what I can't bear about the whole dreary clown-convention. It plays upon some people's mistrust of their own sanity.

Whipstalk. Are you so sure of yours?

Snipe. I'm not so anxious about it that I need a fool to save it for me.

Sophonisba. Oh, the confidence! If you don't fear our retort, you should at least fear that of nemesis.

Snipe. My dear Sophonisba, I have a healthy regard for both. But not on this issue. Besides, for all your offered delight in every bedraggled urchin in literature that sets himself up as a professional puncturer of the illusions of the wise, you wouldn't have any of them in your drawing-room. Their archness would drive you to distraction, and you wouldn't at all find them funny.

Sophonisba. (*Holding out her empty wine-glass for her husband to fill*) You'd be surprised what I've had in my drawing-room. But I don't really see what that has to do with it. It has never occurred to me to use the pages of literature as a guest-list.

Snipe. I don't think that's quite what I had in mind, but let it go. My complaint is that you are all looking for comedy in the wrong places. Antony provides more knockabout farce than any clown. Hamlet is funniest on the subject of corpses. And if it's sourness and wryness you are after, try Macbeth.

Sophonisba. Macbeth! What next!

Sir Affable. Mmm! Mmm! Daggers unmannerly breeched. . . Heaven's cherubim horsed. . .peeping. . .blankets. . .I suppose there is a kind of metaphysical wit there.

Mulligrub. Forget the metaphysical. 'The times has been, That when the brains were out, the man would die, And there an end. . .' How does it go?

Sir Affable. '. . . but now they rise again
With twenty mortal murders on their crowns
And push us from our stools.'

Snipe. 'Stools' is comedy! Has to be comedy! And all the richer for Macbeth's knowing it.

Whipstalk. If that's going to be called comedy, I don't see what isn't. Don't you just mean plain 'good writing'?

Snipe. If you like. All good writing is comic. It would be a strange kind of goodness that could only take itself one way — seriously.

Sophonisba. It would be an even stranger kind that could only take itself comically.

Mulligrub. Ah, but it's your 'one way' that's just the root of the trouble.

Snipe. Hello, I sniff the dreaded ambivalence in the wind.

Mulligrub. What's the matter with you? You won't have things taken one way, and you won't have them ambivalent either. What does that leave?

Sophonisba. I think it leaves 'comedy', dear boy. Of the inadvertent kind.

Whipstalk. Which is decidedly the best kind. Who could be

interested in a Shakespeare utterly in control of his matter? It is the self-division of the creative process that makes for the integrity of. . .

Snipe. Of cant.

Whipstalk. Easily said. But you've given no hostages to date. What's your alternative to ambivalence?

Snipe. A comedy which can afford to take its seriousness for granted and is not forever exhibiting itself on the high wire. If one thought it was the besetting sin of human nature to be frivolous, one might set up shop for earnestness and solemnity. But since those commodities are on sale at every corner—and always have been, and Shakespeare knew it—I propose remaindering them. So does comedy.

Sophonisba. As a consequence of which you are promising us the most serious clown on record? I suppose there is a *kind* of logic in that.

Snipe. Indeed there is. I knew you'd come round.

Bullfinch. Well, it escapes me, but if it means we're ready, I'll buy it. Cushion (*Pats it*). Sword (*Seizes cheese knife*). Where's my Maria?

Mistress Mulligrub. His Maria! He hasn't got one.

All. No Maria! No Maria! Play's off!

Whereupon our party, relieved at not having to perform a play that it felt it had already 'done', began to re-form into small knots. Bullfinch, still sporting a sad cushion in his belly, wandered disconsolately from one to another, and was about to sink, glass in hand, into a private stupor, when the doorbell rang. Instantly, he was gone. There came a sound of voices from the front-door, and Bullfinch re-entered singing, 'Maria, Maria, I've just found a girl called Maria', and leading by the hand an elegant but at present bemused gentleman, known personally to some of the company, but by reputation to all. It was Mr Sottopassagio.

Sottopassagio. Please God, not the singing game. (*Laughs nervously*)

Bullfinch. No, no. I've already won that. (*Throws his arms around Sottopassagio*) How now, my excellent devil of wit.

Sottopassagio. I wish you wouldn't do that.

Bullfinch. (*Hanging on*) Come by and by to my chamber.

Mulligrub. (*Assisting his new guest*) Or *What You Will.*

Sottopassagio. (*With dawning comprehension*) Ah! (*To Mistress Mulligrub*) I wonder, mistress, that you give means for this uncivil rule.

Mistress Mulligrub. Is he being rude? or literary?
Bullfinch. Both! Both!
Mulligrub. He's being Malvolio, love. He has tumbled Bull-
finch's little ruse.
Sophonisba. With, may I say, commendable speed.
Sir Affable. I thought you might have got it earlier. 'Excellent
devil of wit' should have given it you, you know.
Sottopassagio. Yes. I was just making sure it wasn't Dekker.
Bullfinch. Well it wasn't. And you're not Malvolio. We've got
nothing but Malvolios. You're to be Maria.
Sottopassagio. (*Urbanely*) Yes, I understand that. But surely
that's Sophonisba's part.
Sir Affable. What did I tell you, my dear?
Sophonisba. I can't bear it. Am I, even to you, dear Sotto-
passagio, no more than a pert scullery maid?
Mistress Mulligrub. I think I'll do the washing-up.
Sottopassagio. (*Not moving*) Let me help you. No civilised
life is possible without washing-up. Which is where I salute
Maria. She manages her kitchen and her men with decorum.
She knows the value of order in the small affairs of daily
life. I'm grateful to Shakespeare for reminding me of it.
Sophonisba. Oh, your gratitude!
Whipstalk. Oh, your order! It's a poor look-out if that's all
he reminds you of in the way of order. In a consort of
musical, dancing, ceremonious ballet, you notice only the
dirty dishes.
Sottopassagio. Even ballet works better when the dishes are
done.   (*Exit Mistress Mulligrub – balletically*)
Whipstalk. That's no reason for taking them to the theatre.
I really do get irritated by this gratuitous importation of
the everyday.
Sottopassagio. (*With the sweetest of reasonablenesses*) Oh?
Why?
Sir Affable. Why not? 'Nought enters there,
Of what validity and pitch soe'er
But falls into abatement and low price.'
Whipstalk. Yes, yes. Exactly.
Mulligrub. But that's Orsino.
Whipstalk. (*Tearing his hair*) There *is* no Orsino.
Sottopassagio. You're being him now.
Sophonisba. What do you mean 'no Orsino'? Snipe and Mulli-
grub are personally acquainted with him. They can even
tell you who his barber was.
Whipstalk. And who did his washing-up, no doubt!
Snipe. I care about neither barbers nor washers-up. But
neither do I care about your 'ceremonies'. It's all action

and reaction. *They* go haring off in one direction and because there's obviously nothing to be found there, *you* go haring off in the opposite.

Whipstalk. Oh, I suppose it's seeing life steadily and seeing it whole, now?

Snipe. Seeing what's *there*.

(*A general hoot*)

All. Oh! 'There'!

Snipe. Mock on! Mock on! You all know perfectly well what 'there' means. And you also know there's a man called Orsino — or you wouldn't have been arguing about who's to play him.

Sophonisba. Are you suggesting, with your lovable turn for making the usual appear strange, that Shakespeare is all about 'chaps'?

Snipe. Do you know, I've never put it to myself like that before!

Sophonisba. Well now that you *have* put it to yourself. . . .

Snipe. I'm rather fond of it, being a chap myself. But I can't be interested in Orsino's barber because Shakespeare doesn't tell me about him, whereas I can be interested in Orsino's lying in bed all day, because Shakespeare does.

Whipstalk. Shakespeare also 'tells' us, in a dozen ways, about ceremony and order. He introduces a Lord of Misrule. . .

Bullfinch. Me, me. Still me.

Whipstalk. . . . he multiplies confusion, and then, he choreographs his peripeteia into a double *pas de deux*. Mightn't that license *my* interest? Isn't that 'there'?

Sottopassagio. Is it *Les Sylphides* you have in mind? Or *Le Sacre du Printemps*?

Whipstalk. Does that matter?

Sottopassagio. It might. I'm just trying to fathom your analogy.

Snipe. If Shakespeare is 'telling' us things by way of ballerinas in pink tulle (played, of course, by boys!), I give him up.

Whipstalk. It depends what you mean by 'telling' doesn't it? You only like one sort. If he 'tells' you about order and disorder, you go instantly deaf.

Snipe. To answer by the method, it depends what you mean by 'order', doesn't it?

Whipstalk. You know perfectly well what 'order' means.

Snipe. Yes, but humour me a little.

Whipstalk. Very well. It means that in the green world of comic saturnalia, the darkness of misprision and misconstruction (which is Malvolio's darkness as well as the lovers'), there is an invisible economy. And in the final

ceremony of harmonisation, the anarchic energies, the re-
pressions, purge themselves by enactment, and Olivia is
free to love Sebastian (whom she mistook for Viola) and
Orsino can love Viola (whom he mistook for Cesario and
Olivia). Antonio discovers that his latent homosexual
rage. . .

Bullfinch. (*Roaring*)
I believe
For every one who goes astray
Someone will come to show the way.

Snipe.
I believe
That someone in the great somewhere
Hears every word.

All. (*Including, finally, Whipstalk*)
Every time I hear a new-born baby cry
Or touch a leaf or see the sky
Then I know why
I believe.

Whipstalk. Cheap! Cheap! Very funny, but irrelevant.

Snipe. Very funny *because* relevant. Comedy, as I keep
telling you. . .

Mulligrub. Let it go, you two. You couldn't produce your
canons of relevance if you tried. If something interests
you, it's 'there'. If it doesn't, it isn't. Why not try all the
possibilities, and see how they look together?

Bullfinch. Are you granting, or are you taking away?

Whipstalk. Snipe. (*Together*) Both. Both.
(*Laughter*)

Mulligrub. (*Undeterred*) You don't have to reject other
people's interests to assert your own. Let them all shake
down together; and when you have, you'll pretty quickly
see what's worth keeping and what isn't.

Sophonisba. My dear Mulligrub, you're a splendid host but
really this feeble eclecticism is unworthy of you.

Whipstalk. Hear, Hear!

Snipe. (*Reproachfully to Mulligrub*) Even I, who have the
most open of minds, must agree with Whipstalk and
Sophonisba on this one.

Sir Affable. I sometimes wonder whether there shouldn't be
a place for eclecticism, though I don't go in for it myself.

Sottopassagio. I am grateful for any eclecticism if it will call
a halt to this over-collaboration with Shakespeare. We may
talk of our Shakespeare, but it is to each other that we
talk. I'm always conscious, when I read him, of my own
shocking impercipience. And it is always important to

distinguish what we bring—which is little—from what he
bestows—which is often (though not always) much.

Whipstalk. Exactly! If every extravagant ingenuity is to be
fathered upon him, there can be no relevance. It is his
limitation which is our salvation.

Sottopassagio. I'm not sure that was quite my point.

Mulligrub. If the choice is between shocking impercipience
and extravagant ingenuity, I despair of salvation.

Bullfinch. Try extravagant impercipience. I'm quite attached
to my own.

Sophonisba. The pity of it is that everybody *is* so wretchedly
attached to his own. (*Sir Affable stirs in faint demurral*) I
exclude you, of course, my love.

Sottopassagio. Yes. It is always the artist's work that must
shine through.

Mulligrub. But shine through what? We can't all be translucent.

Sottopassagio. But might we not try? Is that not the effort
we make as we sit alone with a book in a lamplit room? Is
it not even more the effort, when we speak to our friends
about a work that has got inside us?

Snipe. You mean, when you bully your friends with your
humility.

Sottopassagio. One hopes to avoid that, though I know I
suffer, like everybody else, from some impurity of response. The effort is always to keep one's mind fresh. Ideal
talk seeks that, just as it seeks freedom from prepossession.
We should keep our minds open to the possibility, for
example, that Shakespeare is often a very shoddy writer.
As Dr. Johnson, with whom one disagrees at one's peril. . .

Sophonisba. Oh, I can't bear it!　　　　　)
Snipe. Oh, no! ·　　　　　　　　　　　)
Mulligrub. I give up!　　　　　　　　　)(*Together*)
Sir Affable. Mmmm. . .Yerz. . .Werll. . .)

Bullfinch. (*Finally removing his cushion and throwing it at
Sottopassagio*) Pistol him. Pistol him somebody.

(*Sottopassagio looks surprised. Mistress Mulligrub enters
with a tray*)

Mistress Mulligrub. Cake? Cake, anybody?

(*Sottopassagio takes a piece, and nibbles thoughtfully*)

Sottopassagio. Is it caraway? With a shade of lemon, perhaps?
No, no, orange. Curaçao, of course! Do you use Normandy
butter? I find it creams more readily, don't you? I was
once given a recipe. . . .

Mistress Mulligrub. Just eat it, Sottopassagio.

II
Hamlet's Sanity

Shakespeare had more magnanimity than any other poet, and he has shown more of it in this play than in any other.

Hazlitt

1 · MILDEWED EARS AND MATRON'S BONES

Unfamiliar with the assurances of Goethe and Coleridge, Claudius, King of Denmark, was not able to sleep soundly in his bed, secure in the knowledge that his nephew had too great an aversion to real action to execute his revenge. Nor was he able wholeheartedly to welcome, as an adornment to his court, his nephew's conversational flair. He found the sweet Prince a persistently trying presence, a ghastly nuisance, and a dangerous opponent. The great love the general gender bear Hamlet is, to Claudius, more a matter for anxiety than for family pride; and anxiety might well turn to fear if that love – 'dipping all his faults in their affection' – is determinedly indiscriminate. Claudius seems to have measured how little, on the other hand, popular opinion might do for *him*, and indeed it has gone against him ever since.

Even when Hamlet's 'faults' have been less genially regarded, his judgements have been allowed to carry. It seems that whatever we make of Hamlet, we make what he makes of Claudius and Gertrude. We seize upon Hamlet's words to Horatio,

> The King doth wake tonight and takes his rouse,
> Keeps wassail, and the swaggering upspring reels,

and pronounce Claudius, in exacerbation of his already great crime, drunkard! We admit that the hand with which Hamlet holds up to his mother the mirror of her nature trembles a little too violently:

> Nay but to live
> In the rank sweat of an enseamed bed,
> Stewed in corruption, honeying and making love
> Over the nasty sty –

but we seldom doubt that the steamy sensuality offered to her view is indeed her own.

If Hamlet had had Falstaff for an uncle and the Wife of Bath for a mother, would his disapprobations have won from us the prompt assent they usually do? Had Gertrude and Claudius rounded upon their fastidious son with something like 'Dost thou think because thou art virtuous there shall be no more cakes and ale?', would we have been tempted to an appreciation of their elemental spirit of revelry? Is it because they have cropped up in the wrong sort of play — what we call a tragedy rather than what we call a comedy — or because they are not sufficiently clamorous on behalf of their own pleasures, that they have been denied that sentimentality of appreciation that we choose to indulge where we have decided to like?

As it is we have listened to Hamlet where he is least to be trusted. Swayed by the eloquence of his hurt sensitivity, we have discounted the evidence of our own eyes. For Claudius does not gratuitously tipple, nor does Gertrude lecher, in our sight. When we see them as a couple they show no signs of preparing for, or recovering from, any scene of lewd riot. What is in play between them is not sensuality but affection and solicitousness. Shakespeare has taken pains to show us what Hamlet will not see, that their regard for one another — whatever the propriety of their *having* a regard for one another — has all the warmth and all the fussiness of a distinctly settled domesticity.

The discrepancy between Hamlet's incensed and lurid imaginings of what his mother and step-father get up to and the amiably domestic reality, is at the heart of the play and is the source of some of its best comedy. It is amusing to discover such tameness when we have been led to expect so much of its opposite, and even more amusing to discover it, with all its fond cares and anxieties, where, even without a Hamlet to prejudice us, we would least expect to find it:

Laertes.   O thou vile king,
　　　Give me my father.
Queen.　　　　　Calmly, good Laertes.
Laertes.
　That drop of blood that's calm proclaims me bastard,
　Cries cuckold to my father, brands the harlot
　Even here between the chaste unsmirched brows
　Of my true mother.
King.　　　　What is the cause, Laertes,
　　That thy rebellion looks so giant-like?

> Let him go, Gertrude. Do not fear our person.
> There's such divinity doth hedge a king
> That treason can but peep to what it would,
> Acts little of his will. Tell me, Laertes,
> Why thou art thus incensed. Let him go, Gertrude.
> Speak, man.
> *Laertes.* Where is my father?
> *King.*   Dead.
> *Queen.*   But not by him.
> *King.* Let him demand his fill.

Poor Claudius! Reduced as he has been by Hamlet's antics to a soft and wary padding about his own court, the opportunity has not often come to him to take the direct magisterial line; and now, with an eminently quellable rebellion to quell, and the sense of his regality resolutely upon him, he must suffer the indignity of being physically protected by a jittery and loving wife. We must suppose that Gertrude falls upon Laertes with the best wifely will in the world, but we must not suppose that Claudius would thank her for it. It always surprises me to see the lines,

> There's such divinity doth hedge a king
> That treason can but peep to what it would,

quoted as evidence of the Elizabethan sense of the inviolability of Kingship, given from whose lips, and in what comic circumstances, they fall. The divinity that doth hedge a king at this moment is the person of Gertrude—and imagination and tradition would have hers ample. As for treason being able only to peep at what it would, the image has a grotesque appositeness if we remember a half-smothered Laertes on tip-toes to deliver the force of his giant-like rebellion in those tones of prolixity and prurience that make him his father's son and Hamlet's contemporary.

In such a manner do the corruptly-crowned heads of the rotten state of Denmark cavort!

If Gertrude, in this scene, is more a woman for being less a Queen, what of Claudius, the ice-cold, omni-competent politician of popular repute? Is he ever any more successfully, chillingly that, than he is here? Don't we at once malign and flatter him, if we hear in his very first words in the play a man in firm control of a situation or in cool possession of himself?

> Though yet of Hamlet our dear brother's death
> The memory be green, and that it us befitted
> To bear our hearts in grief, and our whole kingdom

To be contracted in one brow of woe,
Yet so far hath discretion fought with nature
That we with wisest sorrow think on him
Together with remembrance of ourselves.
Therefore our sometime sister, now our queen,
Th'imperial jointress to this warlike state,
Have we, as 'twere with a defeated joy,
With one auspicious and one dropping eye,
With mirth in funeral and with dirge in marriage,
In equal scale weighing delight and dole,
Taken to wife. Nor have we herein barred
Your better wisdoms, which have freely gone
With this affair along. For all, our thanks.

The verse here is more than usually dedicated, even for
Shakespeare, to the delineation of personality. Nothing that
Claudius is given to say comes from any deep, unknown
source in him; there is not a word that doesn't render up the
man. And that itself is a sign, not perhaps of Shakespeare's
highest inspiration, but of his supreme confidence, his sheer
delight in the exhibition of character. Such a confidence in
a writer will almost always issue in comedy, for its basis is
a freedom from perturbation, and where there is nothing to
fear there is everything to enjoy.

Shakespeare's Claudius is different from Hamlet's Claudius
because he is less unequivocally reprobate; but the difference
is as much in the seeing as in the thing seen. Hamlet is absorbed in Claudius' criminality — and that even before his
prophetic soul can quite locate the crime; Shakespeare enter-
tains the brighter and more varied drama of Claudius'
troubles. There is never to be a time in the play when
Claudius isn't troubled, and his trouble here, in what appears
to be his first public statement on his marriage to Gertrude,
if we cannot yet dignify it by the name of conscience, is at
least a recognition that there are objections to be met, that
there is a delicacy and a tact to be employed. But delicacy
and tact as Claudius employs them can seldom have been so
emptied of their distinguishing virtues. We might allow the
propriety of 'wisest sorrow' as an outcome of discretion's
battle with nature, and we might even feel that he gets away
tolerably with that groped for and judicious-sounding
paradox of 'as 'twere with a defeated joy'; but 'one auspicious
and one dropping eye' is crazily bad — the improbability of
the moral contortion being suggested by the impossibility of
the physical; and when we get to 'mirth in funeral' and 'dirge
in marriage', we do not know where to look. Neither,

presumably, does the assembled court, which is not so far inured to bad taste as to need no menacing reminder that if the form of the apology is all Claudius' own, the affair itself met with a free and a general approval. Has not the whole kingdom, in effect, taken Gertrude to wife?

Whatever else he shows himself for in this attempt to justify the marriage of self-interest to sentiment, Claudius is neither efficient nor cynical. Efficiency would not have so fumbled with the rings, and a cynic would have given away the bride with a finer carelessness. Claudius himself shows us what a confident dismissiveness and an easy disdain look like when he leaves, with what sounds like infinite relief, the question of his marriage for affairs of state:

> Now follows, that you know, young Fortinbras,
> Holding a weak supposal of our worth,
> Or thinking by our late dear brother's death
> Our state to be disjoint and out of frame,
> Colleagued with this dream of his advantage,
> He hath not failed to pester us with message
> Importing the surrender of those lands
> Lost by his father, with all bands of law,
> To our most valiant brother. So much for him.

These are the speech-rhythms of a different man. Here is competence, authority, the most consummate contempt for that which he knows he can contain. Nothing could more exactly measure for us the extent of his earlier unease. But the humour of the scene has not dropped. We register Claudius' masterfulness now, but we are not awed by it. Behind the swelling complacency of a man displaying his happiest expertise we are aware of the mopped brow; his enjoyment of his own powers seems proportionate to his sense of narrow escape. We smile at a vulnerability ill-concealed, and hence at a confidence that is not all it seems; but we smile without malice.

And why should we not go on smiling when Claudius, out of his regained composure, caresses Laertes – the name as much as the man?

> And now, Laertes, what's the news with you?
> You told us of some suit. What is't Laertes?
> You cannot speak of reason to the Dane
> And lose your voice. What wouldst thou beg, Laertes,
> That shall not be my offer, not thy asking?
> The head is not more native to the heart,
> The hand more instrumental to the mouth,

Than is the throne of Denmark to thy father.
What wouldst thou have, Laertes?

He's certainly an emollient monarch at this point, but he is capable of more than one form of address, as we have seen, and if he has chosen here that which is most suitable to its object, he has chosen felicitously. Laertes is easy game for Claudius; he is ever the recipient of that flattery which is contempt, and contempt for Laertes is the proper emotion. In a scene in which Hamlet is often found enjoyable for the inventiveness of his scorn, it seems rather hard on Claudius that he is not given credit for the less pithy but more successfully disguised version of his.

Still, if Claudius is in command of a threatening Fortinbras and a pliant Laertes, he knows there remains the problem of Hamlet. And if we heard him sigh with relief when he was able to leave family matters, it is with a deeper sigh of oppression that he returns to them:

> Take thy fair hour, Laertes. Time be thine,
> And thy best graces spend it at thy will.
> But now, my cousin Hamlet, and my son —

He's lordly, he's expansive, and in his demonstration by means of Laertes and Polonius, of the proper filial relations, he is even subtle. But that mischievous demon that has already whispered into his ear that the best way to be discreet is to be jovial, mutters his infelicities again. 'My cousin Hamlet, and my son' — well, if changes in sensitive relations are to be the theme, Hamlet can ring them more ingeniously: 'A little more than kin and less than kind'. Claudius blunders into trouble, yet I don't believe that we are to cheer Hamlet's ability to discountenance him. Our sympathies do not all line up on the side of Hamlet, for the same genial irony that gives us Claudius' want of nimbleness gives us Hamlet's extravagance of posture. That interpretation of Hamlet offered by Mr Wopsle to the amazement of Pip and Herbert Pocket is not all unhappy. Indeed, when we are told that for this scene Pip's 'gifted townsman stood gloomily apart, with folded arms', we might feel that he has caught exactly the right degree of theatricality, and invited us to precisely the right amount of amused indulgence.

The varied, comic interplay of personality and attitude in this scene works to remind us that, in a general way, a pure sincerity of grief is as rare as gross unfeelingness; that we should not be dismayed if we do not find the one, nor over-anxious to detect the other. Certainly it is not gross unfeelingness that is before us when Gertrude offers to help her new husband and soothe her son:

> Good Hamlet, cast thy nighted colour off,
> And let thine eye look like a friend on Denmark.
> Do not for ever with thy vailed lids
> Seek for thy noble father in the dust.

Her words are not callous, her concern is not perfunctory, her cajolery is not coarse. She is all kindness. She knows that mortality is cruel, but she knows, too, that one can live with it. She searches the serene shallows of her nature for some formulation that will do justice to both the dead and the living, and it is in a spirit of true maternal benevolence that she offers as help, as comfort, as philosophical solace, the little nothingness that she finds:

> Thou know'st 'tis common. All that lives must die,
> Passing through nature to eternity.

'Ay, madam, it is common', Hamlet seethes in return, and what could be more delightful than Gertrude's supposing she has thereby won a concession?

> If it be,
> Why seems it so particular with thee?

She can't, of course, put a foot right. But then, in advancing towards a man so obstreperous in his sense of his own authenticity, who can? 'Seems' is as a red rag to a bull, and the unfortunate, well-meaning Gertrude is treated to a violent disquisition upon appearance and reality:

> Seems, madam? Nay, it is. I know not 'seems.'
> 'Tis not alone my inky cloak, good mother,
> Nor customary suits of solemn black,
> . . . .
> That can denote me truly. These indeed seem,
> For they are actions that a man might play,
> But I have that within which passeth show —
> These but the trappings and the suits of woe.

The inevitable question is: why, in that case, the ostentation of the trappings? A sharper mother than Gertrude might have put that brutally. As it is Gertrude doesn't put it at all, and we, I think, should put it gently. Hamlet's public display of private grief is no better than the frank no-grief-at-all of his mother. But it is no worse. A mature wisdom directs this scene: not a sad recognition of human frailties — that this, alas, is how things are — but a more buoyant conviction that human nature need not be perfect to be sound. We are not to believe that Claudius and Gertrude are gross because they are clumsy, and we are not to doubt that Hamlet's sorrow is genuine because it is conceited.

Dickens, who seems to have found *Hamlet* a most congenial play, knows how extortionate is the demand that the sorrow of loss must be pure to be real. We are not appalled by what David Copperfield feels when he is told of his mother's death:

> I am sensible of having felt that a dignity attached to me among the rest of the boys, and that I was important in my affliction.
> If ever child were stricken with sincere grief, I was. But I remembered that this importance was a kind of satisfaction to me, when I walked in the playground that afternoon while the boys were in school. When I saw them glancing at me out of the windows, as they went up to their classes, I felt distinguished, and looked more melancholy, and walked slower. When school was over, and they came out and spoke to me, I felt it rather good in myself not to be proud to any of them, and to take exactly the same notice of them as before.

David Copperfield is a small boy when he finds himself orphaned, but I do not think we are recalling the self-absorption only of early childhood when we admit, and are encouraged by Dickens to *enjoy* admitting, the justice of the description. Perhaps Hamlet is a shade too old to be feeling important in *his* affliction, but we no more declare his self-consciousness monstrous than we declare David's exceptional. The high expectation that all feelings should run deep, and all affections be unsullied, sits at the centre of Hamlet's affliction; and if we were to judge him by his own demanding standards we would judge him severely. But that generosity which, in other moods, Hamlet knows so much about —

Polonius. My lord, I will use them according to their desert.
Hamlet. God's bodkin, man, much better! Use every man after his desert and who shall scape whipping? Use them after your own honour and dignity. The less they deserve, the more merit is in your bounty

— should no more be denied him in all his common frailties than it should be denied Claudius and Gertrude in theirs.

It's certainly not a frail-sounding Claudius that has one last attempt at reasoning, upbraiding, cajoling, and finally, threatening Hamlet into domestic harmony, but the ensuing silence must be long and painful indeed for Gertrude to feel the need to sink her husband's resounding impressiveness in the bathos of a little motherly coaxing:

> Let not thy mother lose her prayers, Hamlet.
> I pray thee stay with us, go not to Wittenberg.

The two lines manage what Claudius' thirty couldn't. 'I shall in all my best obey you, madam', says Hamlet with a pointed rudeness for Claudius that no longer has the protection of allusiveness or the merit of wit. A moment of fine ludicrousness ensues. Claudius ignores the insult, grabs gratefully at the first words Hamlet has spoken that can in any way be interpreted as pliancy:

> Why, 'tis a loving and a fair reply

—grabs no less hurriedly his lordly magnanimity:

> Be as ourself in Denmark

— his wife ('Madam, come'), and the idea of himself, King, uncle, step-father, basking in the warm glow of restored relations and easy concord (which fiction not even a court of Osrics could believe):

> This gentle and unforced accord of Hamlet
> Sits smiling to my heart —

and, promising to meet Hamlet's grand concessions with even grander celebrations, beats a hasty retreat. 'So much for him' —Claudius, the shrewd political manipulator and schemer!

Claudius, of course, does manipulate and scheme. But just as his drinking, unaccompanied by any defiant philosophy of hedonism, has excited only censoriousness, so his scheming, for which he has neither voracious appetite nor natural aptitude, has earned him only disapprobation unenlivened by that frisson of fascination that some men experience when they confront an Iago or an Edmund. Claudius would have fared better with critics had he behaved worse—and enjoyed himself more while he was at it. As it is, he is not artful by nature. He takes no delight in the ingenuities of intrigue and subterfuge. He looks mournfully upon his own descent into them; never sees them as welcome or inevitable concomitants to his original crime. Hamlet, who knows far more than Claudius about the pleasures of machination, has first to set traps of his own, kill Polonius, discomfort his uncle in a dozen ways. The speedy revenge that Hamlet wishes he could execute would not have tormented Claudius as keenly as do the ingenious forms of his delay. Goaded intolerably, Claudius finally schemes meanly, schemes savagely, but because he is never in control, because Hamlet rages like a hectic in his blood, and because, above all, he is not very good at it, he schemes in panic, without subtlety, and without success.

Neither scheme nor intrigue, however, is the word to describe Claudius and Gertrude's calling in of Rosencrantz and Guildenstern to sound the causes of their son's affliction. There is no good reason for finding that action morally repellent. It is true that the discussion between parents and friends follows hard upon the scene of Polonius' elaborate intrusions into his son's life and clumsy interferences with his daughter's. And if we are determined to share Hamlet's fastidious revulsions we will feel that the juxtaposition of these scenes works to evoke a world that is all for snooping and prying. If we are political, to boot, we will talk about warders and informers, freedoms violated, and passports withheld. But juxtaposition can work to contrast as well as to compound, and it seems to me that Polonius is given room to be himself at this point of the play precisely in order to show us what Claudius and Gertrude are not. We are to notice that parental worry comes in many a guise, and that if interference has to be the word for what happens in both cases, then spying is another word again. Claudius and Gertrude show no signs of taking that vicarious interest in Hamlet's private life which Polonius takes in Laertes', or, come to that, which Hamlet takes in theirs. Nor do they invade it without invitation. An antic disposition is not well calculated to preserve privacy; it will cause anxiety where there is sympathy, and it is always a fine line that divides solicitude and trespass. What would we say of Claudius and Gertrude, as parents, if they took no steps to fathom and minister to their son's distress? And what would we say of them, as King and Queen, if they allowed 'madness in great ones' to go unwatched and untended?

Rosencrantz and Guildenstern, for their part, do not seem to feel that they have been signed on as conspirators, even if they do allow their readiness to help their friend to lose itself somewhat in their enthusiasm for also helping the King and Queen. As their later speeches on kingship remind us, they are avid royalists, awed by authority and thrilled by their fortuitous contact with majesty. The notes they strike with Hamlet are, of course, from the first false, and as there is no profit in speculating whether they have been dubious and superficial friends from way back, we might hazard that it is in the nature of what they have agreed to do that the genuine will never sound. Claudius and Gertrude might have anticipated that. But that they didn't is more a failure of intelligence than a lapse of decency.

However, judgements even of that temperateness do not seem appropriate to the delightful scene in which Claudius and Gertrude first welcome their son's friends, and where Shakespeare seems above all interested in amusing us with the froth of Gertrude's good nature. How easily the queenly in Gertrude,

> Your visitation shall receive such thanks
> As fits a king's remembrance —

too innocent to be really shabby, too intimate to be really grand — accords with her dim but genuine maternal perplexity. And how easily both slip into that womanly warmth that is not quite flirtatiousness, but is not quite, either, the proper tone of a mother to her son's friends:

King. Thanks, Rosencrantz and gentle Guildenstern.
Queen. Thanks, Guildenstern and gentle Rosencrantz.

The soul of Gertrude is distilled into that moment. Claudius' singling out of Guildenstern for blandishment is not discriminatory: as we have seen already, Claudius is weak before the temptation of word play, and the opportunity for alliteration is not to be foregone. Guildenstern is only gentle because his initial is right. Other considerations operate in Gertrude. She, too, has thanks to offer, and she caps her husband not to be witty but to be kind. Poor Rosencrantz must not be left out.

Gertrude seeks to inhabit a cheerful world. She likes to diffuse a warm cordiality of spirits. She is never happier than when everyone is getting on with one another, especially when that everyone is, with the exception of herself, masculine. It is her tiny tragedy that she is to be largely denied that pleasure. She is never really to understand why she is surrounded by so much discord. It distresses and bemuses her. Yet it says much for her spirits that they rouse at the first hint of the harmonious. When Hamlet puts on his play she settles in for a good night:

> Come hither, my dear Hamlet, sit by me.

And she proves to be a lively critic of the play's excesses:

> The lady doth protest too much, methinks.

That is just what Gertrude would notice, but she is no less right for that. Hamlet's

> O, but she'll keep her word,

is a boorish, intention-laden response. There is nothing in his
mother that he can now permit himself to enjoy.

Gertrude is herself to the last. A rapprochement between
Hamlet and Laertes, a fencing match, her son one of the
contestants, wine on the tables, Claudius kingly, the court
itself again: Gertrude is home. All unknowing, she lifts the
poisoned cup and enters, queen and mother, into the spirit
of the thing:

> Here Hamlet, take my napkin, rub thy brows.
> The Queen carouses to thy fortune, Hamlet.

She has no thought that between Hamlet and Laertes, given
all that has happened, there can be no friendship. Here is life
and colour, the gaiety of occasion, the maleness of camara-
derie, the giddy excitement of sport, the sudden fluctuations
of fortune, the whole-hearted involvement of taking the side
which blood and affection dictate. To all that she drinks.
And in her own impercipient, indiscriminate good-naturedness,
she dies.

Claudius' finish is not so blithe. If we choose to adopt
Hamlet's sardonic enjoyment of the

> sport to have the engineer
> Hoist with his own petard,

we will find that finish ironic—Claudius caught in the insufficiency and shabbiness of his own designs. So he is. But
we have not been privy to the small, ignoble drama of
Claudius' life, that queer comic mixture of ambition and in-
competence, perfidy and devotedness, only that we might
be pleased by the neat poetic justice of its close. Whatever
the ironies, there is a wretched poignancy in Claudius' inability, once Gertrude drinks, to offer her help or in any way
acknowledge her calamity. For she was conjunctive to his
life and soul and he can do nothing for her. Worse, he must
actually prevent anything being done for her, there being no
answer, short of a confession, that he can make to Hamlet's

> How does the queen?

but:

> She sounds to see them bleed.

Reduced to that expedient—desperate, ineffective, callous—
he is reduced indeed.

Not, though, to an 'incestuous, murd'rous, damned dane'.
Of course, we do not expect Hamlet, when the moment to
kill Claudius finally comes, to measure his obsequies as he

administers the poison. But his words here, in all their old monotonous implacability, remind us of the one unchanging element in his long, fitful campaign: his ignorance of Claudius. Hamlet has not for one moment known his foe; he has not known him either to show him mercy or to savour the fullness of his own revenge—for a Claudius not rejoicing in his villainies only because he is no longer alive, is a poor thing to triumph over compared to the reality: a Claudius fretful, remorseful, knowingly compromised to the last. We do not, in the hurried actions of the last scene, register it as any kind of joke against Hamlet that he should miss out on that crueller refinement of revenge which a knowledge of his man would give him. Besides, that joke has already been made.

What else is Hamlet's refusal to kill Claudius at prayer, not knowing that the perfect opportunity for that luridly well-timed murder to which he aspires is at hand? The ironies of that scene, though, are not merely circumstantial—lines crossed, chances squandered, purposes mistook. It is not his cue that Hamlet misreads, it is Claudius. He has no idea of what the spectacle of his uncle on his knees betokens. Nor is he curious. There is only one inner drama in Hamlet's world, and there is only one duty. A Christian, remorseful Claudius is not a surprise, only a nuisance—or, as some would have it, a relief.

> Now might I do it pat, now 'a is a-praying,
> And now I'll do't. And so 'a goes to heaven,
> And so am I revenged. That would be scanned.

So it would. Those negligent rhythms serve a strangely perfunctory account of the soul's ascent: a spot of prayer, a thrust of the dagger, and up it goes! His uncle's theology is far more demanding.

The idea of Claudius having a troubled conscience does not appear to excite Shakespeare greatly and he presents it to us in indifferent verse. The life of the speech is elsewhere. It is not in his torment that Claudius is interesting to us but in his fiercely honest appraisal of the small right he has to have that torment assuaged. He would have mercy, and he would pray for it—except that he cannot bring himself to believe in the ludicrous perfunctoriness of a pardon being granted simply because it is implored. The facile moral contract that Hamlet thinks is being signed—'now 'a is a-praying. . . And so goes to heaven'—Claudius scrutinizes only to mock:

> Then I'll look up.
> My fault is past.

Would it were so easy! And would he could say, 'Forgive me my foul murther', and mean it. But only a sardonic mimicry of that ineffectual prayer is possible to him. He can shuffle neither with heaven nor with himself. For he knows that he cannot and will not, even as an act of the mind and for all the peace it might procure him, relinquish what he has won – his crown, his ambition, and his queen.

It is not in the hope of pulling off a passable imitation of repentance that he forces his unwilling knees finally to bend. Nor is his plea to the angels to 'make assay' a request for any special leniency. The help he would have is the help to make him otherwise; the help to find in himself that remorse he knows he should feel but cannot. He is not easy on himself who even acknowledges that there is a difference.

After Hamlet, in his ignorance and impertinence, has been and gone, the last lines of the scene revert to Claudius:

> My words fly up, my thoughts remain below.
> Words without thoughts never to heaven go.

And they have about them a finality that is not just that of a neat, conventional couplet close to a scene. The fall in cadence is an emotional one. Something has settled and closed for Claudius. The attempt to will himself into a state of grace has failed, as he knew it would, and he now knows that there are comforts and tranquillities he will have to do without.

There is little to be achieved by charging that man with worldliness who has had so steely a look at the impossibility of his being spiritual. Worldliness has its rights and its gravities, and the Hamlet that imagines Claudius

> drunk asleep, or in his rage,
> Or in th' incestuous pleasure of his bed,
> At game a-swearing, or about some act
> That has no relish of salvation in't

is no more spiritual a man, and far less serious a one, than the Claudius that confronts, and without extenuation accepts, his imperfect nature.

2 · WHAT SHOULD A MAN DO BUT BE MERRY?

Bitterly cold ramparts, beetling cliffs and pirate ships notwithstanding, the world of *Hamlet* is a domestic one. The action moves through the bright rooms of the bustling court of Denmark; people come and go, fall out of love, leave off their studies, friends meet, courtiers prepare for foreign travel; there are entertainments, sports, parties, funerals. All the ordinary affections and anxieties, suspicions and disappointments operate; brothers worry about sisters, fathers about sons, sons about mothers. And in those moments of vacancy between bouts of libidinous abandon, husband and wife discuss the daily disruptions—now petty, now dangerous —caused by the common passions of their friends and relations. Even the Ghost, so terrifying in his first silent appearances, has only to speak to show himself a familiar inmate of a busy world. Garrulous, peevish and indelicate, he has obviously, in his time, enjoyed long and windy deliberations with Polonius over this or that affair of court management, and enjoyed his Gertrude with no less relish than now, as he imagines, does Claudius. Such a well-lit, sumptuously furnished play does *Hamlet* feel, it comes as a surprise to discover that the dead King had an orchard to sleep in, and even more of a one to learn that Ophelia found so pretty and pastoral a spot—the haunt of liberal shepherds no less—in which to drown.

To such a world, whether he likes it or not, and he mainly doesn't, Hamlet belongs—not simply physically, not because of some cruel accident of time or place, or as a result only of his uncle's obdurate will. The domesticity I unslightingly speak of circumscribes Hamlet's moral world, too. In all his moodiness, dejection and frolic, Hamlet perplexes his friends and family, but he does not suffer on so exalted a plane, so deeply or so irremediably, as to render their concern and worry for him ridiculously inappropriate. The causes of Hamlet's despondency and the possible alleviations of it are not always discovered by this brisk and practical world, but they lie to hand in it for all that. We know that interesting and diverting company would not go a long way to solving Macbeth's problems; we don't, however, write it off as incapable of doing anything for Hamlet's, whatever he says about man delighting him not. Gertrude's belief that Hamlet needs cheering up is innocent but it is not foolish. And if we are inclined to be scornful of such mundane cures for Hamlet's malaise, how do we explain our liking and enjoying Hamlet most when he *is* cheered up?

Cheering a tragic hero up!—that way, we all know, great believers in the piercing power of pessimism as we are, fatuity lies. The very idea is capable of harrowing up the soul and freezing the young blood of the inconsolably modern critic, and the very intention is never safe from that snub which the tragic hero himself, if he is also a misanthropist, loves to administer. If he isn't a misanthropist, what better than a generous dose of the imperturbably sunny to make him one? Certainly Hamlet, at the first scent of it, starts as fearfully as does the Ghost upon the crowing of the cock; and much pleasure does he give us as he sets about exposing now the vacuity and chastising now the insolence of all attempts to win him from his sadness. Vacuous and insolent they sometimes undoubtedly are. But Hamlet is no innocently embattled victim of the world's desire to assault him with optimism. For he that will stand gloomily in corners, heave sighs of oppression, unbrace his doublet and ungarter his stockings, and otherwise publicize his dissatisfactions, cannot intend to escape the notice, or hope to elude the consternation, of his audience. And he that berates the world on the grounds of its commonplace contentments must expect to be with commonplace humoured or with commonplace defied. 'They fool me to the top of my bent', Hamlet grumbles, as if he had not set a hundred subtle snares for folly. Like many a man whose disappointment with mankind does not entail the logic of seclusion, Hamlet busies himself with confrontations contrived to a nicety to disappoint him the more. Badgered and heckled, teased and bewildered, the world yields up its scantiest wisdom. Exasperated then by such wide-eyed incomprehension of his gloom, disgusted by dull quiescence, insulted by easy palliatives, Hamlet is confirmed in his own sense of knowing alone the truth and facing alone the mysteries. Whereupon the circle of hostility and contrariety becomes complete.

The seeming inevitability of such a process is exemplified beautifully in Hamlet's first exchange with Rosencrantz and Guildenstern. The meeting is full of warmth and affection on all sides:

Guildenstern. My honored lord!
Rosencrantz. My most dear lord!
Hamlet. My excellent good friends! How dost thou, Guildenstern? Ah, Rosencrantz! Good lads, how do ye both?

Even Horatio does not receive so enthusiastic a welcome, and Gertrude's certainty that there are not two men living to whom Hamlet more adheres appears to be well founded. What then — for their later removal from the living not to be near Hamlet's conscience — goes wrong?

Something goes wrong almost immediately. Asked how they are, Rosencrantz and Guildenstern make no extravagant claims for the joys of existence:

Rosencrantz. As the indifferent children of the earth.

Guildenstern. Happy in that we are not over-happy.

There is nothing there to jar a sensitive nerve. But when asked for news, Rosencrantz tries his hand at painting a rosier picture:

> None, my lord, but that the world's grown
> honest—

which is not likely to stimulate any fervent wonderment in his friend. And doesn't:

> Then is doomsday near. But your news is not
> true.

Of course it isn't; and it never will be. That is not melancholy speaking: Hamlet replies as any man might. We can only suppose that Rosencrantz's blitheness proceeds from an over-zealous desire to carry out his errand — to draw Hamlet on to pleasures; and the worst that can be said of it is that it is too transparent to succeed. Hamlet himself seems to judge it no more harshly, being curt only to be kind. There are other tones that might more profitably prevail, and Rosencrantz and Guildenstern are given another chance to find them:

> Let me question more in particular. What have
> you, my good friends, deserved at the hands
> of fortune that she sends you to prison hither?

Or are they? What, after all, can they do with that prison idea? Certainly Hamlet's question is one which the unfortunate good friends must dodge, but there is as much perplexity as evasion in Guildenstern's

> Prison, my lord?

It is no less contentious a notion than is the world's growing honest, and not so self-evident as to call for no surprise. Surprise and bemusement, anyway, appear to be what Hamlet is angling for. It is with no desire to open up the topic for free discussion that he proceeds:

Hamlet. Denmark's a prison.
Rosencrantz. Then is the world one.
Hamlet. A goodly one; in which there are many confines, wards, and dungeons, Denmark being one o' th' worst.

Thus far the honours are about equal. Hamlet insists his view, his friends insist theirs. There are designs and obduracies all round. There is not one of them that might not, with reason, feel nettled. Conversations frequently come to such a

point: the outcome might be something or nothing. But that
something can be the very future of a friendship. Too blunt
an intransigence here, too blank an incomprehension there,
and the large allowances of amity sour, in a moment, into
the wariness and mistrust of antagonism. Diversities that
might have been enjoyed become variances that must be detested. Poised finely as this situation is, it is Rosencrantz,
perhaps exasperated by Hamlet's spikiness, perhaps prompted
by too literal an interpretation of his errand, but always less
sensitive than his other half to the climate of Hamlet's moods
— it is Rosencrantz who tips the scales:

> We think not so, my lord.

Modern drama accustoms us to hear a sinister challenge in
such lines, but is there any reason not to believe that Rosencrantz is still acting in the spirit of Guildenstern's declared
hope that Heavens will make their presence and their prac-
tices pleasant and helpful to their friend? That sounded, at
the time, rather like a decision to treat Hamlet as an invalid,
and that such a decision has been taken is what sounds now
in Rosencrantz's horribly clumsy words. Perhaps it's no more
than Hamlet, in this scene, deserves; but friendship should
not deal in deserts. It is not because they are false friends to
Hamlet that Rosencrantz and Guildenstern cannot please or
help him; it is because they cannot believe that anything is
really amiss, that Hamlet has any grounds at all for his distraction. And once that is clear, Hamlet retires from them
forever into a chilly and ultimately vindictive reserve:

> Why, then 'tis none to you, for there is nothing
> either good or bad but thinking makes it so.
> To me it is a prison.

Even more of a one, we must suppose, after what has just
occurred—or rather, after what Hamlet has just *made* occur.

It is not simply because Hamlet has not yet talked to the
Ghost that his first meeting with Horatio goes off so much
more smoothly, nor because Hamlet himself is more amiably
disposed. Horatio's nature is framed to make him at all times
a good friend to Hamlet. Sombre without being cheerless, re-
signed without being flaccid, Horatio neither indulges
Hamlet's fancies and vituperations, nor insults him with the
blank stare of incomprehension. He neither accepts Hamlet's
comprehensive revulsions, nor offers, in their place, an

easy-going breeziness. When Hamlet asks Rosencrantz and Guildenstern their business in Elsinore, Rosencrantz replies,

> To visit you, my lord; no other occasion.

The impression of a world governed wholly by affection is offered for Hamlet's gratification and improvement. Horatio's answer to the same question —

> A truant disposition, good my lord

— is the warmer for eschewing a show of warmth. Its note of wry self-denigration is that of the real world of bruised and imperfect affections, and it touches the most manly, least querulous side of Hamlet's nature:

> I would not hear your enemy say so,
> Nor shall you do my ear that violence
> To make it truster of your own report
> Against yourself. I know you are no truant.
> But what is your affair in Elsinore?

Horatio can no more want to touch upon his reasons for being here than Rosencrantz and Guildenstern want to touch upon theirs; but if he must, he must:

Horatio. My lord, I came to see your father's funeral.
Hamlet. I prithee do not mock me, fellow student. I think it was to see my mother's wedding.
Horatio. Indeed, my lord, it followed hard upon.

It is not for Horatio to join in the bitter fun of Hamlet's joke against his mother, the natural bent of his mind dictating against it as much as propriety and place. Hamlet's way of putting things is not Horatio's way. But Horatio offers, for all that, no resistance to the idea that there has been, in Denmark's royal family, some breach of the finer forms. Without ever pandering to Hamlet and without ever humouring him, Horatio shows at all times a rueful and subdued regard for his friend's distress. And if he thereby spares himself the edge of Hamlet's scorn, something in the order of 'Why, then 'tis none to you', he also spares Hamlet a satisfaction Hamlet can do without.

But even Horatio, with all his sympathetic disenchantment and all his harmonious reticence, is never allowed for long to keep spiritual company with Hamlet. Visionaries do not pursue their mysteries in packs. So when Hamlet is on the scent, poor Horatio must take his place — with no more honours than are granted to Rosencrantz and Guildenstern — within that unreliable and impercipient universe which does not *dare* to comprehend what Hamlet comprehends. Does not dare and must not try! Returned from his ghostly assignation, Hamlet hangs his 'No Trespassing' notice in his unweeded garden and shuts his gate to foe and friend, to antagonist and commiserator alike. 'How is't, my noble lord?', 'What news, my lord?', ask Marcellus and Horatio, alarmed and reverential, on finding Hamlet apparently undamaged by his private initiation into the ghastly secrets of ghosts. Hamlet does not still their curiosity; he teases and coaxes it:

Hamlet. O, wonderful!
Horatio. Good my lord, tell it.
Hamlet.   No, you will reveal it.
Horatio. Not I, my lord, by heaven.
Marcellus.   Nor I, my lord.
Hamlet. How say you then? Would heart of man once think it?
          But you'll be secret?
Both.   Ay, by heaven, my lord.
Hamlet. There's never a villain dwelling in all Denmark
          But he's an arrant knave.

Is that last a riddle? — a deliberate exercise in the art of sinking in story-telling? Or is Hamlet dazzling his friends with what he believes is the hardest gem of truth the ghost has given him? Either way, Horatio's famous reply combines a proper respect for the occasion with a proper impatience with the tone:

> There needs no ghost, my lord, come from
>   the grave
> To tell us this.

For which exquisitely managed demur he is consigned to the ranks of the unimaginative and the merely practical:

> Why, right, you are in the right,
> And so, without more circumstance at all,
> I hold it fit that we shake hands and part:
> You, as your business and desires shall point you,
> For every man hath business and desire
> Such as it is, and for my own poor part,
> Look you, I'll go pray.

In other words: hands off my ghost! In other words: return to the busy world of mean, mundane affairs that you *do* understand and leave the burden of knowledge and perception and suffering to *me*.

Horatio's refusal to take offence only exasperates Hamlet the more, and before he can quit this encounter, Horatio must

hear his perfectly reasonable desire to know what has occurred
caricatured into a greedy and rabid curiosity, a thing to be
o'ermastered; and must hear his own amazement, when once
he has something beyond a riddle and a platitude to be
amazed by, returned contemptuously to him as the very
emblem of the poverty of his experience and the insufficiency
of his philosophy.* Impatient or forgiving, sceptical or
startled, Horatio cannot, to Hamlet's sense, be anything that
is right. But then who that Hamlet knows ever can? The same
fate awaits them all.

What are those more things in heaven and earth that
Horatio dreams not of? The existence of ghosts? But Horatio
now knows of them, even if he has not personally sampled
their stale garrulity. The fact that men kill? Horatio would
know that. The fact that men lust? He would know that, too.
The fact that Claudius does both? Well, here we have him.
But his system can hardly be said to be significantly in-
complete for lack of knowledge of so specific a detail.
Beyond this particular enactment of a general truth, is there
anything that Hamlet knows—anything that we know he
knows—that Horatio doesn't? Or is it Horatio's spiritual
rather than his intellectual limits that Hamlet is reminding
him of? Certainly Hamlet condescends to his friend as the
spiritually adventurous condescend to the spiritually timid.
His parody of the knowingness of men who have their
secrets—'We could, an if we would'—is a tolerable parody
of himself throughout this scene. As he hops excitedly about
the stage, hinting now at this, alluding now to that, making
the ghost a playfellow all of his own, Hamlet offers himself
as some kind of mystic traveller, one who has peered into
the abyss, communed with spirits, become initiate into the
abhorrent mysteries. As is often the case with more terrestrial
travellers, the idea that his auditors are stay-at-homes is in-
dispensably gratifying to him. Poor Horatio might complain
that he hasn't had the opportunity, that no ghost. . .But
perhaps the answer to that would be that ghosts only come
to you if you are fit for them. Anyway, he has been stuck
forever with a reputation for spiritual diffidence and un-
ruffled moral stolidity, chiefly on Hamlet's say-so.

We are, of course—and nobody denies it—meant to admire
Horatio. Hamlet himself shows us the way. Yet Hamlet's

*It does not matter whether or not we substitute the First Folio's 'our philo-
sophy' for the Quartos' 'your philosophy'. We have already seen enough of Hamlet's
present disingenuousness when he is confessing his own inadequacy – 'for my own
poor part' – to distrust him should he be offering to share in another's. In such a
context 'our' can be more coercive than 'your'.

praise of Horatio, when it comes, is not really very different, apart from its being couched in terms of affection, from his disparagement of him. The grounds for both are pretty much the same: Horatio averts his gaze from life's mysteries and is impassive in the face of its sufferings. The contrast between such a man and himself, whichever way he arranges it, is flattering to Hamlet. For after all, there is no tribute less expensive than that paid by the imaginative, the impetuous, and the passionate, to their happier opposites. Nor is there any tribute it is more insulting to receive or more difficult to escape from. It creates what it purports to admire. In that scene in which Horatio receives with scarcely a word — but with that word, reluctantly — the impress of Hamlet's idea of him, he is intensely there in ironic corroboration of Hamlet's tribute — a man put upon and having equally to suffer:

Hamlet. Horatio, thou art e'en as just a man
        As e'er my conversation coped withal.
Horatio. O, my dear lord —
Hamlet.   Nay, do not think I flatter.
   . . . .
              thou hast been
As one in suff'ring all that suffers nothing,
A man that Fortune's buffets and rewards
Hast ta'en with equal thanks; and blest are those
Whose blood and judgement are so well commeddled
That they are not a pipe for Fortune's finger
To sound what stop she please. Give me that man
That is not passion's slave. . .

I have no doubt that all Hamlet does here he does in the name of the warmest good-fellowship. The suddenness of the impulse to have this said, the awareness of the uncomfortableness he is producing and of when to desist, bespeak that tact which is sincerity and convince us his game is not flattery. But he has a game whether he knows it or not, and its prize is the dignifying of his own emotional tumult. It is no accident that critics go to this passage to discover the terms for their commendation of Hamlet himself. For, beautiful as Hamlet's description of his friend's nature is, much as that masterpiece of perfectly harmonized humours earns our respect and our esteem, we incorrigibly reserve our highest admiration for men whose character suffers some intriguing imbalance, men in whom a passion destructively preponderates. We have a fondness for a soaring impatience and a soft spot for a flaw. In declaring himself light in Horatio's virtues Hamlet equips himself for the role of the Tragic Hero.

As for Horatio, as Hamlet represents it such has been his 'character' ever since, notwithstanding the ascendancy his blood wins over his judgement when, with everybody dying around him, he acts in passion and tries to swallow the poison himself. But even there he is denied a major part in the story. His role is to be to *tell* it. To postpone 'felicity' to tell it. All is softened now into a sublime mellifluence, but Hamlet is still insisting that Horatio stay Horatio. As far as this catastrophe is concerned he is to remain an onlooker, consigned yet again to that 'business' and to those 'desires' which Hamlet has decided for him are his. Such is the doom of Horatios. Most men need one and most men find one. Horatios exist relatively, and no doubt, in other circumstances, find Horatios of their own.

Had Hamlet kept company with Macbeth he might have borne such a commission himself. But then Macbeth, who had no reason to doubt the extremity of *his* affliction or the severity of *his* experience, would not have needed him.

When Hamlet drops into his first soliloquy upon the inelegant exit of Claudius, Gertrude and the court, it is as if those who have just left have been no more than a troublesome interruption to his thoughts. Even that discomfiture of Claudius which Hamlet has effected, if he has noticed it, elicits from him no response or satisfaction. His mind, impatient of particulars, seems to return with relief to itself and to that large and general despondency wherein a vague apprehension of wrongness outweighs any sins he can enumerate. As his imagination seeks to reaffirm the hatefulness of the present, a wilful mis-remembering serves the idealization of a happier past:

> That it should come to this,
> But two months dead, nay, not so much, not two,
> So excellent a king, that was to this
> Hyperion to a satyr, so loving to my mother
> That he might not beteem the winds of heaven
> Visit her face too roughly. Heaven and earth,
> Must I remember? Why, she would hang on him
> As if increase of appetite had grown
> By what it fed on. . . .

Hamlet's father might indeed have been a man of great gentleness, and Gertrude, we know, is always affectionate; but we need to know nothing of either of them to know they were not like this. It is not cynicism that tells us such a union never was; the tell-tale sign that these are creatures of Hamlet's imagination is his disposition to make now one thing, now another, of devotion. There is nothing either good or bad but thinking makes it so! Lovingness in his father is almost sexless in its exquisite and fastidious protectiveness; lovingness in his mother is an ugly and insatiable sexual greed. They must have had a strange time of it, those two.

Hamlet's account of the unprofitableness, not just of uncles and mothers but of all the uses of this world, has never wanted for sympathisers; yet I doubt if anyone would have listened to him much if his sense of weariness, staleness, and flatness, had found expression in a matching exhaustion of interest and language. As it is, his despondency is not all enervation. It draws its allusions from history and literature; it is at home with philosophy and religion; it casts an eye both envious and ironic upon the world of action and adventure. It delights in stinging puns and quick rebukes, in rapid combinations of ideas and in urgent quests for general truths. Yet for all that Hamlet's mind is richly stored with those materials, and attended by those natural endowments, which should make for an active perspicacity, it is not a productive energy of thought that we initially see. As Hamlet figures his mother hanging upon her husband, so does his imagination hang upon his own disappointments and revulsions —

> As if increase of appetite had grown
> By what it fed on.

A sickening sense of faculties helplessly frustrating themselves pervades this first soliloquy, so that we come to see why it is that Hamlet finally almost welcomes the inconsequent idea that he is condemned to inactivity and silence:

> It is not, nor it cannot come to good.
> But break my heart, for I must hold my tongue.

If such a constraint has been enjoined upon Hamlet, he shows no sign, before or after, of attending to it; but the idea blessedly simplifies his exasperation. And who would not rather admit to an inability to purposefully act — knowing, as we all do, the crude imperfections of action — than own to an incapacity to purposefully think?

Why then, framed as he is for speculation, accustomed to

reflection, and indubitably a moralist, does he make so little progress through his troubles? If we take the tip from those virtues which the play itself exhibits to the highest degree, we must say that in his first exchanges with Gertrude and Claudius, and in his early conferences with himself, what Hamlet lacks is that combination of good humour and wit, that magnanimity of intelligence which ministers to proportion and connects the imaginary to the real. Something of this kind he almost approaches when he recalls those shoes, still new, in which his mother followed her husband's body. In a speech in which the extravagantly gross makes room, momentarily, only for the extravagantly chaste, so odd and humble a detail reminds us of what a small, sad story of inconstancy it actually is, that lies behind Hamlet's deep distress. It evokes for us that domestic familiarity wherein the disruptive shock of a betrayal is most keenly felt; and it involves us in the drama of a particular woman's easy forgetfulness, as something like 'frailty, thy name is woman' does not. But even Gertrude's shoes do not have Gertrude sufficiently in them for us to feel that Hamlet is allowing the comedy of the actual to play upon his distress. We have to wait for Hamlet's first conversation with Horatio for that, but when it comes it is as if every door in the court has suddenly swung open. Hamlet's abomination of his mother's hasty re-marriage has not abated when he puts to Horatio the reason for its closeness to his father's funeral—

> Thrift, thrift, Horatio. The funeral baked meats
> Did coldly furnish forth the marriage tables

—but he brings the ugly fact out into the daylight, associates it with other familiar frailties, enmeshes the vice of inconstancy in the virtue of economy, locates a ridiculousness in the detail where previously there had been a horribleness in the generality. Claudius and Gertrude do not become less blurred in this sally, but the ordinary world that they like everybody else inhabit, does. These words of Hamlet's, in short, breathe a spirit of comedy. Great thoughts, Doctor Johnson tells us, are always general—an opinion perhaps not unconnected with his gloom of temper and the difficulties he experienced with unpoetic details in Shakespeare. Humorous thoughts are always particular. Comedy, which is the friend of the serious and seeks only to protect it from the preposterous, is the art of seeing the cheerfulness that inheres in all things when they are distinct. Hamlet, the mad, moral miasmatist in all his dealings with Gertrude, Claudius and even the poor Ophelia, none of whom he can see with any distinctness, has only to turn his shrewd, observant eye upon some detail external to his troubles—an Osric or a player's speech, a rotting skull or an unexpected view of himself—to become that sane and merry Prince who might indeed, had he been put on, have proved most royal.

If we are honest I think we must admit that we take a hand in Hamlet's delay. It is precisely during those moments which, Hamlet is to feel, waylay him from his appointed duty, that we attend to him, enjoy him, and believe him, most. We care more for his gibes and his gambols, his songs and his flashes of merriment, than for his censures of womankind and his strictures on villainy. They have more wisdom and they are more truly philosophical. For in truth, despite his restless criticism of the world and its ways, Hamlet is not a great or disturbing seer; no strong, penetrating pessimism develops from his lucubrations. He does not ransack his nature with the violence of a Lear, nor is he ever brought to Macbeth's point of utterly silencing desolation. We feel more comfortable with Hamlet than with men of that kind. He is more our intimate; smaller in his investigations and suspicions, less outraged in his discoveries and corroborations. How strange it is that the ghost of his father, so terrible in its appearance, so compelling in its demands, should yet cause so little turmoil in Hamlet's conception of his universe. He is to talk later, with a lovely wan forgetfulness, of 'that bourne' from which 'no traveller returns'—and that should remind us of what kind of play with what kind of hero this is not. 'Hume himself could not but have faith in *this* Ghost dramatically', Coleridge exclaims, testifying to the marvellously rendered terror it strikes, but testifying also, perhaps, to the absolute worldliness of this other-worldly visitation. In no respect a spirit of health, in every way a goblin damned, the ghost speaks words which are, to a mind already schooling itself in the language of distaste, as a lesson from the master. Apt pupil that he is, Hamlet goes one better than the ghost demands and offers not only to remember his words but to remember nothing else. But what has he learnt? What difference does the knowledge that his uncle is a murderer make?

> O most pernicious woman!
> O villain, villain, smiling, damned villain!
> My tables—meet it is I set it down
> That one may smile, and smile, and be a villain.

Upon the initial reception of the fact of murder, Hamlet cannot be expected to sift his feelings finely. And who is to say that his frenetic parody of his own bookishness is not as good a way of stilling his agitation as any? But what goes down in the note-book is to remain the sum of his research. What is true of Hamlet here is true of him later. The concentrated insistence of vocabulary, the storing up of hateful information for future satisfaction, the speedy passage of his thoughts into that same generality of statement that came easily to him before he knew of ghosts or murder, all bespeak a really rather modest outrage. The appallingness of the idea of murder, the appallingness of *this* murder, does not shake Hamlet to his soul and does not haunt him later. The deep damnation of the taking off is felt as only one of a series of horrors. Even for the ghost it takes its place amongst other resentments, grievances, jealousies, and for those Hamlet has an ear equally attentive. The 'To be or not to be' soliloquy which takes no cognizance of ghosts, takes no cognizance either of those fretting passions and murderous impulses that ghosts are made from. That soliloquy is a classic expression of the wearying effect, upon a sensitive spirit, of the daily injustices and ignobilities and misfortunes of life: fardels. We might wonder what Hamlet knows personally of the law's delay or the proud man's contumely, but it needs no ghost, come from the grave, to publicize them.

Once the ghost has been and gone, the dust settles about his revelations, and Hamlet's wrath runs down again into the old indignation, that sighing over life's hardships, that petty detestation of skulduggery wherein the foremost iniquities and the littlest lapses look the same. Even his revulsion from Claudius suffers no significant increase. He is scarcely a more loathed figure, to Hamlet's imagination, for killing his brother than for being inferior to him. How can Hamlet kill the King when he cannot sufficiently hate the crime? And how can he hate the crime when he cannot sufficiently *feel* it? Here again, I believe, the play invites us to be a party to Hamlet's delay, for whatever we happen to think privately about murders, *this* murder, as it is related by the ghost, as it is travestied in the play scene, and as it is relived in conscience by Claudius himself, does not make us cry out for an instant and a bloody vengeance. We do not easily associate the criminal with the crime, or the crime with anything. And we acquiesce, dramatically, in the drift of Hamlet's feelings away from it. So that when Hamlet mistakenly kills Polonius for Claudius, in a fury at a smaller criminality – when, that is to say, he shows himself eminently capable of decisive action, but sooner able to punish snooping than to punish murder – we recognize something of our common nature in him. Hamlet is not unusual in being unable to cut a clear path through his emotions along which the right detestations for the right crimes might inexorably march.

If Hamlet had succeeded in wiping from the table of his memory

> all trivial fond records,
> All saws of books, all forms, all pressures past
> That youth and observation copied there,

and devoted his thoughts and energies exclusively to the ghost his father's cause, his morality might have been satisfied and the King might have been speedily dispatched, but he would not have been acting in accordance with the soundest promptings of his character and temper. His morality — all for concentration upon remembrance and revenge — pulls him in one direction; the natural vigour of his constitution — finding innumerable occasions for high spirits and exuberance, even in this prison which is Denmark — pulls him in another. He is never that thing of bestial oblivion he accuses himself of being, but the currents of life carry him along. The appearances of friends, the opportunities to exchange ideas and enjoy conversation, the unexpected awakenings of old enthusiasms, the putting on of a play and the setting of traps for Claudius (where the detection is everything and the morality can look after itself), the common pleasures and the common irritations, are all distractions, calls upon his despondency and grief, invitations to forgetfulness. Forgetfulness, when it is a policy, or merely the prompt sequel to a short memory, is odious, but when it is the imperceptible progress of healing tissue it is sound and desirable, the salutary sign of a robust nature. For the possession of which Hamlet can scarcely forgive himself.

Not to feel, not to remember, not to make memory issue into action — what is that but to be no better than his mother? Worse even:

> What is man,
> If his chief good and market of his time
> Be but to sleep and feed? A beast, no more.

Between the beast that only sleeps and feeds and the angel that only loves and avenges, Hamlet is prepared to countenance the existence of no other creature. And there might have been something saintly in that were there not something more approachably human. For if Hamlet is relentless with himself and selects his options absolutely, he is also the first to see the absurdity of his own exorbitant demands. Even as he delivers those lines he stares with wonderment and derision at the particular alternative to slothful bestiality that prompts them: the person of Fortinbras—puffed with divine ambition and ready to find quarrel in a straw. So this is what it means to grasp a purpose and be the author of oneself! Very well then, he will take the part:

> O, from this time forth,
> My thoughts be bloody, or be nothing worth!

—but he does not believe in the play.

Examples gross as earth exhort Hamlet to that fervour of resolution which he longs to have, but they none of them get past the indomitable sagacity of his humour. As with Fortinbras, so with the Player:

> Is it not monstrous that this player here,
> But in a fiction, in a dream of passion,
> Could force his soul so to his own conceit
> That from her working all his visage wanned,
> Tears in his eyes, distraction in his aspect,
> A broken voice, and his whole function suiting
> With forms to his conceit? And all for nothing,
> For Hecuba!
> What's Hecuba to him, or he to Hecuba,
> That he should weep for her?

How irresistibly good-natured that raillery is! And how inevitable it is that the efficacy of the example should lose itself in the consummate mimicry. There is nothing for Hamlet to learn here, and he knows it even as he rehearses the lesson.

It is the same when he witnesses Laertes, demonstrating, with more motive than Fortinbras and more cue than the Player, the magnitude of *his* sorrow. Except that now Hamlet is past the point of tempering with admiration his disdain for the grandiloquent language of passion and the extravagant postures of constancy:

> What is he whose grief
> Bears such an emphasis? whose phrase of sorrow
> Conjures the wand'ring stars, and makes them stand
> Like wonder-wounded hearers?

No watchful, self-reproving soliloquy this time. The wild fantasy of the leap into Ophelia's grave is both parody and performance of what he can no longer pretend to find exemplary:

> Woo't weep? woo't fight? woo't fast? woo't tear thyself?
> Woo't drink up eisel? eat a crocodile?
> I'll do't.

Neither love for Ophelia nor resentment of Laertes has much
to do with this. Ophelia's death is soon forgotten, and Hamlet
knows it is easier to make Laertes look ridiculous in an
apology than in a brawl. The real object of Hamlet's savagery
is himself: the cruel fortuity of his fate, the preposterousness
of his cause. Nothing explains the bitter exasperation of his
buffoonery here, but his knowledge that the high, swift
vindictiveness of passion which everything tells him should,
by right, be his, can be so only by some lunatic distortion of
everything else it is native to him to feel and to believe. What
business has he, that Prince of fine, fastidious sensibility and
broad, discerning wit, who cannot suffer bombast on the
stage and seeks from actors a temperance even in the very
whirlwind of their passion—what business has he contending
for the major role in a vulgar, florid melodrama? Why, the
self-same business he has with meeting ghosts on battlements,
hearing tales of leperous distilments poured into the porches
of his father's ear, and swearing, as a consequence, an eternal
memory and a bloody revenge. So be it. Behold and see:

This is I,
Hamlet the Dane.

Gone is the earlier querulous incertitude, when his obliga-
tions seemed prodigious and his powers frail:

The time is out of joint. O cursed spite
That ever I was born to set it right!

The Hamlet of the antique warrior cry and the leap into the
grave—Herculean at last!—has travelled a long distance from
that. But it has been no descent into the tawdry wrath which
the ghost has urged and which is second nature to Laertes.
If he no longer feels unfitted for his task it is because he now
knows the task itself to be unfitting—no more honoured in
the observance than the breach. Unless burlesque be a way of
honouring it in both.

The struggle with Laertes has few emotional repercussions
for Hamlet. Beyond leaving him with a sense that he owes
Laertes something—an apology, which turns out, in the utterance, to be three parts patronage—it seems to pass quickly
from his mind. The next scene discovers a Hamlet interested
in quite other affairs and careless, almost to insolence, of
what has just occurred. Careless also, for some readers, of
the pressing rights of his revenge. As Hamlet dilates upon
them to Horatio, do we not hear, even at this eleventh hour,
a sad persistence of a familiar irresolution? No—unless we
are the ghost's advocates and have ears only for that which

promises a quick and an efficient performance of his demands:

> Does it not, think thee, stand me now upon —
> He that hath killed my king, and whored my mother,
> Popped in between th'election and my hopes,
> Thrown out his angle for my proper life,
> And with such coz'nage — is't not perfect conscience
> To quit him with this arm?

How far Hamlet's question is rhetorical, seeking to soften Horatio's scarce spoken but much registered disapproval of his friend's mounting tale of impetuous subversion, and how far it is a plea for reassurance (which is noticeably not forthcoming), it is difficult to say, and unnecessary to decide. Belatedness and prevarication might have been the charge against this enumeration, yet again, of lapsed grievances, were it not that those grievances are apprehended very differently now. Almost in proportion as Claudius' crimes have multiplied and swollen have they lost, for Hamlet, their old murkiness. There is a decided jauntiness in his rehearsal of them. Alongside that 'popping' and 'angling' even the 'whoring' sounds fairly jolly. Killing the king is still killing the king, but there is more of king than father now. That murder, the prevented rightful election, the fishing for Hamlet's own life, all seem, in the account, more like impertinences to the state than offences to himself. There is a bright, new impersonality about Hamlet here, an aloofness. The cool requirements of a 'perfect conscience' (relishing more the symmetry than the urgency of justice) have supplanted that dark responsibility of being scourge and minister enjoined upon him by the ghost. The existence of Claudius and his now more seemingly breezy villainies is no longer a test, for Hamlet, of his own courage and constancy and worth. He has left himself out of it, at last.

The care-ridden Hamlet of the first four acts of the play scarcely shows himself in the fifth. As a man who has no more to discover within himself he returns to Denmark with no taste for the introspective soliloquising of earlier days. The memory of the ghost, too, seems to have lapsed, and with it all asseveration of his cause and reiteration of his language. Whether the sea-air has been beneficial to Hamlet, or his adventures have stilled his nerve and deprived action of its mysteries, or whether something long forming in his soul would have made the difference without such stimulants, different he undoubtedly is. Even the graveyard, with all its fatal, morbid allurements, does not induce in him the

melancholy brooding and theatricality that once waited upon
the flourish of his inky cloak. Nor does its tale of human
frailty and vanity call from him any of the immodest cynicism, the self-pleasing disenchantment, which scarred his
former reasoning. The most innocent of artifices were once
dismantled thus:

> I have heard of your paintings, too well enough. God
> hath given you one face, and you make yourselves
> another. You jig, you amble, and you lisp.

But the graveside words that Hamlet utters on a similar
theme, as a challenge to the comic genius of Yorick, are of
another humour altogether:

> Now get you to my lady's chamber, and tell her, let her
> paint an inch thick, to this favor she must come. Make
> her laugh at that.

The voice is no longer that of the fervid satirist, alert to every
wile and snare, and eager to see through illusion and tear
down pretence. There is nothing luridly threatening about
the make-up this time, however thickly applied. If my lady
will not laugh it is not because of her painted duplicity; and
Yorick's failure will say as much about the limited powers of
jesters as it will say about the vain falsities of women. It is
not their endeavours that Hamlet laments, but the piteous
transience which thwarts them.

Things rank and gross in nature do not possess Hamlet's
imagination now. The politician that would circumvent God,
Lord Such-a-one that praised Lord Such-a-one's horse, the
lawyer deprived once for all of his quiddities and quillities
and unable to bring an action for battery against the mad
knave that knocks him about the sconce with a dirty shovel,
Cain, Yorick, Alexander and Caesar—all the graveyard's
inhabitants, possible and impossible, conjured into life and
out of it again with such extraordinary abundance of wit—
are none of them undelightful to Hamlet, quintessential dust
as they now are. He moves about their brief hopes and
fancies as he moves about the graveyard, now with a
poignant, desolate playfulness, now with a haunting quietude,
and now again with a startling train of quick, comic asso-
ciations. The futility of the greatest of aspirations, and the
meanest, can seldom have been demonstrated with so much
exuberance and at the same time so little diminution of the
human nature whose fate such futility is. Hamlet's bones
ache, and his gorge rises, but beneath everything he says and
does there seems to lie some surety, some absolute

collectedness of spirits which, while having nothing in common with the gravedigger's gross inurement or with Horatio's determined taciturnity, enables him to discover a cheerful congruence in the grand democracy he surveys. Even tracing the noble dust of Alexander can be a friendly exercise. And Horatio's famous reproof,

> 'Twere to consider too curiously, to consider so —

does not for a moment halt him in his convolutions:

> No, faith, not a jot, but to follow him thither with modesty enough, and likelihood to lead it.

Not a jot! The dismissal has all the amiability of a perfect assurance. Time was when Horatio's more modest objections were less kindly treated. But that battle has been fought. Alexander's journey can be followed, should be followed, does not entail extravagance and scarcely stretches likelihood. Horatio need not be perturbed for his friend's rationality. His meaning is taken in and passed over in a second. It is no longer to be fiercely resisted, for it is no longer appropriate.

Assured, collected, indifferent to old debates and even, when the time comes, to his own person, the Hamlet of these final scenes has never been so princely. Nor has he ever had so much to say about his realm. In place of denunciations of man's general vileness, alternating with lamentations for his calamitous fortune, there now crops up in his talk a variety of leisurely observations upon the social features of his time. For the first time since we have known him, he seems to have noticed where he lives. And it is with the courteous and casual eye of the aristocrat that he notices. Coriolanus himself would have sympathised with the sentiments of this statement, though he could not have managed its nonchalance:

> By the Lord, Horatio, this three years I have taken note of it,

(but not in our hearing)

> the age is grown so picked that the toe of the peasant comes so near the heel of the courtier he galls his kibe.

Nonchalant, for he is amused by a spectacle. It is not on behalf of the courtiers whose kibes are threatened that Hamlet speaks. A member of that class is soon to appear, and he must stand awkwardly waiting while Hamlet whispers his disdain for him into Horatio's ear:

Hamlet. Dost know this waterfly?

Horatio. No, my good lord.

Hamlet. Thy state is the more gracious, for 'tis a vice to know him. He hath much land, and fertile. Let a beast be a lord of beasts, and his crib shall stand at the king's mess. 'Tis a chough, but, as I say, spacious in the possession of dirt.

The estimate is not gentle, but it is made with the coolest aplomb. Osric does not touch Hamlet nearly. His flourishes and ill-gotten gentilities are parodied with none of the savagery that Hamlet once meted out to less egregious folly. Osric is nothing; the times are more to blame than he:

> Thus has he, and many more of the same bevy that I know the drossy age dotes on, only got the tune of the time and, out of an habit of encounter, a kind of yeasty collection, which carries them through and through the most fanned and winnowed opinions; and do but blow them to their trial, the bubbles are out.

But even the times, discerned with such nice particularity – the 'drossy age' has a reality the 'unweeded garden' never had – do not earn from Hamlet anything but an equable, a passing contempt. There is much in them to notice, much to dislike, much to be amused by, but they are not for Hamlet to put right. Let the *stricken* deer go weep!

So, with little enthusiasm for his deed, but with less for its postponement, Hamlet as much allows as effects his revenge. Thereby failing neither his morality, which for so long clamoured for its rights, nor his humour – his intelligence – which could only grow careless of them. The achievement is not spectacular; it has not so far exceeded the common as to confer any awesome nobility upon our human capacities and devices. But that which is common need by no means be negligible; and for Hamlet to have attained some such recognition himself, to have assented without cynicism to the general imperfections of action and nature, is a prodigious achievement for *him*. Which other tragic hero in Shakespeare makes such a good job of healing his own divisions?

But perhaps the final effects of the play are not tragic at all. There seems to be so much propriety in all that happens. Hamlet prophesies the election will light on Fortinbras and gives him his dying voice – a decision in favour of an active, practical man which consorts perfectly with those lenient accommodations to a middling world which Hamlet was making right up to his quitting it. Fortinbras duly arrives, refers with solemnity – as how could he do otherwise? – to

Death's gluttony, and knowing nothing of Hamlet personally, but being himself a soldier, pays Hamlet the finest tribute a soldier knows, and prepares for him a military funeral. For those of us who would have order restored, order is restored; and for those who would have a little final piquancy, there is the odd inappropriateness of Hamlet's funeral. But that latter is only very slightly odd and is not, certainly, ironic. We do not feel that Fortinbras has made some telling error, or that the soldiers' music and the rites or war either serve Hamlet too generously, or pay him scant respect. Do we not feel, rather, that while everything that is passing before us is not exquisitely right, it is perfectly satisfactory? and that while Hamlet might have proved most royal, and was indeed proving so, Denmark will still be the better for having Fortinbras at its helm? A politic and a worldly appraisal, perhaps, but also a considerate one, fitting both to the character of Hamlet and to the talents of Fortinbras. As it is magnanimous to the world they have variously inhabited.

III

Macbeth
What's Done, Is Done

1 · SCOTLAND, NOT ENGLAND

Were the Japanese makers of the film, *Throne of Blood,* so very wrong about this play? Is Macbeth not as strange to us, and just as grotesque a hero, as any grunting, howling, arrow-bequilled samurai could ever be? A man of lurid and bloody imaginings, repulsive to the point of bestiality, a prey to superstitions which would be ludicrous if their consequences were not so grisly, his proper place would seem to be in a casebook of criminal pathology — with Jack the Ripper on one side and the Kray brothers on the other — not in a Great Paradigm Tragedy. The very operations of conscience in him look like chicken-hearted vacillation. His only consistency is the maniacal pursuit of — by the worst means — the worst. And the only thing he perceives with any steadiness is, at the last, the desert of unmeaning he has made of his world. What strange theatrical confidence-trick has Shakespeare pulled, to make us feel the great bond of a common humanity with him?

The temptation, which every reader must have felt at some time, is to invent some mysterious virtue in the man which (mysteriously) counteracts all that is repellent in him — be it conscience, or courage, or contempt of fortune. And the temptation is strong because, somehow, we have to account for the fact that this barbarian butcher has always been regarded as a classic tragic hero, and will, I daresay, go on being so regarded. There is no getting round the fact of Macbeth's stature. And yet all the attempts to rationalise that stature as a personal attribute of his nature remain specious: they have to turn their backs on the criminal, in order to discover the hero.*

There is a naive transposition of bloody violence into innocuous mental-moral event to which we sedentary critical gentlemen ('Persons with gold-rimmed spectacles whose usual occupation is to spy upon the obvious', as Conrad has it) are

* (I include the attempt I made myself ten years ago.)

peculiarly prone—the unconscious vengeance of Mind, perhaps it is, upon the most threatening variety of Mindlessness.
We can very swiftly make over your blood into 'an image',
your man of blood into 'a study in conscience', and the
action of *Macbeth* into a statement of evil. Shakespeare is
thereby made safe for literature. But it can never be safe to
hear, in Lady Macbeth's voice, the mixture of drunken
gloating and horrified loathing which is murder—

> yet who would have thought the old man to have had
> so much blood in him—

and when we call it 'evil' (or even 'Evil') we express little
more than the incomprehension of our necessary outrage.
The criminal in someone like Claudius may be elusive. It
is possible to remain in a state of bemused bafflement as to
what, precisely, happened in the orchard of Elsinore. But one
can entertain no such doubts as to what happened in Duncan's
chamber, or as to the state in which Macbeth's hired thugs
left Banquo's skull. And Lady Macduff's screams are not
open to variety of interpretation. What, in heaven's name,
would a compensating virtue look like which would compen-
sate for all this?

It is not much of an advance, either, to apply the household solvent 'Dramatic Poem' to the fabric of the drama—
pretending that the play's power has not much to do with
'characters' and very much to do with an imaginative structure of Ideas and Values. It has everything to do with character—and with Macbeth's character above all. Dissolve that,
and you have nothing recognisable left. Yet Macbeth, for
much of his stage life, is despicable as only the moral coward
turned bully-tyrant can be.

So one casts about for the enabling-ennobling precedent—
disdaining, of course, the sentimental duplicity of the
Western badman (who is never really bad anyway), to toy
with the Clytemnestras and Electras of Greek drama (but the
individual crime is held, for the Greeks, firmly within the
substantive categories of family, state, and race, and conscience is profoundly social). Norse saga, then? Woyzeck
(except that Büchner has already saturated himself in *Macbeth*)? Or there is Dostoevsky. . . .

But Macbeth is no Raskolnikov in a kilt, either. Raskolnikov's criminality is a feverish ague that shakes his moral
adolescence for four hundred pages, but it has its climacteric,
and there is some expectation, at its end, that Sonya and
Siberia will steady his pulses, lower his temperature, and cure
his delirium. Whereupon the interest of his case lapses: for,

for all the virtuosity of the handling, Raskolnikov remains a case. But Macbeth is no case. He is presented to us with that commanding mastery which creates, by assuming, a human centrality for its subject. With his kind of criminality the notion of cure is an impertinence. Throw physic to the dogs: he'll none of it.

Try (if you doubt it) to imagine a 'healthy' Macbeth – one who is able to rest in the impeccable logic of

> If chance will have me king,
> Why chance may crown me,
> Without my stir.

A Macbeth who, having answered his wife's persuasions with

> I dare do all that may become a man,
> Who dares do more, is none

(a complete answer!), firmly declines further argument, and amuses himself thereafter with occasional sallies from Cawdor Castle to unseam a passing Norwegian; who becomes a loyal and trusted liegeman to the boy Malcolm, when he succeeds to the throne; is to be seen at his own fireside on winter evenings, deep in conference with his old battle-comrade Banquo, with whom he enjoys metaphysical discussions on dreams and prophecies, free-will and necessity, spiced with reminiscences about witches of their acquaintance; until at a ripe old age he is elected to the throne (Malcolm having died of the combined avarice, gluttony and lechery he had promised to disclose once in power). I'm not just being facetious. Isn't it impossible (a) to feel that this calmly rational accommodation is *available* in the world we're shown? and (b) to pretend that it would be half as grand and gripping as what we are shown? This Macbeth would be so much *less* the man.

Interestingly, the play does give us just such a grizzled old warrior: Seyward is the Macbeth-that-might-have-been, who enjoys the honour, love, obedience, troops of friends that should accompany old age. But Seyward's leaf has yellowed in autumnal, Christian England. And Seyward is peripheral to the main design.

Macbeth falls into the sere in pagan Scotland, where – everything combines to suggest – humane statute is far from having purged the gentle weal.

This Scotland is a climate, a landscape, a moral ambience, a political entity, and a structure of social habituations. And it is not England. Indeed one way of phrasing one's objections to the all-too-numerous *Macbeths moralisés* one has met, would be to remark that they seem to think it *is* England. They want it cosy, well-hedged and benignly arable. Whereas Shakespeare has given us something colder, wilder, and more frightening. Not however in some unfocussed atmospheric way. I know I'm not the only reader of the *Journey to the Western Isles* who has been struck by the way Johnson's factuality keeps adumbrating a Scottishness very close to that projected by Shakespeare's creativity. Johnson, plumped on a bank amid his blasted heath, for instance, seems to be feeling some such subversive drag upon his humane habituations as shook Macbeth's footing so drastically:

> We were in this place at ease and by choice, and had no evils to suffer or to fear; yet the imaginations excited by the view of an unknown and untravelled wilderness are not such as arise in the artificial solitude of parks and gardens, a flattering notion of self-sufficiency, a placid indulgence of voluntary delusions, a secure expansion of the fancy, or a cool concentration of the mental powers. The phantoms which haunt a desert are want, and misery, and danger; the evils of dereliction rush upon the thoughts; man is made unwillingly acquainted with his own weakness, and meditation shews him only how little he can sustain, and how little he can perform. There were no traces of inhabitants, except perhaps a rude pile of clods called a summer hut, in which a herdsman had rested in the favourable seasons. Whoever had been in the place where I then sat, unprovided with provisions, and ignorant of the country, might, at least before roads were made, have wandered among the rocks, till he had perished with hardship, before he could have found either food or shelter.

Very much the place, that, where, on a foul-fair day, one wraps one's cloak about one and shudders one's distaste: 'How far is't call'd to Forres?' (Understood: the nearer the better). In this place, Johnson tells us, he first conceived the idea of his narrative. There was something about this Scotland that challenged explanation.

Shakespeare does not show Johnson's explicit interest in socio-economic process: poverty of soil producing sparsity of population, which in turn promotes savagery of manners and suspicion of temper—which, further intensified by a difficult terrain, gives rise to chronic banditry and clan feud. But the chain of interlaced causes lies behind the fierce warrior society we are introduced to in the second scene, and Shakespeare seems as well aware as Johnson of the way a national temper is shaped by these conditions.

Among a warlike people, the quality of highest esteem is personal courage, and with the ostentatious display of courage are closely connected promptitude of offence, and quickness of resentment.

'O valiant cousin, worthy gentleman!' is Duncan's salute to that quality in his General. And in its unconsciousness of oddity, the remark reveals a society where being 'too full o'th'milk of humane kindness' is bound to be felt as a weakness, and where treachery will excite minimal comment. Standing before a Scottish castle Johnson had no difficulty imagining himself

> interrogated from the battlements, admitted with caution at the gate, introduced to a petty monarch, fierce with habitual hostility, and vigilant with ignorant suspicion; who, according to his general temper, or accidental humour, would have seated a stranger as his guest at the table, or as a spy confined him in the dungeon.

He did not have to stick at imagining it, either, for everywhere he went, Johnson heard tales of clan feud, massacre, conspiracy, and dynastic butchery – tales not so very different from the ones Shakespeare found in his Holinshed, and out of which he stitched together *his* tale of Macbeth.

The Scotland of that play is no mere 'country of the mind'. It is as real, as historical a place as the one Johnson visited. And Shakespeare's interest in it is as properly historical as Johnson's. He wants to understand its essential dynamic. For he is writing the moral history of a peculiar phase of culture – the barbarian, warrior phase, 'ere humane statute purg'd the gentle weal' – and Scotland was the classic case that lay on his own doorstep.

The moral history of a culture will always involve some account of the peculiar ways a people feels itself to exist within its environment. And in Scotland, Shakespeare's or Johnson's, humanity's hold on the country feels forever tenuous. So that the sudden passage from 'the ruggedness of moors, to seats of plenty, gaiety, and magnificence' can strike the traveller with a surprise 'analogous to that which is felt at an unexpected emersion from darkness into light.' The surprise of Duncan, perhaps, at the hautboys, torches and martlets of Macbeth's castle –

> This castle hath a pleasant seat, the air
> Nimbly and sweetly recommends itself
> Unto our gentle senses.

The celebration has all the premature lyricism of relief. Such places are rare. Their hospitable solidity, warmth, light and music is the blessed exception to a nearly universal wilderness. As Egdon Heath is the imaginative co-ordinant of Hardy's novel, so the blasted heath of the Witches is the imaginative heartland of Shakespeare's Scotland. Humanity is a mere excrescence. The two Generals we see trudging across it, dwarfed and stoical, accompanied only by an offstage drum, represent the victorious army; and they are indistinguishable from a pair of straggling fugitives. From time to time the heath reverberates to the sound of unseen galloping horsemen, but the sounds only deepen the sense of solitude, just as the appearance of the Witches increases the isolation of Macbeth and Banquo:

> What are these,
> So wither'd and so wild in their attire,
> That look not like th' inhabitants o'th' earth
> And yet are on it?

They are, as Banquo, mastering his surprise, quickly realises, the very spirit of this soil:

> The earth hath bubbles, as the water has,
> And these are of them.

Heath-dwellers must learn not to be too startled by them.

Doctor Johnson reports, with some complacence that *he* met no witches on the road to Forres. But he did inquire earnestly into the 'Second Sight' he heard everywhere discussed, and finished up willing to credit 'the local frequency of a power which is nowhere totally unknown'. Somehow it didn't seem so foolish, this 'indistinct cry of national persuasion', as it might have done from the rational security of Fleet Street. It was not some fey, whimsical, spinsterish superstition, but something grimly primitive, with which he found himself unaccountably in touch, 'on the heath'.

It doesn't seem arbitrary there, for instance, to interpret '*prediction*/Of noble having, and of royal hope' as a 'supernatural *soliciting*' to crime. Even the civilised Banquo is pretty prompt to name the solicitors as 'instruments of darkness', and to wonder whether the whole thing isn't some devilish trap for the unwary. He counters, that is to say, one superstition by appealing to another. There is no question of laughing it all off. And it is a troubled rationalist who, on the

fulfilment of the first head of the prophecy, blurts out,
'What, can the devil speak true?'

In this place, scoured with violent winds and barbarically
resistant to humanisation, superstition and insight tend to
fuse: so that a man may glimpse, out of the corner of his
eye (as it were), 'a naked newborn babe,/Striding the blast',
or contend against 'the sightless couriers of the air' which
'blow the horrid deed in every eye' so that tears 'drown
the wind'. The force of the metaphor arises from the daily
experience of struggling with streaming eyes into a violent,
naked wind. This is Nature, for the play—not the only
nature, but the one most potently operative from the start.
Macbeth did not make it, and cannot change it. He, together with the other Scots, inherits it. And it is radically
hostile to the human.

It is the way they all take this world for granted that is
so potent for the play's 'climate'. When a common soldier
tries to account for the rash of rebellion that has broken
out, he can only say (of one traitorous chieftain) that he is

> Worthy to be a rebel, for to that
> The multiplying villainies of *nature*
> Do swarm upon him.

In a similarly unthinking way Lady Macbeth invokes the
murdering ministers that wait on '*Nature's* mischief'. The
shadowy malignance of the Witches is given us as being there
before the palpable malignance of rebellion; and both are
preceded by thunder and lightning, fog and filthy air—eman-
ations as it were, of Scotland's soil and sky. The reporter of
the battle appeals naturally to the same treacherous climate
for his account of military treachery, as if it were all one:

> As whence the sun 'gins his reflection
> Shipwracking storms and direful thunders [break]:
> So from that spring, whence comfort seem'd to come,
> Discomfort swells.

While nature swarms, discomfort swells. Multiplying villainies.
Dawn itself, in these latitudes, is a ghastly and comfortless
prefiguring of the day's violence. The cheerless Fife sky,
under which the dismal conflict rages, is described as if it
were full of apocalyptic armies with streaming banners:

> Where the Norweyan banners flout the sky,
> And fan our people cold.

It is a very 'northern' imagination at work, creating a place
where what seemed corporal can melt into the air 'as breath

into the wind'. And Coleridge was not, as he feared, being 'too minute' when he noticed the appropriateness of this image 'in a cold climate'. It is one of the innumerable fine touches by which Shakespeare is naturalising his audience to the Scottish 'Nature'.

Looking beyond the foul weather and filthy air, however, even when all goes calm, this nature is felt as ominous, populous with prowling presences—stealthy, abusing sleep. Nature seems dead, but its death, like its life, constitutes a continuous menace. And repeatedly, in the play, we are given this nightly engulfing, when the stars themselves hide their fires.

Banquo, a man very susceptible to the subtler oppressions of his native climate, finds it hard, at these times, to feel that all is well. His speech is full of the starts and pauses of a man listening intently to silence.

Banquo. How goes the night, boy?
Fleance. The moon is down: I have not heard the clock.
Banquo. And she goes down at twelve.
Fleance. I take't, 'tis later, sir.
Banquo. Hold, take my sword.
　　　　There's husbandry in heaven,
　　　　Their candles are all out: take thee that too.
　　　　A heavy summons lies like lead upon me,
　　　　And yet I would not sleep:
　　　　Merciful powers, restrain in me the cursed thoughts
　　　　That nature gives way to in repose.
Enter Macbeth, and a Servant with a Torch.
　　　　Give me my sword: who's there?
Macbeth.　　　　　　　　　　　　A friend.

Conscience and climate are continuous here. Conscience is both mirrored and elicited by the sultry clouded night which lies like lead on the body and the spirit, and induces an apprehensive agitation where a man will lunge for his sword at the slightest noise. And Shakespeare has given us the oppression as felt by others besides Macbeth—has given it as air, weather, atmosphere, an affair of the lungs, and all the more powerful metaphorically for being very concretely that, first. Banquo's state is clearly related to the smothering sensations, the knocking heart, 'against the use of nature', which Macbeth suffers from; just as his lunge for his sword is related to Macbeth's 'start' when he instinctively seems to fear 'things that do sound so fair'. In Scotland these reflexes of mistrust are almost native to the air.

One could multiply examples of this unnatural nature—

light thickening, seeling night scarfing up the tender eye of
pitiful day. But they are among the most memorable things
in the play. What lies behind them is a complex reality, topo-
graphical, political, social, meteorological even. Let Macbeth's
hired assassin epitomise it in his blunt, commonplace way, as
he stands at his post, awaiting Banquo:

> The west yet glimmers with some streaks of day.
> Now spurs the lated traveller apace,
> To gain the timely inn.

The timely inn—a little beleaguered pocket of light and
warmth in a vast blasted landscape: it is unthinkable that one
should not spur apace, to reach it before nightfall. 'It will be
rain tonight', Banquo remarks, glad to be within reach of *his*
timely inn. 'Let it come down!' howls the Murderer, making
the inevitable connexion between the impersonal violence of
the skies and the lawless violence which is Scotland.

2 · HEATH-DWELLERS

Of course there is no gap between the landscape, the 'weather'
of Scotland, and its political condition. They are most
powerfully coalescent.

Shakespeare has specified a particular historical phase: a
society riven with faction, teeming with rebellious chieftains
—the merciless Macdonwald and his skipping kerns, Sueno
the Norway's king with terrible numbers, and that most dis-
loyal traitor, Cawdor, profiting by the seditious anarchy—
each horde breaking in successive waves against the kingdom.
(No wonder the Sergeant feels nature as villainously
swarming when all these fall on him in the space of a single
day.) It is a society given over to the bloodiness of tribal
violence, to ripping and unseaming, its swords smoking with
bloody execution and its battlements regularly ornamented
with severed heads; and it honours supremely the supreme
exponent of the prevailing ferocity—the super-barbarian
upon whom the meek Duncan is utterly dependent (as
Duncan himself is the first, meekly, to admit).

Most alarming is the endlessness of it all: you may build
your absolute trust where you will, but you may always pick
the wrong gentleman. Cawdors are endemic. Or perhaps we
should call it 'the Cawdor disease'. For once the savage fit is
past Cawdor becomes again the gentleman Duncan had
trusted:

> very frankly he
> Confess'd his treasons, implor'd your Highness' pardon,
> And set forth a deep repentance.

It is the behaviour of a man who has no account of his treachery to offer, beyond the fact that it was possible, and therefore attempted. He lives in a society where the overturning of kingdoms and the wresting of sceptres from established power is so familiar, and the sanctions against it so weak, that practicality becomes the only impediment—'If we should fail?' Deal with that solid matter, and objection is all but stilled. The mind settles and bends up to the feat. Morality offers no more resistance than a pile of dust. We should not be surprised that Macbeth is able to contemplate murdering Duncan. We should be surprised with what horror his mind recoils from the thought. It makes him, at once, a man apart.

Morality, we know, is never a private matter—never an *in camera* negotiation between the individual and his conscience, followed by the issue of a communiqué. It is forever being shaped by the moralities and immoralities that press upon it. It is forever social, conditioned by the expectations of the men it lives with.

The expectations of the men Macbeth lives with strike us from the start as abnormal, unusual. They are only half-civilised. The fangs and iron of a barbarian warrior-culture keep showing through the garments of polity and public order, as do the manners of 'heath-dwellers'. Smoking swords and unseamed enemies aside, there is the way these things are taken for granted—even by Duncan.

Is it not striking how, on the King's murder, everybody knows, with grim promptitude, where they are?—fighting against the undivulged pretence of treasonous malice, surrounded by the brewed tears of unfelt sorrow, and discerning daggers in men's smiles. They all live on the edge of chronic mutual suspicion, and on the Red Alert, their ears become preternaturally sharp:

> Woe, alas:
> What, in our house?

laments Lady Macbeth. Comes Banquo's swift retort:

> Too cruel anywhere.

That is not a reproach delivered sadly to the lady's tactlessness. It is the taut vigilance of the hunted animal who hears a twig snap.

> O, yet I do repent me of my fury,
> That I did kill them,

cries Macbeth. And again there is the rapier-swift reflex —
from Macduff this time:

> Wherefore did you so?

Not a question: an accusation. It is all too horribly known.
Which is probably why Macduff bursts from the murder-
chamber with such an implausible extravagance of bombast:

> O horror, horror, horror!
> Tongue nor heart cannot conceive nor name thee.

'What's the matter?' ask Macbeth and Lennox together, with
beautifully pitched bathos.

> Confusion now hath made his masterpiece:
> Most sacrilegious murther hath broke ope
> The Lord's anointed temple, and stole thence
> The life o' th' building.

The life of the building, indeed! Macduff proclaims horror
because he cannot feel it. Nobody can. They are all frozen
in postures of self-preserving wariness.

Consider Malcolm's classic response to the news, 'Your
royal father's murther'd.' It is

> Oh, by whom?

Well, he needs to know.

Integrity, in such a world, is subject to powerfully dis-
torting pressures. One may intend, like Banquo, to stand in
the great hand of God and fight; but private counsels of self-
preservation have a horrid knack of swamping public fears
and scruples. As we discover on his next appearance:

> Thou hast it now, King, Cawdor, Glamis, all
> As the weird woman promis'd, and I fear
> Thou play'st most foully for it: yet. . .

(even Banquo, a man of palpable integrity, feels the under-
tow of criminal licence)

> . . .yet it was said
> It should not stand in thy posterity
> But that myself should be the root and father
> Of many Kings. If there come truth from them. . .
> Why. . .may they not. . .But hush, no more.

In Scotland you may cry hush to these impulses, yet still go
on entertaining them, with your 'ifs' and 'whys'. Just as

you may understand perfectly what is meant by

> If you shall cleave to my consent,
> When 'tis, it shall make honour for you,

yet encounter it, not with a categorical negative, but with a cautious conditional:

> So I lose none,
> In seeking to augment it, but still keep
> My bosom franchis'd, and allegiance clear,
> I shall be counsell'd.

Banquo is showing, as always, the fearlessness of a clear spirit (also issuing a tactful warning). Yet the urbane accommodation is muddied, ominous with incipient compromise. He *wants* his children to be kings. 'Good repose the while', replies Macbeth. But neither Banquo nor he is to have much of that. It is a mockery in this Scotland. Macbeth is not the only murderer of sleep.

The minor characters who, we are sometimes told, are only minimally characterised, show this same guarded wariness. Macduff's reading of the post-murder situation—so contemptibly easy to make—though it may brush aside the superstitious maunderings of Ross and the Old Man, nevertheless swathes itself in protective double-talk:

> *Ross.* Will you to Scone?
> *Macduff.* No cousin, I'll to Fife.
> *Ross.* Well, I will thither.
> *Macduff.* Well may you see things well done there: Adieu.
>   Lest our old robes sit easier than our new.

He returns to skulk in Fife. It is the negative self-preservation of a man who knows the reality of power when he breaks his shins against it, and who chooses the evasion of 'a low profile'. He, like Banquo, is to pay a stunning price for his thoroughly natural pusillanimity—though, unlike Banquo, he lives to whip himself for it. The debate as to whether he is, or is not, a traitor is no mere verbal misunderstanding. It is a real question which he is to answer categorically:

> Sinful Macduff,
> They were all strook for thee: naught that I am,
> Not for their own demerits, but for mine
> Fell slaughter on their souls.

Or there is Ross, paralysed by the fear of his own fears, and suffering the same submission to obscure compulsion:

> But cruel are the times, when we are traitors
> And do not know ourselves.

As just such a traitor, he leaves Lady Macduff to her fore-
boding and her fate. Like the Messenger—another 'homely
man'—'he dare abide no longer'.

Or there is Lennox, whom we see alleviating his impotence
by ferocious sarcasm: forgotten and betraying circumstances
are beginning to come back to him, about those few stunned
minutes he spent in the royal chamber with Macbeth.

> Did he not straight
> In pious rage, the two delinquents tear,
> That were the slaves of drink, and thralls of sleep?
> Was not that nobly done? Ay, and wisely, too:
> For 'twould have anger'd any heart alive
> To hear the men deny't. So that I say,
> He has borne all things well, and I do think,
> That had he Duncan's sons under his key,
> (As, and't please heaven he shall not) they should find
> What 'twere to kill a father: so should Fleance.
> But peace. . . .

'But hush, no more'. 'But peace'. And Lennox remains in the
service of Macbeth, seeing all, doing nothing. Unless you
count his invocation of 'some holy angel' to fly to the court
of England, as 'doing'.

These attitudes and conditions have not been created
single-handed by a wicked tyrant. They are brutally known —
known to the point of stupefaction, as Lennox's tone makes
plain. And if anybody does manage to

> Give to our tables meat, sleep to our nights:
> Free from our feasts and banquets bloody knives;
> Do faithful homage, and receive free honours,

he will have effected a major revolution. There is no sign that
the Scots have much experience of such conditions.

No, I am not forgetting Duncan, 'so clear in his great
office'. I am just trying to remember what minimal effect
that clearness appears to have upon Sueno, Macdonwald,
Cawdor, and is to have on the man who comments upon it.
In this world Duncan is, for all his courage, frankness and
decency—indeed, *because* of them—an anomaly. Shakespeare has suppressed all Holinshed's references to his weakness and inefficiency in order to heighten the anomaly. His
subjects hardly know what to make of him, except as some
inexplicably blessed hiatus in the long tale of rebellion,
murder and mistrust.

But one subject above all is *trying* to make sense of his reactions to the appalling trustfulness:

> He's here in double trust;
> First, as I am his kinsman, and his subject,
> Strong both against the deed: then, as his host,
> Who should against his murtherer shut the door,
> Not bear the knife myself. Besides, this Duncan
> Hath borne his faculties so meek; hath been
> So clear in his great office, that his virtues
> Will plead like angels, trumpet-tongu'd against
> The deep damnation of his taking off.

It is strange that none of these impediments proves really 'strong against the deed'. But is it very strange? As one hears in Macbeth's voice the involuntary rise of pitying contempt, does one not also understand how it may be the 'virtues' themselves which elicit the contempt? – 'Besides, this. . .this (what can I call the phenomenon?). . .this *Duncan*. . .hath borne his faculties so. . .(what is the word to do justice to its simultaneous integrity and feebleness?). . .so *meek!*' Macbeth strains every nerve, but he cannot respect meekness. He cannot put his own energy of being into felt subjugation to meekness. It is not ambition that demands the murder – ambition is mere foredoomed and foreseen miscalculation, an overleaping of itself. It is some primal disquality of being which cannot be wished away. Macbeth wishes with every fibre of his being; he concludes, 'We will proceed no further in this business.' But 'this business' has a momentum deeper than any such conscious, prudential decision-making. Duncan – and this is a paradox to which the play allows every possible grimness – is a standing provocation to all that is murderous in Macbeth's nature: and the murderous in his nature, such is the state of his country, is inseparable from his manhood. In England this would be preposterous, monstrous; for there, humane statute has purged the gentle weal, and a different conception of manhood has been made viable. Macbeth could be a Seyward, in England. In Scotland he cannot.

And Duncan shows every sign of knowing this – of knowing, I mean, that his trust, whether in Cawdor or Macbeth, is a moral candle held aloft in a gale, shedding little light, and threatened permanently with extinction. Connoisseurs of 'dramatic irony' will have it that he turns, from his melancholy reflections on Cawdor's treachery to the embracing of Macbeth's treachery, with a sublime unconsciousness – exclaiming 'Oh worthiest cousin!' Irony seems rather an honorific title for so crude an effect. And what is dramatic about it? It is equally possible that Duncan *knows* the Cawdor-pestilence may strike again at any time. Why may not the irony of his trustfulness be one that he has fully absorbed? He just knows there is no alternative:

> Though all things foul would wear the brows of grace,
> Yet grace must still look so.

So he appeals winningly to Macbeth's magnanimity, saying, as it were, 'It is not by sovereignty of nature I am king. It is not because I can finally awe, intimidate, or command you. I cannot even rule without you. But I *am* king.' It is very magnanimous, very honest, very courageous.

Yet his appeal is on a fatal basis. For it concedes the sovereignty of nature which is Macbeth's torment and temptation, and thus reinforces the criminal soliciting. He says the one thing you do *not* say to a Macbeth:

> More is thy due, than more than all can pay.

Macbeth can only mutter his reply. It is a thing he knows all too well. A thing he can only *un*know at the price of living a coward in his own esteem, like the poor cat in the adage, letting I dare not wait upon I would. And feeling himself, consequently, so much less the man.

If there were some socially supportive morality; if honour meant something more than the pervasive and barbaric warrior-honour; if Macbeth did not have to invent his own apocalyptic terrors of retribution to stand in for the just social retribution of his peers; if he didn't know with fatal contempt that these peers will tell the clock to any business that he says befits the hour – dogs all, with various qualities and functions, but uniform servility to *de facto* power; if only he were not so solitary, he would *not* have to kill Duncan. But in Scotland – and by nature – he is solitary. He has to forge his morality single-handed – an impossible task. So, blindly, futilely, he struggles, within and for his culture – trying to make the transition from savage barbarism into humanity, acting all the parts, including that of a criminal so sickening that the country finally surfeits itself on its violence, and purges itself of him and his kind, purges him, also, of himself.

The cure is, of course, not total. In the resultant convulsion, Duncan is replaced by the cagey young master of *Realpolitik,* his eldest son. This one has made a science of the mistrust he finds foisted upon him. Anything, for Malcolm, will serve as a whetstone for the sword – including the distress of a bereaved man. There is, after all, no substitute

for accurately directed Force. So that there is some irony,
and much fitness in the concluding tableau of the play —
where the new king, consecrating the end of barbarism and
the inauguration of 'faithful homage', is overlooked by the
severed head of Macbeth. The spirit of the new monarchy
may be different, but the methods are age-old: Scotland is
still proposing to solve its political problems by fixing heads
on battlements.

Violence, we know, cannot be purged by violence. But
neither can it be purged without it.

3 · COME ON, GENTLE MY LORD. . .

When one claims that Macbeth 'has to' kill Duncan, one
expects to be misunderstood (deserves to be, possibly). But
I don't know how else to put it. He 'has to' in exactly the
same sense, and with the same necessity, as he 'has to' be
himself. One is not 'endorsing' the act, or the being (to use
the language of the bank-clerk). One is simply trying to
characterise something special about both act and being, and
about the world they inhabit — I mean Macbeth's air of per-
forming, in Bradley's phrase, 'an appalling duty'. Certainly
it is difficult to specify what it could be a duty *towards,*
but there's no mistaking the fact that, in an important sense
of the word 'want', Macbeth does not want to do it, yet feels
he must — *must* settle and bend up each corporal agent to this
terrible feat. The 'feat' is a test of his manhood which he dare
not fail.

No doubt he feels it that way because of the absence of
any 'socially supportive morality', or any cogent alternative
definition of manhood. So I've been arguing. But can one
talk about his 'forging his morality singlehanded' when there
are recurrent, comradely offers of assistance coming — to look
no further — from Banquo? Why are these offers never taken
up?

Here, I think, we approach the most poignant aspect of
Macbeth's solitude. For it seems pretty clear that he simply
cannot understand an offer of moral companionship — whether
it comes from Banquo, from his wife, or from Duncan himself. It merely embarrasses and flusters his barbarian integrity
of a man of action. In these matters he is both child and
savage.

I've already mentioned his muttered response to the gift
of Duncan's gratitude, dependence and trust. We are right to
detect in it the accents of guilt. But is there not also a

straightforward embarrassment at the personal nature of the appeal, and an attempt, very clumsy, to recover some simpler, more soldierly footing?

> The service and the loyalty I owe
> In doing it, pays itself.
> Your Highness' part, is to receive our duties. . .

And he stirs uneasily to find they are not being received simply—as duties. It feels all wrong to him. If only Duncan would command. The transformation of feudal subordination into personal relation is one he can't handle.

Banquo can. And as if to sharpen the image, we see him doing so, as Duncan embraces him:

> Let me enfold thee,
> And hold thee to my heart.
> *Banquo.*   There if I grow
> The harvest is your own.

That, in its warm-hearted urbanity, is the note Macbeth should have struck.

Except that it is unthinkable. A call upon the simplest social competences makes him sweat with labour. He will withdraw from the royal banquet, of which he is host, and then be surprised when he is missed:

Lady Macbeth. Why have you left the chamber?
Macbeth. Hath he ask'd for me?
Lady Macbeth. Know you not, he has?

Assailed by an urgent internal problem, he simply withdraws, becomes 'rapt'—so conspicuously so, that his friends must make his excuses:

> New honours come upon him
> Like our strange garments, cleave not to their mould
> But with the aid of use.

It's a good thing Banquo is there to apologise for him, for his own attempts at camouflage are hopelessly inept:

> My dull brain was wrought with things forgotten.

More 'social' creatures may, when the occasion demands, make their faces vizards to their hearts, and do it with enviable facility: the mere attempt fills Macbeth's mind with scorpions. He loathes it with a deep and unremovable loathing.

Consequently he goes through the motions of social deceit like an ill-oiled marionette. He supposes that a manifested intention to reassure will have the immediate effect of reassuring:

> Do not muse at me my most worthy friends,
> I have a strange infirmity, which is nothing
> To those that know me.

This after he has staggered from the table, roared defiance at a stool, and given the most stunning demonstration of guilt-ridden terror!

Now all this is the behaviour of a man who has no conception of the common ground of human desire and impulse. What is personal to him is, by that token, unknowable to anybody else.

So of course he 'starts' when someone speaks aloud the thought he was hardly conscious of entertaining—'All hail Macbeth, that shalt be king hereafter.' The fact that they speak it is decisive proof that they 'have more in them than mortal knowledge.' How else could they know his secret aspiration?

It is poignant in its incomprehension. How, from where we sit, could anybody in Scotland *not* know it? Once Duncan is dead, he is the almost automatic choice for the throne. Even those, like Macduff and Banquo, who have their misgivings, do not well see how they can deny it him. There would have been no point in murdering Duncan, if he had not known it to be the case. Yet, in such portentous moral isolation does Macbeth live, that he imagines he is invisible in his desires. Invisible even to his wife.

> My dearest love,
> Duncan comes here tonight.
> *Lady Macbeth.* And when goes hence?
> *Macbeth.* Tomorrow, as he purposes.
> *Lady Macbeth.* O never
> Shall sun that morrow see.
> Your face, my thane, is as a book, where men
> May read strange matters.

Strange matters indeed! But a strange book, too: for her 'reading' has more than half created the text—just as her innuendo ('And when goes hence?') has elicited the tic of guilty self-correction which seems to license her construction ('Tomorrow. . . .as he purposes'). Is that evasion, or truthfulness? Is it clear, in any case, what he is evading, or being truthful about? Macbeth's social ineptitude and his moral naivety rest, both of them, upon a terrified unacquaintedness with his own desires. We do not offer to pronounce, therefore, on what he knows, because we see *he* does not know. And the unacquaintedness can issue, at one moment, in the articulate torture of a mind full of scorpions, or, as here, in some trivial scruple of fact, grotesque in its pointlessness—a pattern which repeats itself after the murder:

Lennox. Goes the King hence today?
Macbeth. He does: he did appoint so.

To see his maladroit dealings with the commonplace necessities of veracity in everyday life, is to realise that, for him, the commonplace and the everyday scarcely exist. There is only a vast shadowed region of inchoate forms and un-realised actions, horrid images which startle and unman him the moment their bubbles rise and burst in consciousness.

Banquo's offer of friendly comprehension is an offer to naturalise this underworld of unacted desire and to neutralise its terrors—by accepting them as normal. He brushes aside Macbeth's twice repeated, clumsy pretence that the main drift of the prophecy concerns his (Banquo's) children, and goes with a probing tactfulness direct to the problematical thought which must be—what could be more natural?—exercising his friend's mind. *My* children shall be kings?

> That trusted home,
> Might yet enkindle *you* unto the crown,
> Besides the Thane of Cawdor.

(The verb 'enkindle' is scrupulously poised between its active and its passive connotations—there is no accusation, and no censure.)

> But 'tis strange:
> And oftentimes, to win us to our harms
> The instruments of darkness tell us truths,
> Win us with honest trifles, to betray's
> In deepest consequence.

(Whatever he is doing with his eyes, Banquo is certainly gazing right into Macbeth's soul here.)

> Cousins, a word I pray you.

He turns to the cousins for a word, presumably because he sees no word forthcoming from his partner. He is already 'rapt'; already so plunged into furious soliloquy that he has to wrench himself back when he remembers (some thirty lines too late) that he has not yet thanked the gentlemen. Banquo's kindly penetration has not been rebuffed. His shrewd gaze has simply met the blank stare of Macbeth's self-obsession. The offer has not even been perceived.

Macbeth is unable to go Banquo's way, though it is by far

the better way. It is not in his nature. He must find his own way. In time, he *will* 'naturalise the underworld of unacted desires' — by acting the desires. He will make direness familiar to his slaughterous thoughts — by way of slaughter. And when his impulses can no longer 'start' him, as they so unmanningly do in the early part of the play, he will look back across the wilderness his 'way' has created, without remorse or self-pity. For it had to be thus. His fit will not come again. He is perfect,

> Whole as the marble, founded as the rock,
> As broad, and general, as the casing air.

Signifying nothing.

It is in his dealings with Banquo's 'royalty of nature' (Macbeth's own phrase of esteem) that we are most keenly conscious of the better way which can never be taken. Macbeth has a terrible hunger to be known, and an equally terrible mistrust of anyone who looks as if he might. He is at once fascinated and apprehensive when he sees 'considerate eyes' turned upon his inner world. And he lurches, then, from a clumsy confidentiality to a clumsy repelling of confidences, a fatal stiffness coming over him at the very moment he most desperately needs the supple language of friendship.

Banquo. What sir, not yet at rest? The King's abed.
> . . .This diamond he greets your wife withal,
> By the name of most kind hostess,
> And shut up in measureless content.
Macbeth.   Being unprepar'd,
> Our will became the servant to defect,
> Which else should free have wrought.
Banquo.   All's well.

With his usual percipience, Banquo cuts straight through the affectation of hostly over-anxiety, to the anxiety which is not affected:

> I dreamt last night of the three weird sisters:
> To you they have show'd some truth.
Macbeth. I think not of them.

(The grossly transparent lie — also the needless one, for Banquo has already confessed that he does, and wants to share his thoughts.) But Macbeth's retrieval of the blunder is, if anything, worse than the blunder, being cast egregiously in the royal plural and the royal manner:

> Yet when we can entreat an hour to serve,
> We would spend it in some words upon that business. . .

(then, remembering he is not king, yet)

>   . . .If you would grant the time.
> *Banquo.*   At your kind'st leisure.

He waits. The hour serves now. And his expectancy makes
Macbeth blurt out everything he meant to conceal.

> If you shall cleave to my consent,
> When 'tis, it shall make honour for you.

(Not that there *is* any 'consent', or is like to be. . .No, no. . .
and it is certainly not now; but 'when 'tis'. . .) It is a way of
opening the matter which effectively declares it closed. Yet·
who could say that Macbeth does not want desperately, at
this moment, to unburden himself about the whole hideous
affair?

Of course he is also obsessed with the coming murder, and
only attending with half his mind. In a moment he will be
seeing daggers in the air. But it would make little difference if
he were not. He inhabits so much the world of superstitious
terror and hallucination, that he can never respond to
Banquo's urbane candour of a man of reason. It gains no
lodgement in his mind, except as a threat of exposure, or a
promise of complicity.

It is the same when his wife comes to him, her hands full
of a yearning pitying tenderness which she wants to bestow
on him – on them both.

> How now, my lord, why do you keep alone?
> Of sorriest fancies your companions making,
> Using those thoughts, which should indeed have died
> With them they think on? things without all remedy
> Should be without regard: what's done, is done.

She needs no one to interpret his growing taste for solitude
to her.

>   Come on:
> Gentle my lord, sleek o'er your rugged looks.

Smoothing the lion's mane. Whereupon the lion makes a
convulsive attempt at. . .what is it? Candid confession? or
furtive concealment? A heart-rending appeal for sympathy?
or a brusque rebuff of the sympathy she has already offered?
Is he securing her complicity in Banquo's murder? or sparing
his dearest chuck any complicity in it whatsoever? He doesn't
know, and we can only sense that it is all these things by
starts and nothing constantly. 'So prithee go with me', he
concludes; but he has made it impossible for anyone to go

with him. He takes his way alone.

It is in this perspective that one may feel that the Macbeth of Act V has finally 'grown up'.

> My way of life
> Has fall'n into the sere, the yellow leaf,
> And that which should accompany old age,
> As honour, love, obedience, troops of friends,
> I must not look to have.

It has always been so. Only now he knows it. He does not feverishly exhort himself against unreasonable expectations: 'must' has none of that self-correcting urgency, only a desolated calm of acquiescence. The reckoning is steady, unemotive, laconic.

Is there, after all, so very great a difference between knowing everything there is to be known about your world, and knowing there is nothing to be known? Who was more the man, the one who went in primal terror of the avenging spectres of his own conscience? or the one who takes it all on his own shoulders?

> But let the frame of things disjoint,
> Both the worlds suffer,
> Ere we will eat our meal in fear, and sleep
> In the affliction of these terrible dreams
> That shake us nightly: better be with the dead,
> Whom we, to gain our peace, have sent to peace,
> Than on the torture of the mind to lie
> In restless ecstasy.

Is that not a man to the fullest capacity?

I ask, not because I know the answer, but because I am sure there is a question.

4 · TO KNOW MY DEED. . .

I suppose the feature of the play I've been trying hardest to account for is this: the fact that all the most powerful and impressive things in it are negative things. Reckonings with what we 'must not look to have'. Acquiescences in unmeaning. Commitments to action which is certainly futile, but 'At least we'll die with harness on our back.' The sardonic shrug in the face of the irremediable. We may judge Macbeth as harshly as we choose, and the more harshly the better, but there still remains his extraordinary capacity – his extraordinary and *growing* capacity – to live unblinkingly with the consequences of his own deed. And the tune goes manly.

It is possible that Macbeth made the 'wrong' choice, when he concluded

> To know my deed, 'twere best not know myself.

Knowing oneself, certainly, is one prime duty of the individual; and it is not unconnected, either, with knowing one's deeds. But must patients always therein minister to themselves—applying endless salves and plasters to their sick consciences? Is it necessarily the ultimate blasphemy to throw that particular physic to the dogs?

The case is far from clear. For it might be the ultimate courage. It might be perfect conscience to 'stand up to' the conscience that is making a coward of you—especially if you know yourself no true coward?* And would it not be equally 'wrong', if Macbeth were to stick where he finds himself immediately after the murder?

> I am afraid to think what I have done:
> Look on't again I dare not.

Is that not truly ignominious, immoral?

However we answer these questions (and, though they may find no simple solution, we *will* answer them), this thing we call conscience is a strange commodity. The conscience Macbeth displays so much of, in the early part of the play, is little better than a fever of superstition which shakes his single state of man till function is smothered in surmise. It populates his moral world with spectres of delirium. It deranges him until he is actually hallucinating, snatching at air-drawn daggers, and being physically shoved from his stool by figments of his own fear. But it can hardly be said to make him more moral? The dagger marshals him to Duncan's murder. His initiate's fear at the ghost makes him resolve upon 'hard use' to overcome it. This version of conscience is craven, panic-ridden, a disorder of the mind, quite, quite inoperative. It behaves and feels like guilt. He is ashamed of it. You might almost say that it's only when he has less of it, only when he has cauterised its over-sensitive tissue, that it is able to function properly at all.

And the incipient moral adult in Macbeth, the one who is

---

*Cf. 'A man should stand up to his bad luck, to his mistakes, to his conscience, and all that sort of thing. Why—what else would you have to fight against?' Captain Giles's query, and its place in Conrad's tale (*The Shadow Line*) is very relevant here. *Macbeth*, one might say, is the most Conradian of Shakespeare's plays—and not least in the sober respect it accords to negative sentiments.

not a child-savage, fights against it for his self-possession:

> There's no such thing!
> It is the bloody business that informs
> Thus to mine eyes.

Being gone, he is a man again. The barbarian morality of the 'horrid image' must be forcibly denied as the 'strange and self-abuse' that it is. And when it is burnt away to nothing, then perhaps the truly binding conscience, which exists in the clear daylight of a common humanity, may come into being.

The process is inevitably one of disillusion. Because with the superstition went illusions of self-importance which are bitter to relinquish. But slowly he is acknowledging the plain outlines of the common reality. 'Fate and metaphysical aid' turn out to be grandiose misnomers for three juggling hags who have paltered with him in a double sense. They are not the 'fiends' his disappointed delusion wants to believe them. They should never have been taken seriously. Part of his mind never did take them seriously—filthy, black and midnight hags that they were. Nor their 'masters' for that matter:

> *Apparition.* Macbeth! Macbeth! Macbeth!
> *Macbeth.* Had I three ears, I'd hear thee.

Progressively he is shedding his needless dreads. All these 'ministers of fate' have done, after all, is to foretell a state of affairs which is (once *he* has brought it about) crushingly, bruisingly obvious. And in the play's final phase, the recognition of this bathos comes with leaden redundancy to a man who has at last seen the point of an exceedingly bad joke; and the spirit of his reviving intelligence mocks his expiring credulity:

> 'Fear not, till Birnam Wood
> Do come to Dunsinane.' And now a wood
> Comes toward Dunsinane. Arm, arm and out. . . .

The forest he had envisioned, mystically, impossibly unfixing its earthbound root and marching on his castle, turns out to be the oldest camouflage trick in the military manual. What is there to say but 'Arm, arm and out'? Yet in that clangour of a sardonic defiance lies much of the music of Act V—and strangely stirring music it is.

He does, of course, right to the end, persist in believing himself bound by the prophecies whose origins and agency he nevertheless holds in contempt. The annals of superstition yield many of these unconstant starts and strange infirmities; and Shakespeare is no peddler of miracle cures. It is part of

his rigour to show us that the man who creates, all unknowing, 'a clearness' for his country, can never possess it
for himself. His country's purge and the true 'Med'cine of
the sickly weal' he may be, but he nevertheless remains
sickly himself to the end—as in the contemptuous remark he
throws at Macduff, before 'trying the last':

> But get thee back, my soul is too much charg'd
> With blood of thine already.

Yet it is not *just* sickly. The component of guilt is minimal,
and of remorse (that tinkling personal irrelevance beside
the resounding impersonal sorrows of Scotland) there is
scarcely a trace. Grimly, calmly he acknowledges the charge
upon his soul. It is, in its cool resumption of responsibility,
the voice of the moral adult.

'Maturity', I know, is too often a plume that critics use to
tickle their own esteem. I should like to use it to raise
Shakespeare's esteem. For, it seems to me, the portrait of a
maturity which has learned to live with the consequences of
actions catastrophic and destructive in the extreme, is of
commanding interest—and altogether a much more ab-
sorbing thing than the study in guilty disintegration which is
often, critically, substituted for it. And Shakespeare gives
it to us nowhere else: Hamlet, with a high grace of intelligent
percipience, sidesteps; Othello tumbles into self-pity; Antony
makes drama; and even the austere Coriolanus falls back on
an earlier and simpler persona, in order to die 'nobly'. Whereas Macbeth goes on steadily knowing his deed—a dedication,
apparently barren, which determines the whole temper of the
play's final Act.

But to see of what undaunted metal that Act is made, one
need only consider the very different temper of *King Lear*'s
close:

> Vex not his ghost. O, let him pass. He hates him
> That would upon the rack of this tough world
> Stretch him out longer.

Verse eloquently wrought from the tarnished silver of regret
and pathos. But, if the world is indeed 'tough', these racked
and elegaic cadences hold their own peculiar peril. There is
something faintly nerveless, if not unnerved, about the *Lear*
accommodation of the unaccommodable. And if one were
pressed to say what 'nerve' could possibly mean in a world
where 'all's cheerless, dark, and deadly', one might point to
the temper with which Macbeth confronts an equally
universal cheerlessness:

It is a tale
Told by an idiot, full of sound and fury,
Signifying nothing.

5 · ARM, ARM AND OUT . . .

Of course, the stoic nihilist of Act V is not the only Macbeth in whom we can take a mature interest. But there
are ways of being interested in the earlier Macbeth which
make much more sense of the stoic nihilist when he eventually
emerges.

I've suggested that Macbeth comes to regard the killing of
Duncan as a crucial test. And I have suggested why. By its
means he attempts to make murder, whose thought is at best
'fantastical', real to himself. For, in common with most of
the Scots, he finds it difficult to believe that any act is truly
heinous: the 'embarquements of fury' (in Tullus Aufidius's
phrase) have been too often overborne for their privilege to
feel anything but 'rotten'. And he needs, as we all do, to have
some limit set to his overweening potency of act; because
without it he cannot be moral.

But all the impediments he can find in himself fall under
the withering rubric of his wife's scorn—letting I dare not
wait upon I would—the poor cat's pusillanimity. Whether it
is the fear of bloody instructions returned upon his own
head, the fear of social condemnation, the prudent husbanding of golden opinions, or a simple fear of failure—they
are all 'weak' reasons, and they cannot make up the absolute
prohibition of an ineluctable wrongness in the deed itself.
This he cannot feel—or if he does feel it, it is as just one
more fear to be overcome if he is not to live a coward in his
own esteem.

But the ineluctable wrongness discloses itself with
astonishing power in the wake of the murder. And such is
the power, that we find ourselves wondering whether, if it
had disclosed itself in any other way, it could have been half
so real. Did he have to murder Duncan in order to become
moral?

> Perhaps the most marvellous moment in *Macbeth*
> [writes Middleton Murry] is when the two actors
> suddenly emerge from their madness, and look upon
> their deed with the same naivety as we of the audience.
> . . .Suddenly Macbeth and Lady Macbeth *see them-*
> *selves,* with an absolute and terrible naivety. This power

that is in them to see themselves, manifested as they manifest it, convinces us, as nothing else could now convince us, of their essential nobility of soul. And by this turn the situation becomes bottomless in profundity. That a man and a woman should, in the very act of heinous and diabolical murder, reveal themselves as naive and innocent, convulses our morality and awakens in us thoughts beyond the reaches of our souls. So that it seems that the wonderful imagination of

> Pity, like a naked new-born babe,
> Striding the blast

is embodied in the sudden birth of childlike astonishment in the eyes of the murderers themselves.

'Innocent' may seem to be coming it a bit strong however convulsed our morality; but Murry has put his finger on something haunting about the royal murderers, something we have all dimly felt—and which persists throughout the play. The very last exit of Macbeth's queen—a woman every bit as 'fiend-like' as Malcolm will have her—has an irreducible component of childlike sweetness about it:

> To bed, to bed: there's knocking at the gate: Come, come, come, come, give me your hand: What's done cannot be undone. To bed, to bed, to bed.

Half-submerged in the remembered horrors of the murder-night lies the picture of two shining, well-scrubbed children in their nightgowns, saying goodnight to the adults. With the fiend-like queen as elder sister. There are echoes still of 'innocence'.

Murry's subsequent account of Act II Scene ii is so nearly right, and so suggestive when wrong, that I shall give it at length:

> The short scene which follows the murder is beyond criticism or comparison. It is a revelation—of depths hitherto quite hidden in the two accomplices. The first crack of the surface, the first glimpse beneath, comes with Lady Macbeth's:
>
> > Had he not resembled
> > My father as he slept, *I* had done't.
>
> The second follows instantly when, as Macbeth enters with bloody hands, she cries—never before, never after, but only now—'My *husband*!'

These cracks are the more ominous, in that her sur-
face had seemed the more steely. Suddenly, we know
all that was concealed in her injunction 'to screw your
courage to the sticking-place'. . .
When you turn the little wooden screw on a violin. . .
to tighten the string, your fingers feel delicately for 'the
sticking-place', where the screw is tight and the string is
taut; and you feel for it with a faint and subtle apprehension lest the string should snap. That is Shakespeare's
figure and that is what Lady Macbeth has been doing to
her soul, and by her example to her husband's. And her
words: 'Had he not resembled my father as he slept, *I*
had don't', tell us that the screw has given way, or that
the string has snapped.
The snapping of the strings. Almost we hear them go.
The very words break sudden and abrupt.

Enter Macbeth
Lady M. My husband!
Macb. I have done the deed. Did'st thou not hear a noise?
Lady M. I heard the owl scream and the crickets cry.
   Did you not speak?
Macb.   When?
Lady M.   Now.
Macb.   As I descended?
Lady M. Ay!
Macb. Hark! Who lies i' th' second chamber?
Lady M.   Donalbain.
Macb. This is a sorry sight. [*Looking on his hands*.]
Lady M. A foolish thought, to say a sorry sight.

After the staccato dialogue, the weakness of that last
line is wonderful. It is almost like a nursery rhyme. We
see the pitiful and helpless smile. Then Macbeth begins
to manifest the same amazing, terrible naivety which
has taken possession of his wife. As with her, this
naivety is not in his words alone, but in the very texture
of the verse: like a child telling a ghost-story.

Macb.
There's one did laugh in's sleep, and one cried 'Murder!'
That they did wake each other: I stood and heard them:
But they did say their prayers, and address'd them
Again to sleep.
Lady M. There are two lodg'd together.

We hear the vacant laugh. Whose is the 'foolish thought'
now?

Macb. One cried 'God bless us!' and 'Amen' the other;
  As they had seen me with these hangman's hands.
  Listening their fear, I could not say 'Amen',
  When they did say 'God bless us!'
Lady M.   Consider it not so deeply.
Macb. *But wherefore could not I pronounce 'Amen'?*
  I had most need of blessing, and 'Amen'
  Stuck in my throat.
Lady M.   These deeds must not be thought
  After these ways; so, it will make us mad.

'After these ways' now, not 'deeply' any more. At first,
while she is fumbling for the broken string, to screw it
tight again, she speaks at random: 'consider it not so
deeply.' But as she gathers control, she knows that he is
not considering it deeply at all. He is considering it
simply, and strangely, and fatally, as she also has been
considering it. There is no word for that kind of con-
templation, when two creatures, become themselves,
look on the irremediable thing they did when they were
not themselves. 'Not after these ways', says Lady Macbeth – that is, 'as we are doing now': that is, not deeply,
but simply and terribly, with a child's staring eyes. 'So
it will make us mad.' And it does.*

But that is just where Murry is wrong. It doesn't make
Macbeth mad. Macbeth is not seen wringing his hands because nought's had, all's spent. He calls fate into the lists to
champion him to the utterance. Terrible dreams may shake
him nightly, but we do not hear that he has light continually
by him, nor do we see him walking unquietly in his sleep. He
looks upon the irremediable thing he has done, and he refuses the specious comfort that it was done when he was 'not
himself'. There is no fumbling for broken strings, because the
string has not broken. This man we see striding from one
butchery to the next is 'terrible' to watch, because the
striding is invincibly sane. His grasp upon the humane values
he is violating becomes fiercer with every violation:

      if't be so,
  For Banquo's issue have I fil'd my mind,
  For them, the gracious Duncan have I murther'd,
  Put rancours in the vessel of my peace
  Only for them, and mine eternal jewel
  Given to the common enemy of man

*J. Middleton Murry, *Shakespeare* (1936), Chapter xiv.

To make them Kings, the seeds of Banquo Kings!
Rather than so, come fate into the lists. . .

Listening to those energetic tones, at once tormented and
sardonic, I cannot escape the feeling that it is precisely in the
ironic futility of his action that Macbeth is discovering his
resources of fortitude. He is passing beyond the state of
heroic self-regard to one of insolent insouciance – the worse
things are, the better it pleases him. That's right: that's the
way it should be. It's a vindication.

Not an unfamiliar state of mind, I imagine: you can, at
the blackest of moments, feel a grim relish for the sym-
metries of even-handed justice – even while you are scheming
(with small expectation of success) to circumvent them. And
there is a kind of zest in knowing that, whatever falls upon
you, you have earned it all, every last bit. It is an oblique way
that integrity has, of affirming the justice it defies. The faci-
lities of remorse, of course, always lie near to hand. But they
would involve Macbeth in denying the absoluteness of the
deed, whining and grovelling before the boy Malcolm: 'I
was wrong and wicked; I should not have done it.' To what
end? It would be 'tedious'. Everything is tedious. And it
would change nothing. What's done is done. Things without
all remedy should be without regard.

The one proud tribute he can pay to the morality he discovered in Duncan's chamber, is indifference to his own fate.

Yet it is out of Macbeth's refusal to see anything tragic in
his predicament, out of his rejection of all heroism (beyond
the minimal heroism of dying with harness on his back), that
this play generates its unique kind of tragedy and heroism. It
is often on the brink of unmeaning farce, and we are not in
the least surprised when that current of feeling crystallises
rock-hard into the sentiment that nothing whatsoever matters,
nothing 'signifies'. Something nevertheless persists in 'signifying'. What is it?

I can see no point in giving it a name – though many an
abstract noun presses forward for adoption. So let me
answer, instead, the more pertinent question: Where is it?

It is there in the curious mixture of hilarity and despair,
pity and contempt he unleashes on the unfortunate cream-
faced loon:

Go prick thy face, and over-red thy fear
Thou lily-liver'd boy. What soldiers, patch?

> Death of thy soul, those linen cheeks of thine
> Are counsellors to fear. What soldiers, whey-face?
> *Servant.* The English force, so please you.
> *Macbeth.* Take thy face hence.

The public joke has its solaces. Sick at heart himself, he knows well enough where this 'poor heart' got his goose-look. Somewhere in his soul, he stands at an infinite distance from 'this push', and is coldly amused.

It is there in his farcical dealings (in the same scene) with his armourer. And it is there in the conversation with the Doctor who, like all medical men, knows far more than he has any business to, and evinces an odious kind of tact in imperfectly concealing the fact. Macbeth is facing his Pharsalia —the contemptible 'push' that will 'cheer him ever', or disseat him now. Not that he cares—deserted by his supposed allies, surrounded by whisperers and lack-hearts whose curses (not loud, but deep) are as distinct to his ears as if they were his own, unable to do anything for his sick wife except employ a moralist in medic's clothing. No, he has lived long enough.

And yet this man succeeds in being ordinary, cheerful and indeed, jocular. He neither hides the magnitude of his problems, nor burdens other people with them. With a quick mobility and a sardonic ease of transition he paces about the small cage of closed options his life has become, his voice and his movements instinct with unabateable energy.

> Give me my armour.
> *Seyton.*   'Tis not needed yet.
> *Macbeth.* I'll put it on:
> Send out moe horses, skirr the country round,
> Hang those that talk of fear. Give me mine armour:
> How does your patient, Doctor?
> *Doctor.*   Not so sick my lord,
> As she is troubled with thick-coming fancies
> That keep her from her rest.
> *Macbeth.*   Cure her of that:
> Cans't thou not minister to a mind diseas'd,
> Pluck from the memory a rooted sorrow,
> Raze out the written troubles of the brain,
> And with some sweet oblivious antidote
> Cleanse the stufft bosom of that perilous stuff
> Which weighs upon the heart?

Doctor.   Therein the patient
        Must minister to himself.
Macbeth. Throw physic to the dogs, I'll none of it.
    Come, put mine armour on: give me my staff:
    Seyton, send out: Doctor, the Thanes fly from me:
    Come sir, dispatch. If thou could'st, Doctor, cast
    The water of my land, find her disease,
    And purge it to a sound and pristine health,
    I would applaud thee to the very echo,
    That should applaud again. Pull't off I say!
    What rhubarb, cyme, or what purgative drug
    Would scour these English hence? hear'st thou of them?
Doctor. Ay my good lord: your royal preparation
        Makes us hear something.
Macbeth.   Bring it after me!

   The Doctor offers to lead him back into the quagmire of
remorse, scruple and self-examination, proposing a bed in the
hospital where patients lie, on the torture of the mind,
ministering to themselves in restless ecstasy. But though
Macbeth perceives the shrewd thrust, is even a little amused
by it, his refusal is unhesitating: 'Throw physic to the dogs,
I'll none of it.' The remark is not petulant. It's just that if
that is the only alternative going, then, frankly, he had rather
have his armour on and his staff in his hand. It's too late in
the day to be indulging in the luxuries of private conscience.
Surely the Doctor can do better than that. How about a
purge for Scotland? Scotland is sick enough. Or can medics
only minister to the already convalescent? And he turns a
grin of good-humoured mockery on the Doctor's offered
superiority: What, in your professional opinion, Doctor,
would scour these English hence? You have *heard* about the
English?
   The spirit of that gibe—for all its time-honoured, man-of-
the-worldish cynicism about medicine—is very curious and
very potent. It has the stamina of health, the stamina of
'How much, after all, does it all matter?' The stamina which
concludes 'I have lived long enough; I 'gin to be aweary of
the sun', and then cries out, 'Give me mine armour.' And
even if there is some comic anarchy about the way he gets his
armour on, and some contempt for those who think it
matters whether it's on or not (the spectacle of that poor
armour-bearer hopping and crawling after this pacing,
shouting, restless animal, and then exiting, panting, with his
arms full of jumbled ironware—'Bring it after me!'—is on the

verge of slapstick), nevertheless one does feel that the man is
armed, is 'in harness', is in the state where he can decently
meet his anti-climactic nemesis. It's best, when all is marred,
to go with a swagger, a jingle, a joke. Much, much better (to
make the point sharply) than to go Antony's way—lachry-
mose, self-pitying, ignominious. No, do it in pert rhyme:

> Lay on Macduff!
> And damn'd be him, that first cries 'Hold! Enough!'

Here lies the authentic core of the warrior-ethic: clean as
polished steel, admirable, shallow, magnificent.

It is in keeping with that devil-may-care spirit that Shakespeare winds up the Doctor's surgery for the day. The patient
exits ranting:

> I will not be afraid of death and bane,
> Till Birnam Forest come to Dunsinane;

and the doctor muses parodically:

> Were *I* from Dunsinane away and clear,
> Profit again should hardly draw *me* here.

The Doctor is free to patronise the last vestige of superstitious folly in Macbeth's accommodation to an impossible
world: he has no Pharsalia impending, so he can *afford* to
be rational. But there are distinct signs, in his chirpy riposte,
that Macbeth's spiritedness has lifted a load from his spirits.
He has been relieved, even, of the burden of feeling sorry for
his employer. With a bit of luck he will also get 'away and
clear'.

Which leaves Macbeth—who most certainly will not—to
make his final ·reckoning of the zero sum his life has added
up to.

In the character of that reckoning, as Dr Johnson might
have remarked, 'I rejoice to concur with the common reader.'
It is, very obviously, one of the great moments in literature.
It will not, therefore, suffer any diminution if I approach it
from an oblique angle.

Suppose the famous soliloquy is not a soliloquy (whatever
a soliloquy may be). Throughout this Act, Macbeth has been
talking simultaneously to himself and to anybody else who
happens to be standing about. He is careless who hears since
there is nothing he cares, any longer, to conceal. (His portentous isolation has given way to this strange, blank publicity.) And Seyton, who has already been used as a sounding-
board for his master's self-communings, is standing about in
Act V Scene v. Which makes a change, for in the preceding

scene, he had to be bawled for three times before he appeared ('Sey-TON!'), and then he did so with an ill-concealed smirk:

What's your gracious pleasure?

It's much of a piece with his general insolence. His response to 'Give me my armour' was ''Tis not needed yet' – without so much as a 'Sir' appended! And it is this curser-not-loud-but-deep who brings Macbeth word of his wife's death. It might well generate constraint, and I suppose among the hundred feelings embodied in 'She should have died here-after' there is a feeling of constraint in Seyton's presence – a need to contain emotion. But I cannot detect in the next remark ('There would have been a time for such a word') any shy shrinking back into privacy. The voice is rising in contempt for the everything of which Seyton is the nearest representative. 'Here you', says Macbeth, 'since you're standing there with your half-hearted sympathy and your whole-hearted indifference, you may as well hear the ripened wisdom of my life-experience. . .and much good may it do you. Talk to you, talk to the Doctor, talk to the air. . .what difference is there?'

And then into that starved air, and to those grudging ears, he speaks the great annihilating truths that we all, some-where, live with, and all *know* we live with, sometimes. The effect, in its mixture of casual disdain and burning ferocity, is riveting.

It helps if we remember, too, that it is a bereaved man speaking. He has lost his dearest partner of greatness, a woman of undaunted mettle, his dearest chuck. And numbed though he has become, we have seen him holding steady cognizance, still, of her rooted sorrow, of the written troubles of the brain; and his demand for 'some sweet oblivious anti-dote' has been full of an impotent solicitude for her. Well, that is all needless now. But he is, nonetheless, in the queer oblique way of grief, talking about his loss, with his 'To-morrow, and tomorrow, and tomorrow'. When the blow comes out of the dark, it is as inevitable as life itself, that the felled man will scramble up, fists squared, ready to pummel the universe, or, failing that, jeer at the fools who think they see some significance in it. Significance! What would they know? picking their way to dusty death, their brief candles about to be snuffed out at any moment. . .as hers has just been. The only possible triumph over that is a limitless con-tempt. And the contempt blazes in the pausing, the stressing, the very breathing of his summation:

> It is a tale
> Told by an idiot, full of sound and fury,
> Signifying nothing.

He is seeking solace in insensibility, you may say. It has been said. But that is odd, because he was reflecting, just a moment before, that insensibility has become a permanent condition with him — has been congratulating himself on it, almost: 'I have almost forgot the taste of fears.' Odd, but very human. The reflection arose because, just this once, he *had* the old taste of fear; at the 'cry of women', whose cause is so easy to guess, his fell of hair *did* rouse and stir as life were in it. Surprised by grief, he remembers that he has forgotten — and then remembers *what* he has forgotten. Life — or is it death? — can still lay a finger on him, still reach him when he least expects it; and he hardly knows if he resents being forced into feeling, or resents feeling so little.

It is not insensibility that produces his unique response to the 'common tale' of mortality, this 'ordinary sorrow of man's life' —

> The Queen, my lord, is dead.

If roads have ends, this is the end of his. But in the pause that follows the announcement, there is the marvellously evoked, breathing presence of a man who gathers himself to say everything there is left in him to say — though he begins (as the magnitude of his provocation requires) with studied carelessness: he owes that to himself, and to her.

> She should have died hereafter;
> There would have been a time for such a word.

'Should'? queries a pertly superficial part of one's mind. Would have died anyway? or ought to have died then? And again. . .time for 'such a word' as which? He hasn't mentioned any. But we understand him well enough. There is no meaningful distinction between the futile sense that it would have happened sooner or later anyway, and the instinctive rebellion against its happening now. It can make no difference when it happens: it makes every difference now — for it has happened. Death is all, and death is a nothing. The attempt to articulate callous indifference voices an involuntary protest: She would have died. . .But when?

There is the same expressive indeterminacy about the word he stumbles upon as he tries to imagine a time when she *should* have died: 'hereafter'. It confesses its own helplessness and disbelief — prepares, in its inefficacy, for the bitter recognition, one line later, that there is no meaningful 'hereafter' when things could happen decently and decorously – only weary tomorrows – creeping, anonymous, indistinguishable. So the 'word' never gets named. Where would be the point, in the shadow of the impending tomorrows? Instead his mind shies, sidesteps, in a manner now familiar. One recalls the last occasion this happened: 'I am sick at heart when I behold. . .Seyton, I say!' One doesn't ask *what* he beholds. It is the impossibility (or the futility) of saying that cuts off the sentence. His own formulations mock him: there would have been a time for such a word, would there? when time is an infinite regress of degenerating samenesses, only less pointless than the 'syllables' that record it? and words go the same downhill way to dusty death, through the rant of a player to the mouthings of an imbecile? There would have been 'a time' only for 'such words' as that. Everything Macbeth feels, about his wife, his bereavement, his predicament, 'Life', is spoken by way of this multiple-reference-in-indeterminacy. His distraction, grief, contempt, absentness, numbness, rage, express themselves in things not said, unable to be said, not worth saying. And yet there is a kind of mastery, we feel, in being able so finally to disdain the saying.

For you cannot call it a failure of expression. It is in the grip of the most desolating clarity; and it communicates it. It is the triumphant declaration of the 'clearness' Macbeth has made for himself – the clearness of the 'conscience' mastered, and the deed known.

> And, to conclude, he knows himself a man,
> Which is a proud, and yet a wretched thing.

And within minutes, the blurring of outline, the fog and filthy air of a blood-drunken self-hypnosis have cleared away, and as we look toward Birnam we see – 'within this three mile', the air is so clear – the green boughs of Malcolm's army descending the opposite slope. Living light kisses the face of the earth. Relief has arrived – as much for Macbeth, as for Scotland. Enough. An end.

> Arm, arm and out!

It's perfectly true that uglinesses persist. We don't lose sight of the coarsening of moral fibre that Macbeth has undergone – has indeed chosen to undergo. The slaying of Young Seyward is particularly offensive, because it is done to the tune of that idiot witches' rant – the last echoes of Macbeth's superstitious puerility. It sticks to his last sand. Shakespeare is not mitigating anything. Indeed it is in this connexion, very near the end of his undertaking, that he chooses to show us the alternative warrior – modest, Christian, invincible:

Ross. Your son my lord, has paid a soldier's debt.
He only liv'd but till he was a man,
The which no sooner had his prowess confirm'd
In the unshrinking station where he fought,
But like a man he died.
Seyward.   Then he is dead?
Ross.

Ay, and brought off the field: your cause of sorrow
Must not be measur'd by his worth, for then
It hath no end.
Seyward.   Had he his hurts before?
Ross. Ay, on the front.
Seyward.   Why then, God's soldier be he:
Had I as many sons as I have hairs,
I would not wish them to a fairer death:
And so his knell is knoll'd.
Malcolm.   He's worth more sorrow,
And that I'll spend for him.
Seyward.   He's worth no more.
They say he parted well, and paid his score,
And so God be with him.

Old Seyward's soldierly grief is nicely counterpointed against Malcolm's slightly self-preening version of humanity and sympathy – a contrast which reveals how little the old soldier's emotion needs to be buttressed by tragic posturings. In its resolved obduracy of understatement, his voice is very close to Macbeth's – the Macbeth who is now dead. In a happier time, in another country, he might have been this grizzled warrior. And to what end was he ever anything else? What was all this furious close of civil butchery designed to clarify? Why write a play about this Macbeth fellow – dead butcher that he is?

One answer to this question, critically, has been to impose upon him the civilised conscience of self-approving Englishness – and to treat as his greatest virtue, and his claim upon our humanity, the very qualities which he least respects and is most plagued by in himself. With the consequence that his last hours are represented as largely admonitory: see and tremble, this is what happens when a man defies his conscience – his English conscience.

If however we are impressed by that courage in extremity, by that relentless knowing of his deed, we must think again. Wonder perhaps if a Scottish conscience might not be bound

by laws equally imperative, but not so readily assimilable to
our moral habituations. Is it a coincidence that English
consciousness, whenever it is struck with a sudden doubt
of its own stamina, courage, or vitality, whenever it catches
itself suspecting itself of effeteness, habitually looks to the
barbarian north for some intimation of the lost energies?
Doesn't the pagan-heroic past of a race, whatever the present
level of civility, always retain that haunting suggestion of
some lost manliness — so that we feel an inconsequent
nostalgia for the very tough-minded imperviousness which we
think it is our distinction to have outgrown?

The bloody horrors of the House of Atreus seem to have
struck the Athenian Aeschylus that way, when he composed
his myth of origin: no Apollonian enlightenment could
humanise his city, he saw, until the implacable and great
goddesses of ancient night were held in due awe. In honouring
them one became, not less, but more fully Athenian.

The savage weal of Scotland, where murthering ministers
waited perennially on nature's mischief, may have served
that stabilising, rectifying function, for Shakespeare's English
imagination.

IV

Antony and Cleopatra
Gentle Madam, No

1 · THE COMMON LIAR

What is it that Demetrius says to Philo which, as the play begins, we are just too late to hear? That, of course, is not the sort of question we are supposed to ask any more. But an actor, wanting to kick the play off by making the most of the few lines he has, might put it to himself. So might a reader who feels that while speeches such as Philo's offer representative judgements upon the lovers, they are also themselves elements of the drama, fragments of that buzz of gossip and speculation and fascination that Antony and Cleopatra excite. It is of the essence of the comedy of the first half of the play that the lovers should love in a great glare of publicity; and equally, that we should be delighted by what we see of human nature as it offers itself as appalled or intoxicated by the spectacle. We are tossed, from the first words, into the agitated passions of critics:

> Nay, but this dotage of our general's
> O'erflows the measure.

That can only be a response to a check; a forced withdrawal to the last line of any censure—a condemnation of excess. We might guess that Demetrius has resisted the flow of Philo's witty disapproval with some show of easy tolerance. Philo's judgement has been questioned, and Philo is a man proud of his perceptions:

> Look where they come.
> Take but good note and you shall see in him
> The triple pillar of the world transform'd
> Into a strumpet's fool: behold and see.

A something proprietorial there? At any rate he has a stake in the performance; he is the moral impresario of the show. That does not necessarily discredit his acumen, nor does it remove from his words their possibly generalising force. But the rightness of a judgement is not entirely separable from

the satisfactions of making it. And how right, anyway, is
Philo? How good a critic is he of the scene which, to clinch
his point, he confidently presents to Demetrius? 'Behold
and see' —

Cleopatra. If it be love indeed, tell me how much.
Antony. There's beggary in the love that can be reckon'd.
Cleopatra. I'll set a bourn how far to be belov'd.
Antony. Then must thou needs find out new heaven,
        new earth.
Attendant. News, my good lord, from Rome.
Antony.   Grates me, the sum.
Cleopatra.Nay, hear them, Antony:
        Fulvia perchance is angry; or who knows
        If the scarce-bearded Caesar have not sent
        His powerful mandate to you, 'Do this, or this;
        Take in that kingdom, and enfranchise that;
        Perform't, or else we damn thee.'
Antony.   How, my love?
Cleopatra.Perchance? nay, and most like:
        You must not stay here longer, your dismission
        Is come from Caesar, therefore hear it, Antony.

If Cleopatra starts this teasing, bantering charade, she it is
that most knows its lightness and insists upon its limits.
Antony certainly looks somebody's fool here, but there is
little call for us to be stern about that: the greatest of men
might permit themselves some extravagant folly in this area
and not expect to be taken as propounding their deepest
philosophy. We need too, I think, to stretch our notions of
strumpets and gypsies to accommodate the shrewdness and
wit that plays up in Cleopatra throughout this scene and,
what is more, plays through what looks like a real anxiety as
to Antony's unsettled and possibly impermanent presence.
To insist that a witty strumpet is still a strumpet seems to
me poor morality. The more so if the wit is not mere decora-
tive accomplishment but quick sense controlling quick
emotion. And even dotage is less contemptible if the object
be worthy.
    The gypsy's lust, according to Philo, is in a constant state
of being cooled by Antony, which might account for why we
are not treated to any torridity in this scene. Except in the
reporting, we never are. The one thing not present in this
exchange, not in her, not in him, not as howsoever subtly
given off between them, is lust. Certainly there are grand
protestations of devotion:

Let Rome in Tiber melt, and the wide arch
Of the rang'd empire fall! Here is my space.
Kingdoms are clay: our dungy earth alike
Feeds beast as man; the nobleness of life
Is to do thus: when such a mutual pair,
And such a twain can do't, in which I bind,
On pain of punishment, the world to weet
We stand up peerless.

But the time has passed when such spirited defiance was seen by critics to reduce Rome to nothing and to make, for the imagination, even reality tremble. The pendulum has swung, and we now have Antonys—the accounts quite out-Philo Philo—lost not only to temper but to nature herself.* Sometimes it seems as if the chief good and market of the critic's time is but to scruple and demur. The hapless Shakespearean hero, swollen with self-indulgence, blown with grandiosity, vaunts himself in vain today before an audience coolly discerning in matters of intelligence. Yet rather than rebuke Antony for the high irresponsibility of his declamation, might we not hazard, to catch what most distinguishes it, the word innocence?—leaning, if you will, rather to the word's implications of guilelessness than to its implications of purity. Is not the kiss implanted during that speech one of the most innocent kisses in literature? 'Bellows and fan to cool a gypsy's lust'? 'Bellows and fan'?

There is, it is true, a certain sensual drowsiness in Antony's description of the pleasurable life to which he declares himself addicted:

Now for the love of Love, and her soft hours,
Let's not confound the time with conference harsh:
There's not a minute of our lives should stretch
Without some pleasure new. What sport tonight?

But that would never find its way into Mario Praz. Which but makes it, I suppose, the more likeable. We are not to register any outrage as to behaviour here; it is enough that we are reminded that declared hedonism will always be doomed to infelicity of expression. What just about saves it in this instance or rather makes of it something else, neither utterly repugnant nor hopelessly effete, is Antony's boyishness. 'What sport tonight?' is a request quite literally for that: fun and games. There is no dark 'act of sport' implied here. What Antony has in mind is this:

*For Antony as nincompoop, Shakespeare as botcher, and only the critic with no nonsense about him, see A.L. French: *Shakespeare and the Critics*.

No messenger but thine, and all alone,
To-night we'll wander through the streets, and note
The qualities of people. Come, my queen,
Last night you did desire it.

I do not think we need to be too censorious about the innocuous slumming that Antony proposes, beyond noting that,
like bad critics, they take the wrong sort of interest in
character.
That Cleopatra accompanied Antony in these jaunts
Plutarch tells us, and the idea with which he leaves us is that
she fell in, as much as Antony could want, with his ingenuities of pleasure. Shakespeare's slight shift of emphasis determines a nicer inference:

Come, my queen,
Last night you did desire it.

We need not yet have felt the restless power of Cleopatra's
infinite variety to register something a little less rapid and
inventive in Antony. His appeal to an earlier whim of Cleopatra's is, in this world of quickly shifting pleasures, a sad
attempt to strike the note of perfect mutuality. Indeed, as
one half of the 'mutual pair', Antony might strike us as liable
rather to lag. Perhaps it is too early, or at any time less than
tactful to complain of some disharmony or inequality in the
relations of the lovers, but this opening scene involves us in
what they are like together in terms other than those which
Philo provides. Shakespeare's interest in sensuality in this
play is almost entirely a matter of looking at the ways
sensuality interests spectators of it. It exists primarily, as it
always will, in men's fancy, and fancies are various, even
amongst Romans. Rome might not be Egypt, but it has
fertilities of its own. As witness another Roman, Pompey,
not at all like Philo, straining his imagination towards the
exotic:

        but all the charms of love,
Salt Cleopatra, soften thy wan'd lip!
Let witchcraft join with beauty, lust with both,
Tie up the libertine in a field of feasts,
Keep his brain fuming; Epicurean cooks
Sharpen with cloyless sauce his appetite,
That sleep and feeding may prorogue his honour,
Even till a Lethe'd dulness—
        Enter Varrius
                How now, Varrius?

And who could say that he doesn't reach it? There is nothing of Philo's confident knowingness here. Pompey is a perfect stranger to the world of the senses which he hopes will keep Antony occupied. An Antony too addicted to pleasure to move is a calculation important to Pompey's ambitions; but an Antony charmed, dazzled, bewitched, overfed, over-loved, drunk, senseless and stupefied, is a figure that exceeds the requirements of political expedience. Goodness knows what further extravagant fantasies Pompey might have called to his aid had not Varrius interrupted him. But even the interruption, the news that, Epicurean cooks notwithstanding, Antony is hourly expected in Rome, does not affect Pompey's estimate of his rival. He chooses, reasonably enough, to find cause for pride in Antony's renewed activity:

> but let us rear
> The higher our opinion, that our stirring
> Can from the lap of Egypt's widow pluck
> The ne'er-lust-wearied Antony.

But not for any reconsideration of the man. Antony's reputation, it seems, will be a long time dying. Not because there is a malevolent will in a man like Pompey to keep it alive, but because it never occurs to him to question it. 'Ne'er-lust-wearied' is simply what Antony is. There is, in the end, a kind of tribute in it. For Pompey is fascinated by Antony and the unceasing pleasures he himself can only wildly imagine.

In some brilliant comic touches in the galley scene — more brilliant and more comic than the political satire of that scene which, in its ridicule of the great, is merely consoling to the small — Shakespeare portrays the Pompey who isn't sure whether he loves or hates that which he knows so little about, rising to the opportunity to keep up with the 'ne'er-lust-wearied Antony', and seeing to it that his own brain fumes as it should. Given Antony's reputation, and Pompey has partly given it to him, the business of drinking with him is a supreme test of Pompey's manhood. It is Pompey, host and competitor, who offers Antony the bold taunt:

> This is not yet an Alexandrian feast.

No, and according to Pompey's idea of what one of those is like, this never could be. Nonetheless Antony and Enobarbus do their best for him. They all take hands and a remarkably irreproachable song is sung to a Bacchus who is more cherub than god. Even that is a little too much for Caesar, but Pompey is there to the last, undisgraced and challenging Antony to a further bout on shore.

Much is often made of that moment in the galley scene
where Menas puts to Pompey his scheme of assassination and
is told that the deed should have been done but not mentioned. Much is made of the exchange because it lends itself
to that argument that so bedevils criticism of this play, that
we are to contrast the cynicism of political life and its pre-
varications over honour and so on with the quick fertility of
Egyptian passion. Leaving aside the question of whether so
manufactured an antithesis could seriously test our initial
priorities, we can find more than an exposure of political
dishonesty to interest us here, if we remember how much
the entertaining of Antony matters to the Pompey we have
already seen. Pompey's reply to Menas is a fairly faithful
transcript of Plutarch. What Shakespeare has added is
Pompey's zest for the drunkenness of the occasion, Menas's
difficulty in drawing him away from the revelry, and Pompey's final words to Menas, 'desist and drink' – his hostly
ministrations seeming to count more than thoughts about
power. There is to be no sign that Pompey's lost opportunity preys upon his mind or spoils the present, less political one. In short, what Shakespeare has created is a Pompey
more interested in cupping it with the best of them than in
running the world single-handed. His words to Menas, in this
context, seem more like a kindly and properly grateful way
of fobbing him off, than a paltering with honour. If this
play were about the world well lost for pleasure, Pompey
needs must be its hero, for it is he who is offered a chance
Antony never has, and he it is who, for pleasure's sake,
spurns it with never a regret. But perhaps, for the romantic
critic, the sacrifice is made on behalf of the wrong pleasure.

Pompey's final words in this scene are worth nothing. How
well these lines –

> O Antony
> You have my father's house. But what, we are friends?
> Come down into the boat –

catch a man not knowing his resentments from his affections,
as he slides into drunken and maudlin bonhomie. There is a
more deadly indictment of the power of drink and surfeit
implied in that than any 'Roman view' ever manages. And
indeed if there is anything specifically Roman in this play,
it is not moral censure or political practicality, but maudlin-
ness. Pompey suffers from it, Lepidus lives and dies on it,
Antony becomes consumed by it, even Caesar has the odd
bout, and finally it strikes, where we would least have suspected its efficacy, at Enobarbus. The Egyptians, as it

turns out, are far less sentimental.

If Pompey is far gone in Alexandrian revelry and Roman sentiment by the end of this scene, Caesar resists the powerful influences. Nonetheless it is a fairly wobbly and tipsy Caesar that thus excuses himself:

> What would you more? Pompey, good-night. Good brother,
> Let me request you off: our graver business
> Frowns at this levity. Gentle lords, let's part,
> You see we have burnt our cheeks. Strong Enobarb
> Is weaker than the wine, and mine own tongue
> Splits what it speaks: the wild disguise hath almost
> Antick'd us all. What needs more words? Good night.
> Good Antony, your hand.

He is clearly not the best person to enjoy a gaudy night with. His description of the general condition sounds accurate enough, but such accuracy is not always welcome. Still, there is nothing awesomely chilling about the man here; if he chooses to withdraw he has not been disgustingly immune. Caesar's reputation for cool, political competence and icy unemotionalness has been established in despite of the play. It serves the thesis that Antony is a noble and generous loser, the finer for not winning when winning is what Caesars do. Even Bradley who makes, I think, the proper observation that 'Shakespeare took little interest in the character of Octavius, and he has not made it wholly clear', yet finds it clear enough to detect in it something 'as hard and smooth as polished steel'. Bradley is thinking specifically of Caesar's calling Antony 'the old ruffian', in response to Antony's challenging him to single combat: 'There is a horrid aptness in the phrase, but it disgusts us.' The issue need not be of how much we care for Antony, and hence of just how horrid the aptness is. Is it not sufficient to say that if the phrase is apt it is also to a degree affectionate? It is said in temper; it registers—and this inevitably entails Caesar's knowledge of the limits of his own capabilities as a soldier—the impotence of Antony's gesture; but the words are those of an old friend, they carry the intimacy of regret as well as the exasperate hostility of an old affection. That Caesar should end the episode in question, a mere dozen lines later, with 'Poor Antony' is unsurprising and consistent.

When we first meet Caesar it is to hear his version of the Egyptian adventure. He begins with fairly top-of-the-head disapprovals of time wasting:

> he fishes, drinks, and wastes

> The lamps of night in revel; is not more manlike
> Than Cleopatra —

and allows the logic of his exasperation to carry him to an exorbitant dismissal —

> You shall find there
> A man who is the abstract of all faults
> That all men follow —

from which even the mild Lepidus demurs:

> I must not think there are
> Evils enow to darken all his goodness:
> His faults, in him, seem as the spots of heaven,
> More fiery by night's blackness; hereditary,
> Rather than purchas'd; what he cannot change,
> Than what he chooses.

That is kindly meant, though it cannot be said to shed much light. Still, it forces Caesar to be less lazy-minded about what his real objections are. We might not admire all his thoughts nor trust all his concessions, but this is a man working towards some clarity of attitude:

> You are too indulgent. Let's grant it is not
> Amiss to tumble on the bed of Ptolemy,
> To give a kingdom for a mirth, to sit
> And keep the turn of tippling with a slave,
> To reel the streets at noon, and stand the buffet
> With knaves that smells of sweat: say this becomes
>   him, —
> As his composure must be rare indeed
> Whom these things cannot blemish, — yet must Antony
> No way excuse his foils, when we do bear
> So great weight in his lightness. If he fill'd
> His vacancy with his voluptuousness,
> Full surfeits, and the dryness of his bones
> Call on him for't. But to confound such time,
> That drums him from his sport, and speaks as loud
> As his own state, and ours, — 'tis to be chid.

There is a pleasing asperity in Caesar's dismissal of Lepidus's decent feebleness, and we need not share Caesar's sense of what makes for indecorousness to find his depiction of it vigorous — a long way from the heated imaginings of Pompey and the flourished sagacities of Philo. Certainly he is not really granting what, in the way of tolerance, he offers to grant, nor can he resist a nicely tart description of the penalties of voluptuousness. But he is working for some discrimination between what it is fairly open to him to feel as grievance and what is finally a matter all for Antony himself to deal with and, yes, pay the price for. Or *would* be all for Antony himself to deal with, were it not that he has been for Caesar a friend and hero as well as an unreliable ally. A personal regret for what Antony has become is never far from Caesar's mind; it is as much a disappointment to him as it is a trouble. The rush of news telling of Pompey's growing influence has clearly much to do with Caesar's returning again to the question of Antony's indulgences:

> Antony,
> Leave thy lascivious wassails.

But while we hear in that the urgency of a man in need of all his allies, can we say that we do not also hear in the sudden intimacy of the address the deep sigh of a nostalgic yearning for the Antony that was? The speech that follows, relating Antony's retreat from Modena and his ability to drink what 'beasts would cough at' and to eat what 'some did die to look on', is for many readers only evidence the more of Caesar's fastidious austerity. Yet the Antony he remembers, the Antony we must even say he creates—so loving and so lyrical is the depiction:

> Yea, like the stag, when snow the pasture sheets,
> The barks of trees thou browsed—

is more extraordinary than it would come within the compass of a merely austere mind to apprehend. If it is austerity that is before us in this speech then it is austerity wrought to splendour. There is, without doubt, something queerly inapt in the expenditure of so much lyricism upon such uninviting virtues; something humourless in so ceremonious a glamorising of the unglamorous. But the celebration of Antony, which begins and ends in a lament, proceeds from an imagination that cherishes a passion. The greatness that is celebrated might conform less easily to our idea of what greatness should be, than do Cleopatra's more lavish and more conventional accounts of her lover, but it is greatness for all that. Caesar is quick to shake off these thoughts and to return, in an earlier manner, to the pressing affairs of Empire:

> Let his shames quickly
> Drive him to Rome, 'tis time we twain
> Did show ourselves i' the field, and to that end
> Assemble we immediate council; Pompey
> Thrives in our idleness.

But he speaks with all the brusqueness of a man who will not permit himself for long the luxury and indeed the distress of an old veneration: not with the dismissiveness of a man who scorns in himself an idle fancy. Astute politician he may be, but Caesar too has been quickened by a grandeur, and he will honour its memory — seasonably.

We lose much if we see the words of Philos and Pompeys and Caesars only as guiding commentaries upon the love of Antony and Cleopatra, no matter whether we concur with those commentaries or disown them. Part of what we lose is Shakespeare's enjoyment of the ways men half-create the legend they are offering to judge. His spokesman in the play, on behalf of such enjoyment, is Enobarbus, and it is he who is most alive to the power of the story, who is most responsive to what men want from it, and who can most wring from it its lessons and seductions. In the great comic scene in which he delivers up Cleopatra on her barge, he is given every help by an audience every raconteur dreams of. Having aided in the rapprochement between Antony and Caesar and the formal and public marrying off of Antony to Octavia, Maecenas and Agrippa seize the opportunity of having Enobarbus all to themselves and, with almost indecent haste, pump him for stories:

Maecenas. We have cause to be glad, that matters are so well digested. You stay'd well by't in Egypt.
Enobarbus. Ay, sir, we did sleep day out of countenance; and made the night light with drinking.
Maecenas. Eight wild-boars roasted whole at breakfast, and but twelve persons there; is this true?
Enobarbus. This was but as a fly by an eagle: we had much more monstrous matter of feast, which worthily deserved noting.
Maecenas. She's a most triumphant lady, if report be square to her.
Enobarbus. When she first met Mark Antony, she purs'd up his heart upon the river of Cydnus.
Agrippa. There she appear'd indeed; or my reporter devis'd well for her.
Enobarbus. I will tell you.

Well, these are Romans, and Romans close to the centre of power at that. If I find it difficult anywhere, I am especially hard-pressed here, to discover a Shakespeare in the grip of a vast imaginative contrast between a vital Alexandria and a desiccated Rome. What this scene tells me is that if Romans can be censorious they can also be excited. Their imaginations,

essentially masculine in these moments, are no more proof
against the rumours of Cleopatra's sumptuousness than are
those of the most Alexandrian of literary critics. If it be
argued that Maecenas and Agrippa are distinctly off-duty
here, that they have shifted from the forum to the bar-
room as it were, then that but alerts us to the kind of Cleopatra Enobarbus is providing for them. I would not care to
hazard which is the most real Roman—he that will publicly
pronounce upon the 'beauty, wisdom, modesty' of an Octavia, or he that privately sweats over Cleopatra; but that these
Romans do sweat and drool and ogle – 'O rare for Antony',
'Rare Egyptian', 'Royal wench' – Enobarbus sees to.

By the time Enobarbus silences the eager promptings of
Maecenas and Agrippa with his 'I will tell you', we know that
he is going to play the story for all it is worth. So far he has
rationed out his information, keeping them waiting with
grand intimations of what he has seen and what he could
tell: 'This was but as a fly by an eagle.' Falstaff would have
been proud of that. The report, when it comes, has after all
this to be good; nor, I think, are we aware for the space of a
single line of Enobarbus's not making it so. What description
itself might fail of, Enobarbus coins paradox upon paradox
to provide. They come thick:

> whose wind did seem
> To glow the delicate cheeks which they did cool,
> And what they undid did;

and fast:

> That she did make defect perfection
> And, breathless, power breathe forth.

Until we start to get the trick of it, so that we are tutored in
the convention that Enobarbus will exploit for his final
coup:

> For vilest things
> Become themselves in her, that the holy priests
> Bless her, when she is riggish.

We can only applaud the witty blasphemy of that, calculated
to a nicety to give Maecenas and Agrippa the Cleopatra they
want, and a little more to boot. That commentators should
find here the Cleopatra *they* most want would be surprising
were it not for the presence especially of Agrippa to remind
us of men's insatiable need to gape. Strange it still is though,
given the comic circumstances of Enobarbus's utterance, that
so many critics should alight upon his words for the rare

occasion of their writing most unembarrassedly as men, just when we would have them write most moderately as critics.* It is not, after all, to be unchivalrous to Cleopatra here, to keep rather more of our appreciation in reserve than Agrippa can, and to be less eccentric in our benedictions than are the holy priests; nor is it to be unresponsive to Cleopatra's powers to feel them to be, in Enobarbus's account, less remarkable and commanding than we have, at other times, seen them. The Cleopatra in her universally love-sick-making barge with whom Enobarbus captures the gasps of his hearers is a Cleopatra all for spectacle. Enobarbus has been, so far in the play, a stringent if genial ironist; I see nothing in his descriptions of Cleopatra to make us change our sense of him. The highest appreciation of a spectacle will always be an ironist's; only he can simultaneously measure the folly of its ingenuities and relish the grandeur of its success. Enobarbus could not have written all of *Antony and Cleopatra,* but where much is performed with an eye to effect there is much that we rely upon Enobarbus to give us. If we feel that there is, for our sense of the lovers, something too precious to be left only to Enobarbus's humour, then we must keenly divide the reality from the gesture. If we feel that the reality *is* the gesture, we deliver ourselves up to Enobarbus—worse, we find ourselves wrangling with Philo and Pompey.

2 · E L'ALTRO PIANGEA

The second scene of *Antony and Cleopatra* sinks us at once into what feels like an Egyptian Sunday afternoon—a time too languorous even for the languid. Cleopatra's attendants idly twit one another with saucy revelations conned from nature's infinite book of secrecy. Enobarbus lolls about, aloof from the general inactivity and a party to it. Cleopatra enters, looking for Antony, unsure of his present disposition which, in her account, is subject to a trifling changeability:

> He was dispos'd to mirth; but on the sudden
> A Roman thought hath struck him.

And when Antony approaches she disappears. The tedious weight of the passing moment is upon everybody. But things are precarious as well as flat. Cleopatra is more anxious

*See even D.J. Enright: 'This *is* Cleopatra.' (*Shakespeare and the Students.*)

than she admits, and rightly so; for if Antony's protestations
were exorbitant — 'Here is my space' — so are his reversals, in
these stretches of unremarkable time that mock all attempts
to live grandly, likely to be freakish and violent.

If Cleopatra doesn't know what Antony is feeling, neither
does Antony. As the news from Rome crowds in upon his
idleness he tries out a churlish imperturbability:

Antony.   Well, what worst?
Messenger. The nature of bad news infects the teller.
Antony.   When it concerns the fool or coward. On:
             Things that are past are done with me. 'Tis thus,
             Who tells me true, though in his tale lie death,
             I hear him as he flatter'd.
Messenger.   Labienus —
             This is stiff news — hath. . . . .

—which does not convince the messenger. Messengers would
have encountered such vapouring before. And although
Antony is more the susceptible man he claimed he wasn't,
when he learns from another messenger of Fulvia's death,
we cannot be sure he is now himself:

             There's a great spirit gone! Thus did I desire it:
             What our contempts doth often hurl from us,
             We wish it ours again. The present pleasure,
             By revolution lowering, does become
             The opposite of itself: she's good, being gone,
             The hand could pluck her back that shov'd her on.

That sounds as though it would like to be remorse. But it
isn't. We do not have to be champions of the rights of Fulvia
to notice how Antony floats his liabilities only to let them
sink in the shallow waters of rumination. Detached and dis-
tant, he muses merely upon the oddity of things, the strange
inconsistency of human passions, the impermanence of all
desires. He toys with compunction as he toyed with indifference, plausible in neither.

Nothing is safe in these distracted fluctuations; not
Fulvia's memory, not Cleopatra's allure, least of all Antony's
sense of himself. The death of Fulvia, the removal of a major
impediment to his easy sojourn in Egypt, might have been
welcomed. That it should be regretted is perverse, just as its
lesson —

             I must from this enchanting queen break off —

is inconsequent. The only virtue of that idea, amidst all this
instability, is that it at least feels definite. Throughout

Enobarbus's astute prattle Antony holds on to his idea tightly, as if it too could slip through his fingers: 'I must with haste from hence'; 'I must be gone'; 'Would I had never seen her'; 'She is cunning past man's thought'. All of which Enobarbus imperturbably parries as though they were light and passing disturbances, mere flaps of conscience that he has had to deal with many times before. But on Antony's production of his trump-card — 'Fulvia is dead' — Enobarbus pricks his ear to some new mendacity in his friend:

Why sir, give the gods a thankful sacrifice. When it pleaseth their deities to take the wife of a man from him, it shows to man the tailors of the earth; comforting therein, that when old robes are worn out, there are members to make new. If there were no more women but Fulvia, then had you indeed a cut, and the case to be lamented: this grief is crown'd with consolation, your old smock brings forth a new petticoat, and indeed the tears live in an onion that should water this sorrow.

We can take the measure of what in the way of love and respect for Fulvia has *not* previously figured in the intimacy of the two men, from Enobarbus's seeing no cause to deliver an epitaph and no need to administer a comfort. The jaunty callousness does not invite, and does not encounter, controversy. In response to the firm reminder that a guilty conscience, in this instance, could only be spurious, Antony shifts his tone to the formal and his emphasis from feeling to affairs:

The business she hath broached in the state
Cannot endure my absence.

He has not been talked out of a guilty conscience, for a guilty conscience is not quite what he had. But his justifications are one by one discredited. If they will not bear scrutiny, then scrutiny they shall not receive. He silences Enobarbus only by pulling rank on him and withdrawing the personal nature of his resolve from publicity.

At no time during this scene has our sense of Antony's predicament, if that is not too small a word, entailed our making up our minds which way we want him to jump. Had he been able to reply to Enobarbus's words about 'the tears that live in an onion' with a firm denial of their truth and returned with conviction to Rome, we might have applauded his decision; had he risen to the challenge of Enobarbus's urbane tranquillity and stayed delightedly where he was, we might likewise have applauded, despite the fact that in either event we would not have had a story. The story we do have tells of Antony returning to Rome now for this reason, now for that; even, as he is to put it when he takes his uncomfortable leave of Cleopatra, for her greater glory. Of course, despite all resistance, he does get away, and if getting away is the chief thing it might matter little how compromised he becomes in the process. But the grounds for the decision have not been cleared. By reducing what holds him in Egypt to 'enchantment', what calls him away to 'business', and by acting to-day on his hankering for the latter, he is creating an antithesis which in other moods will determine another preference. In so far as his leaving Egypt is a matter of making important choices about himself, it is not a decision at all.

So, we are not to be surprised when, in Rome, something equally unlike a decision prompts his return to Egypt. On a hint from Plutarch, Shakespeare turns Antony's rapid conference with the Egyptian Soothsayer to sharp account.

'Now sirrah; you do wish yourself in Egypt?' Antony half asks and half tells the Soothsayer who, seeming to have reasons of his own for wishing a speedy return, knows how to further his cause. He warns Antony that Caesar's fortune shall rise higher than his, and offers some consoling thoughts about the spiritual odiousness of comparisons:

> Thy lustre thickens,
> When he shines by: I say again, thy spirit
> Is all afraid to govern thee near him;
> But he away, 'tis noble.

Believe that and resolution can go sleep; events will take care of themselves. The temptation is irresistible to Antony:

> Be it art or hap,
> He hath spoken true. The very dice obey him,
> And in our sports my better cunning faints
> Under his chance: if we draw lots, he speeds,
> His cocks do win the battle still of mine
> When it is all to nought; and his quails ever
> Beat mine, inhoop'd, at odds. I will to Egypt:
> And though I make this marriage for my peace,
> I' the east my pleasure lies.

(Note that Rome is not so dedicated to the sobrieties as to preclude the usual forms of idling away the time – it is not Rome's fault that Antony's bad luck precludes him from enjoying them.) Had not Antony, a moment· earlier, lulled

Octavia into security with an assurance, not exacted but bountifully given, that although he had not kept his square he would now act 'by the rule'; had he weighed the choice of Egypt, against the rights of Rome, against his own best interests, against anything rather than the one thing he can argue is not his to influence – Fortune's desertion of him; had he thought of Cleopatra as she, in Egypt, thinks of him – then his decision to return might have had some mettle in it. But as he left Egypt, so he plans to leave Rome – out of a flat reversal of spirits; torpid rather than impulsive, yielding to change rather than effecting it. The dull insipidity of the moment masters him now as it mastered him in Alexandria.

The remainder of Antony's time in Rome and Athens is, not surprisingly after this, the subject of little dramatic interest. He undertakes his marriage to Octavia in a rather trance-like state and packs her off back to Caesar – though being no Cleopatra she is not quick to detect his intentions – discomfort in his lips and eyes, guilt in his brows' bent. He enunciates the causes of his resentment of her brother, dripping with unease:

> Nay, nay, Octavia, not only that, –
> That were excusable, that and thousands more
> Of semblable import, – but he hath wag'd
> New wars 'gainst Pompey; made his will, and read it
> To public ear;
> Spoke scantly of me: when perforce he could not
> But pay me terms of honour, cold and sickly
> He vented them; most narrow measure lent me:
> When the best hint was given him, he not took't,
> Or did it from his teeth.

Caesar himself is to complain of Antony frequently in the play, but he is never as feebly querulous as that. Antony, of course, is scratching for a quarrel and a pretext for Octavia's departure as go-between. Her preparedness to go to Caesar in that role gives Antony the opportunity of recovering himself in a show of grand munificence:

> Provide your going,
> Choose your own company, and command what cost
> Your heart has mind to.

Which, whatever the expense incurred, ensures Antony a cheap let-off. Antony's givingness is famous, but he might have treated Octavia more roughly and been kinder.

However, the play does not work hard to interest us in Octavia. And the very fact that if she excites anything at all

in us she excites pity, recalls to us the superior attractions of
Cleopatra who excites so much else. We grant, on that
account, a large leniency to Antony, part of which entails our
not expecting too much of him while he is in the west; it is
in Egypt that his best self has now to show. Indeed it is there
that we next meet him, and I think we detect a something
changed in the tenor of his relations with Cleopatra from the
first moments. Shakespeare has chosen not to show us the
moment of their reunion; but he does show us that the lovers
have not merely picked up where they last left off, that
Antony's absence and return, involving him in something
more like a commitment, have made for a new element.
Enobarbus was all for staying in Egypt in the first place, and
his expressed concern now over the projected conduct of the
wars takes the measure of the new recklessness that is in the
air. There's a new solicitousness, too, in Antony's bearing
towards Cleopatra. Remarking on the extraordinary speed
of Caesar's movements he bends to her, in pointed defiance
of Enobarbus and Canidius who are happy with neither her
military strategy nor her military presence:

> Is it not strange, Canidius,
> That from Tarentum, and Brundusium
> He could so quickly cut the Ionian sea,
> And take in Toryne? You have heard on't, sweet?

Antony's conscientious inclusion of Cleopatra in conferences
of war might irritate the other men, but his drop into the
language of endearment clearly irritates Cleopatra. It is not
as anybody's 'sweet' that she replies:

> Celerity is never more admir'd
> Than by the negligent.

She has already been provoked by Enobarbus into a denial
of her mere femininity, so that her killing sententiousness is
directed as much at Antony's untimely uxoriousness as it is
at his military negligence. But there's no shaking off a proud
and attentive husband:

> A good rebuke,
> Which might have well becom'd the best of men,
> To taunt at slackness. Canidius, we
> Will fight with him by sea.

With a genial oafishness Antony shows that he has mastered
her meaning, and makes certain that it does not go unnoticed
by Enobarbus and Canidius. Cleopatra has to say little more
to have her way. Antony defends the decision to fight at sea

as a man defending the honour of his lady—no matter if his lady is being, for the moment, manly. Assiduous in his ministrations to her as he is, mindful and deferential, it is no surprise when, come the battle, Cleopatra draws him after her irresistibly.

The scene in which Scarus recounts the shamefulness of that act leaves us in no doubt as to what our feelings must be. The graphic descriptions of Cleopatra hoisting sails and flying 'like a cow in June', and Antony clapping on his sea-wing and flying after her 'like a doting mallard', do not brook disagreement. There is no other account to be offered. Enobarbus is stunned and abates Scarus's verdict not a jot.

Yet the very decisiveness of the judgement clears a space in our minds; we no longer have to go on weighing and balancing the rights of the two things Antony has seemed best at. The impending collision has finally happened. Excessive devotion to the business of being a lover has destroyed Antony as a soldier. But what if that is only as terrible as being a soldier is important? Antony has claimed other realities. Well then, if he is sunk as a soldier, might he not soar as a man? I don't think we entertain that eventuality with an entirely open mind, but rather like Enobarbus we follow the wounded chance of Antony, though reason sits in the wind against us.

Perhaps here though, one must speak only for oneself; for there are those whose optimism is not only quickened by what follows, but even vindicated. Indeed for many readers the wait is not at all long before they breathe, in the company of Antony, the finer element. From his speech to his followers after Actium to his death, Antony is most lovably there for them in his warmth and liberality. Bradley, whose good nature hates not to find good nature in others, speaks feelingly of what endears Antony to him:

> How beautiful is his affection for his followers and even for his servants, and the devotion they return! How noble his reception of the news that Enobarbus has deserted him! How touchingly significant the refusal of Eros either to kill him or survive him!

This is the first of the episodes that give us such an Antony:

Antony.
>   Hark, the land bids me tread no more upon't,
>   It is asham'd to bear me. Friends, come hither:
>   I am so lated in the world that I
>   Have lost my way for ever. I have a ship,

> Laden with gold, take that, divide it; fly,
> And make your peace with Caesar.

All.   Fly? Not we.

Antony.
> I have fled myself, and have instructed cowards
> To run, and show their shoulders. Friends, be gone,
> I have myself resolv'd upon a course,
> Which has no need of you. Be gone,
> My treasure's in the harbour. Take it: O,
> I follow'd that I blush to look upon:
> My very hairs do mutiny; for the white
> Reprove the brown for rashness, and they them
> For fear, and doting. Friends, be gone, you shall
> Have letters from me to some friends, that will
> Sweep your way for you. Pray you, look not sad,
> Nor make replies of loathness; take the hint
> Which my despair proclaims. Let that be left
> Which leaves itself: to the sea-side straightway;
> I will possess you of that ship and treasure.
> Leave me, I pray, a little: pray you now,
> Nay, do so: for indeed I have lost command,
> Therefore I pray you: I'll see you by and by.

Can we, without risk of churlishness, resist Bradley's 'How beautiful is his affection for his followers' here? Antony has fled in pursuit of Cleopatra and lost a battle he might have won. His shame is all upon him, and yet he has time to think about the welfare of his followers, offer to provide for them, even recommend that they blamelessly desert him and join sides with Caesar. Can we deny the names of generosity and affection to the manner and the import of the words that at such a time show such a considerateness? We cannot. Yet there are reasons to withhold from Antony a tribute so full as Bradley's. For as we look at the beautiful modulations of Antony's speech, the exquisite placings of that word 'friends', the subdued mystery of his nonetheless advertised 'resolve', are we not to doubt whether his manner of address is at all likely to produce the result he desires: the escape and welfare of his attendants? We must assume that that really is what Antony wants, and that he is not showing his concern for them and making his offer only that they might demonstrate, in return, the depth of their devotion—for there would be no beauty in that. Nor do I detect in his words anything that smacks of such sinister design. But his attendants do not leave him and accept his offer, and it is hard to imagine, given the nature of Antony's speech, how they could. Even the most circumspect generosity, the most responsible affection, might not have known the way to make desertion easy for a loyal nature; but could desertion be harder for his men than Antony all unwittingly makes it? The spectacle of the ruins of a once great soldier is a melancholy one; and that melancholy should be the word — that it is not more sickening on the one hand or more agonizing on the other — is an effect all of Antony's making. For the note he most strikes is the elegiac one. And nothing more melts both our severest judgements and our clearest sympathies than the sad strains of elegy. It is beautiful and bewitching. It dignifies defeat and it neutralizes anger; it reduces the sharp pains of remorse to the sweet pangs of regret. Its province is an exquisitely diffused sadness. 'Pray you, look not sad', Antony gently requests, and we know the likely effect of that. Ships and treasures have little reality in this atmosphere; when everything human is rendered so frail and insubstantial, they are as nothing. It would take an uncommon toughness in a follower of Antony, or an uncommon insusceptibility, to resist the seductive tearfulness of the moment and remember the attractions of treasure, or reason the permissibility of desertion. What might have been forgivable practicality can now be only monstrous betrayal; that Antony himself will not see it as betrayal will but make it the more of a one. That, of course, is to be Enobarbus's problem. And it is in his story that we are to see more fully what it is like for a follower of Antony to be the recipient of his melancholy considerateness, how hard it is either to remain with him manfully or to leave him boldly.

Antony, of course, in this speech to his followers, is only half-aware of them; just as, in his slow recognition of Cleopatra and his putting to her, more as a tribute than a reproach, the absolute fact of his devotion to her, he is away somewhere on his own. His words all through this scene are partly addressed as if to the unseen forces of the air. We do not complain of that. Given what has happened we might the rather complain that he is as aware of followers and of Cleopatra as he is. There are times when a warm, human attentiveness ought not to operate. And even those unseen forces are not addressed as appalled witnesses but as things of compassion; what they are privy to, as Antony muses over what has become of him, is a wistful nostalgia. If it was affection that made Antony's sword weak at Actium, it is affection that softly diffuses itself through all his words after it. It seems that one of the penalties of Antony's having made himself, to the exclusion of all else, a creature of warm susceptibility, is that he should be deprived of the dignity and even the consolation of regarding himself with severity.

There is nothing in the play that invites us to speculate, in this fashion, upon Cleopatra. Indeed, in so far as the question is of penalties, she is remarkable for not noticeably paying any. That's a subject for later discussion; but it does seem to me significant that from this stage of the play onwards the pair suffer an odd estrangement. We see Cleopatra often in the company of Enobarbus discussing an Antony whose moods are foreign to her. We have a sense of her, a little bemused, watching and waiting and not always liking. There are, of course, to be great moments yet, and if Antony is to make some brave shows of recovering his manly vigour, nothing is more touching than the brave show Cleopatra makes of believing in them. Her words at the end of that delightful scene where she helps Antony into his armour, remind us that the liveliness with which she enters into his enthusiasm has yet some caution in reserve:

> He goes forth gallantly: that he and Caesar might
> Determine this great war in single fight!
> Then Antony –; but now – Well on.

Yet when Antony returns successfully from his skirmish she rises indeed:

> Lord of lords,
> O infinite virtue, com'st thou smiling from
> The world's great snare uncaught?

It is a magnificent reception. Cleopatra is all queen and all responsive woman; and what does it matter if Antony seems to have had a rather more boisterous and athletic welcome in mind?

> O thou day o' the world,
> Chain mine arm'd neck, leap thou, attire and all,
> Through proof of harness to my heart, and there
> Ride on the pants triumphing!

It only adds to our gratification that *his* idea of what the occasion requires should be an exuberant boyishness rather than a lofty majesty:

> My nightingale,
> We have beat them to their beds. What girl, though grey
> Do something mingle with our younger brown, yet ha' we
> A brain that nourishes our nerves, and can
> Get goal for goal of youth.

Cleopatra nonetheless remains a queen as she promises to
bestow upon Scarus a king's armour, all of gold—just one,
she seems to imply, of many that she has to give. And
Antony, requesting Cleopatra's hand for 'a jolly march'
through Alexandria, remains himself. The delight they take
in one another's style of grandeur could not be more innocent or more winning.

However, unless we believe that Shakespeare allows
Plutarch to determine him to an arbitrary tragedy just when
all is glorious between the lovers, we must admit that something like sadness attends our reception of such scenes. The
glory is that of the last throw of the dice, and their commitment to it, even then, is unequal. Cleopatra is splendidly alert
to Antony's demands, and she seldom fails him; but she is, as
it were, waiting for her cue. We marvel at her ready cheerfulness, at her resourcefulness, at the patience with which
she works to raise Antony's wilting spirits ('That's my brave
lord'); but we are not surprised, though some critics are a
little hurt, that Antony's death does not for long diminish
her vigour. Despite fluctuations and eruptions of passion,
noble and otherwise, they seem to me never so separated,
never so far from blissful identity of impulse, never so little
of a 'mutual pair', as they are in all their dealings after
Actium.

For much of Acts III and IV, Cleopatra remains on the
peripheries of the main action. It is not that she isn't a vivid
presence now, but rather that she feels herself to be extraneous on many occasions; unable to see what she has to do
with either the savagery of Antony's jealousies or the dole-
fulness of his affections. 'Call to me all my sad captains',
Antony demands, after the whipping of Thidias. 'Call all his
noble captains to my lord', Cleopatra corrects him, dis-
associating herself from any melancholy. Egyptians, we are
told, are committed to feeling—but not, it seems, to feelings
of this dolorous cast. It is certainly Antony the lover who is
most present to us throughout this section of the play, but
even so Cleopatra's attendance is not indispensable; for as
scene after scene discloses, Antony is a lover now—not
sensually but sentimentally—in all his relations. Friends,
followers, attendants—they none of them escape Antony's
relentlessly bountiful affection. For Antony, being a lover
has always found most of its justification in a grand and
public expansiveness of spirit; many of his pleasures have
been for the general gratefully to share, and those that have
not, have been for the general delightedly to observe. Love is
most love for him when it declares its power to make the

world — the outside world — a different place; and that kiss
is sweetest that melts Rome in Tiber or rates everything that
has been won or lost. We never arrive at an inwardness with
Antony's sense of his passion because passion for Antony
does not itself reside interiorly. As we have seen, his deci-
sions for or against it have been matters of sudden starts and
impulses, not reflection. Away from Cleopatra, the best
Antony can do is recall that i' the east his pleasure lies. While
Cleopatra can every day concoct and improvise an Antony,
accumulating around them both a living history of things that
were and never were. We do not have to look outside Cleopatra to find vindication of her passion; the activity of
loving repays itself in her by quickening her inner life, providing her with necessary nourishment for her wit no less
than for her fancy. But not even the most partial of Antony's
admirers would talk about his love as a thing that enjoys
rapport with the active faculties of memory and invention,
or has the power to stir him even in his vacancies. In accordance with Antony's own idea of himself, we go instead to
outward manifestations, to that affection which is so un-
reserved in its expression, so democratic in its distribution.
Above all we go to the love his friends and followers and
attendants bear him: the devotion he inspires. We seem, in
fact, after the shame and shock of Actium, to go nowhere
else. For Antony is available to us almost entirely in terms of
his effect upon others. It is as if the play is asking that we
bring all our disparate thoughts about Antony in love to bear
upon the question of what he occasions in those who love
him, what he causes them to feel, what his givingness gives.
By this are we to know what he has made of love or, if there
is a difference, what love has made of him.

It is always difficult to know, when affections are hemmed
in by sorrows, how far a person should be accountable for
his words. And in this play, where the stakes have been high
and the passions always capricious, the difficulty is especially
great. Enobarbus shows us the way to a proper reservation
of judgement when attempting to account to a bewildered
Cleopatra for an Antony in this mood:

Call forth my household servants, let's tonight
          Enter three or four Servitors.
Be bounteous at our meal. Give me thy hand,
Thou hast been rightly honest; — so hast thou, —
Thou, — and thou, — and thou: you have serv'd me well,
And kings have been your fellows.

'What means this?' asks Cleopatra, and Enobarbus's

explanation is charitably off-hand:

> 'Tis one of those odd tricks which sorrow shoots
> Out of the mind.

That restrains us; perhaps 'this' is but freakish, perhaps it adheres in no inevitable way to Antony. But the need so to separate the action from the man takes the measure of the perturbation—whatever Antony is doing, neither Cleopatra nor Enobarbus likes it. They are not moved to an admiration of Antony's 'beautiful affection', and their disquiet intensifies as Antony continues to melt all about him:

Antony. And thou art honest too.
I wish I could be made so many men,
And all of you clapp'd up together in
An Antony; that I might do you service,
So good as you have done.
All. The gods forbid!
Antony. Well, my good fellows, wait on me tonight:
Scant not my cups, and make as much of me
As when mine empire was your fellow too,
And suffer'd my command.
Cleopatra. (Aside to Enobarbus.) What does he mean?
Enobarbus. (Aside to Cleopatra.) To make his followers weep.
Antony. Tend me tonight;
May be it is the period of your duty,
Haply you shall not see me more, or if,
A mangled shadow. Perchance to-morrow
You'll serve another master. I look on you,
As one that takes his leave. Mine honest friends,
I turn you not away, but like a master
Married to your good service, stay till death:
Tend me to-night two hours, I ask no more,
And the gods yield you for't!
Enobarbus. What mean you, sir,
To give them this discomfort? Look, they weep,
And I, an ass, am onion-ey'd; for shame,
Transform us not to women.

I have seen accounts of this scene by critics who blush for Cleopatra's ignorance of Antony's 'meaning' here, not because Antony is too horribly clear but because she, in her incomprehension of his benevolent intent, is too horribly unfeeling. But in an excess of its opposite unfeelingness can look lovely; and Cleopatra is seldom more impressive to me than she is, in her blankness, here: a total stranger to the need to be either the creator of tears or their object.

Enobarbus, too, reaches heights in this scene. Not simply because he is astute in his criticism, but because he is astute in his generosity. Generosity of affection is the issue in this scene, and it is Enobarbus, in his, who shows us how far Antony might be said to fail of it. How tactful his final appeal to Antony is! We have seen him in his asides to Cleopatra aloof from what Antony is doing and finally critical of it, yet without incurring Antony's wrath or injuring his feelings, he brings the performance to an end by speaking as one most affected by it; he conceals his distaste for that performance in an attestation of its success; he muffles rebuke in tribute. He shuts Antony up and eases him off. The effort, on both accounts, is to spare a dignity. The generosity is purposeful and adroit.

Whereas Antony? Well, he weaves a wonderful spell. He singles out the meanest of his men; he is individually attentive; he pays the warmest of tributes to their loyalty. When he wishes that he could reciprocate their good service, their protest sounds of the sincerest. On such an evening, after such an address, perhaps it could not have been otherwise, but who would say that Antony has only caught the thing he angled for? He is bewitching too, as he requests that they serve him for one night more, perhaps the last night of their employ: an appeal of such lenity and apology that it seems to dispel all idea of the obligation of service and asks instead only for the charity of a little — a last — forbearance. His intimation that they may soon be Caesar's men is scarred with no suggestion of reproach; and all is suffused with that melancholy insubstantiality which characterised his earlier speech to his followers after Actium—an insubstantiality that, strangely, does not blur the human but renders it the more exposed and vulnerable:

> Haply you shall not see me more, or if,
> A mangled shadow.

I suppose a man has a right to see his own finish as only melancholy; but why inspire melancholy in others? How, after all, does that serve them? What does it help them to, what comfort does it administer, what courage to face a desolate, Antonyless future does it teach the trick of? I think of Coriolanus taking leave of his family and friends at the gates of Rome, and his sound intuition that if his going is not to be heartbreaking for them he must show them a self vigorous and confident: Coriolanus, of course, has at that time such a self to call upon. Antony, to do him justice, once he is tipped the wink by Enobarbus, has a go at trying to recall his:

Ho, ho, ho!
Now the witch take me, if I meant it thus!
Grace grow where those drops fall, my hearty friends;
You take me in too dolorous a sense,
For I spake to you for your comfort, did desire you
To burn this night with torches: know, my hearts,
I hope well of to-morrow, and will lead you
Where rather I'll expect victorious life,
Than death, and honour.

But who would now believe that?

There is no call to be exasperated by Antony's bluster; it takes an honest man to dissemble so badly. It is what he does well that we are to blush for. His 'Ho, ho, ho!' has at least the merit of recognising—albeit dimly through the moisture and the tears—what a more strenuously inspiring generosity would have looked like. No exaggerated sympathy for the discomforted, weeping, but anonymous servants occasions our criticism here. Antony does nothing useful for them, but the greater question—it is to be asked more pointedly later—is of what, for his good or his credit, they do for him. What kind of tribute to him is it that their tearful devotion to his noble and shadowy ruin pays? If the affection Antony wins from his attendants is the affection he invites, does not this scene compel us to say, with a backward glance at Cleopatra's first words in the play—her cautionary reminder that there should be limits even to love—that he wins too much? Too much, of the wrong kind? There are tears and tears. Cleopatra's ignorance of Antony's meaning in this scene speaks well for her, just as Enobarbus's annulment of it speaks well for him; but their refusal to be moved is no disrespect to Antony; they show what a proper regard should *not* entail. Cleopatra is never to dissolve over Antony; Enobarbus, of course, is. That latter fact is often taken as a further triumph of Antony's loving munificence. But are we not to wonder, after what we have so far seen, whether it is not a defeat for it?

With the desertion of Enobarbus and his dying unreproached and all forgiven, we look further at the way Antony lodges in the hearts of others. I see little sign in Enobarbus's dying speeches of Shakespeare's being interested in giving us a study of remorse; nor does he seem gripped by the moral questions that attend disloyalty. Enobarbus's words, when he discovers how graciously and generously Antony has behaved towards him—

O Antony,

> Thou mine of bounty, how wouldst thou have paid
> My better service, when my turpitude
> Thou dost so crown with gold! This blows my heart—

evoke more of Antony than Enobarbus. It is the inescapable
bounty of Antony that swells Enobarbus's heart, his love and
magnanimity that have found a passage even through the
enemy ranks and moved a rival soldier, however busy in his
office, to mouth their greatness and by so doing taunt
Enobarbus for his unfaithfulness:

> > > > > Your emperor
> > Continues still a Jove.

The long arm of Antony's godlike givingness stretches out to
Enobarbus—and Enobarbus as a consequence goes 'seek/
Some ditch, wherein to die.' Such was certainly never
Antony's intention when, with men deserting all about him,
he received without remonstrance the news that Enobarbus
too had gone, and sent love and treasure after him:

> *Antony.* Who's gone this morning?
> *Soldier.*   Who?
> > One ever near thee; call for Enobarbus,
> > He shall not hear thee, or from Caesar's camp
> > Say 'I am none of thine.'
> *Antony.*   What sayest thou?
> *Soldier.*   Sir,
> > He is with Caesar.
> *Eros.*   Sir, his chests and treasure
> > He has not with him.
> *Antony.*   Is he gone?
> *Soldier.*   Most certain.
> *Antony.*
> > Go, Eros, send his treasure after, do it,
> > Detain no jot, I charge thee: write to him—
> > I will subscribe—gentle adieus, and greetings;
> > Say, that I wish he never find more cause
> > To change a master. O, my fortunes have
> > Corrupted honest men. Despatch.—Enobarbus.

The mine of bounty might be bottomless, but it is an infinitely jaded Antony that crowns his old friend's turpitude
with gold. There is no time for grief now, no point in repro-
bation. Even surprise does not have space in which to breathe.
'—Enobarbus'—the name, at the last, is thrown away; the
memory and the affliction postponed. There is no display of
any passion, no grand decision taken to favour forgiveness.

Antony does not calm himself to justice, or bestir himself to bounty; and the liberality is more exquisite for having all the spontaneity of a half-attention. Even the letter that Antony will have written, he will not write himself; the loving words are dictated, and as they immediately come to Antony so they will suffice. In all his thoughts and actions there is not a trace of calculation.

But, as we have had cause to ask before, might he not have calculated more and made Enobarbus suffer less? Is it too much to ask of generosity that it seek the best way to effect the thing it most intends? That this is not the best way I think we know even before we have the proof of it in Enobarbus's exacerbated remorse. At the very moment that we are moved by Antony's instinctive kindness we also start from it in dread, for we know that the return of his treasure will only open up the wounds of Enobarbus's guilt, and that those 'gentle adieus and greetings' will be as a knife in them. The greatest of men might, over such a matter, miscalculate, or be the nobler for not calculating at all; but if we are beginning to feel, having seen much of it now, that Antony's generosity is something it might be better not to be on the receiving end of, it is not only on account of its splendid carelessness that we pronounce it dangerous. For what we have been shown in those scenes where Antony chokes the power he offers to generate—the power in his followers to leave him and accept reward; the power in his servants to find comfort and face the possibility of a mangled master and an end to service; and now in Enobarbus the power to feel let off and free—is that there attaches to his givingness a fatally unmanning sadness, that there is a moral infection of weary piteousness in it. We cannot propose, unless we would be critically cute, that Antony kills Enobarbus with kindness. Even before he received back his treasure, Enobarbus had weighed the political inadvisability of what he had done and accused himself so sorely that he would 'joy no more'. But it does seem to say more about the inevitable effects of Antony's good intentions than it does about Enobarbus's character that the latter should die of melancholy, that he should call down the poisonous damp of night to disponge upon him, that he should not so much take his life as permit it to melt away.

It comes back, this failure of Antony's to invigorate those who love him or to disburden them of himself, to the fact that a man cannot emotionally any more than materially give more than he has to give. Antony has no purposiveness to pass on, just as his spectacle—the spectacle as he evokes it — has no power to inspire wonder or fear. For what flavours his affection and his bounty, even if it does not solely determine them, is his own melancholy apprehension of himself, his own bewildered sense of the extreme sadness of what has befallen him. The subtle wrongness of those 'gentle adieus and greetings' lies not in any design behind them, but in their exorbitance, in their exceeding what a proper understanding and a decent forgiveness demand. They embrace the betrayal. Antony's assessment of the significance of Enobarbus's defection —

> O, my fortunes have
> Corrupted honest men —

begs a question; perhaps it even begs two. Yet for all that he shuffles off responsibility, he is quiescent. He is severe neither on himself nor on his fortunes. There is no fight left in him. And how can one feel more for a man than he feels for himself? That question is soon to present itself, fatally, to Eros — the man whose very name must, in this context, spell trouble.

After the final defeat of his forces we see Antony, alone with Eros, weaving once again his wonderful spell:

Antony. Eros, thou yet behold'st me?
Eros.   Ay, noble lord.
Antony. Sometime we see a cloud that's dragonish,
    A vapour sometime, like a bear, or lion,
    A tower'd citadel, a pendent rock,
    A forked mountain, or blue promontory
    With trees upon't, that nod unto the world,
    And mock our eyes with air. Thou hast seen these signs,
    They are black vesper's pageants.
Eros.   Ay, my lord.
Antony.
    That which is now a horse, even with a thought
    The rack dislimns, and makes it indistinct
    As water is in water.
Eros.   It does, my lord.
Antony.
    My good knave Eros, now thy captain is
    Even such a body: here I am Antony,
    Yet cannot hold this visible shape, my knave.

Poor Eros, having to listen to that. No wonder — and certainly no surprise for us by now — he is soon weeping. 'Dim, unstable, unsubstantial', is how Hazlitt describes the imagery of these speeches by way of catching their beauty. And magical they are in rendering the shifting shapes and shadows of things. But we have seen Antony evoking his own beautiful insubstantiality too often to wonder whether this is but another 'odd trick'; clearly this is now the habit of his soul. Finally there are limits to how much beauty a man has a right to bathe his own dimness in. When Macbeth discovers that 'life's but a walking shadow' there is nothing wistful and lovely in the utterance; he has known enough of distinctness for his apprehension of its opposite to be hateful. Antony makes sad music out of his shadowiness. The string he plucks is that of plangency; the feeling man is still alive and thrills to the exquisite shimmer of indefinite sensation. But if Antony is not Macbeth he is not Cleopatra either. We might think of the alertness of mind that she brings to her final moments, how much she is still fascinatedly finding out, and we might ponder then whether, as far as his consciousness can register it, anything is happening to Antony at all. Even the belief that Cleopatra has not, as he had thought, betrayed him, but has died with his name on her lips, makes no intrusion into his mood; he summons his energies only for a further drop into a sublime lassitude:

> Unarm, Eros, the long day's task is done
> And we must sleep.

— It could easily have been 'weep'.

Everything that happens to Antony now is humiliating. The events are taken largely from Plutarch, but Shakespeare shows him how much better a story he had than he knew. It is not a comic scene: there is too awful an indignity in the prolongation of Antony's reluctant life for it to be that; but it is not a painful scene either, for the strange inconsequentiality of what happens, or rather of what doesn't, prevents our being moved deeply. Our nerves are jangled, we seem to be teased where we are fastidious. And we are asked, as well, to acquiesce in a judgement of unusual harshness — but not an arbitrary or a sudden one; we have been pushed towards it over many scenes. Bradley has all along resisted that pressure, yet around the issue of Eros's refusal to kill Antony — and the question of the devotion Antony inspires is inescapably before us and before Antony now — he does seem to wriggle: 'How touchingly significant the refusal of Eros either to kill him or survive him!' That could mean many things. I would like to think that Bradley was in two minds about the touching significance of what Eros does and does not do, but I suspect he would have sympathised with these words of D. J. Enright's:

> Eros's inability to kill Antony, his killing of himself
> instead, is further testimony to one kind of greatness
> in Antony (who would do this for Caesar?), working
> in the same way as Enobarbus's death. Undeniably
> Antony has one characteristic of the tragic hero: he
> does not leave this world unattended.

'Unattended' is perhaps an unfortunate word, for while
Antony's passage by no means goes unnoticed or unmourned,
the last thing Eros or the later guards want is to be present
at it or to ease it. There is a degree of having it both ways
in the argument: Antony is great because his men see his
death through with him, and he is also great because they
don't. We need not, I suppose, where such greatness is the
question, press for consistency; but would it not have been
greater in a Roman, or perhaps in any man in this need, to
have known the way to help Eros to his painful task, or
greater still to have had that in his very presence that would
ensure its performance? We are, of course, on fairly alien
moral territory here. So, we must suppose, was Shakespeare.
But there is evidence enough to suggest that the 'Roman
way' interested him, and that he put his mind to the problem
of what for Romans, in such a situation, the highest duty
would comprise; what a noble Roman could properly ask for,
and what a devoted one would properly return. In *Julius
Caesar*, neither Cassius nor Brutus is thought to be less the
man for successfully persuading an attendant to help him to
his death. They both acknowledge the enormity of what they
ask, but they both know the quick way to steel a man to it.
On both occasions the act has some love in it; it has none of
that delighted alacrity which, we might deduce from some
accounts, would be expected to accompany the sword into
Caesar.

Antony, as we have seen, has not been good at steeling
men for a long time now; making them weep is where he is
strong. Eros is already well softened when Antony puts his
awful request to him, and his initial reluctance is countered
thus:

> Eros,
> Wouldst thou be window'd in great Rome, and see
> Thy master thus with pleach'd arms, bending down
> His corrigible neck, his face subdued
> To penetrative shame; whilst the wheel'd seat
> Of fortunate Caesar, drawn before him, branded
> His baseness that ensued?

There is a strange, rather fleshly vividness in Antony's conjured image of himself and his shame here — 'pleach'd arms',
'corrigible neck', 'face subdued to penetrative shame'. It is
an effect partly of imagining the compassion that there is
to be felt on his behalf by another, of his knowing perhaps
too well what a devotion to his own person is like and where
it is susceptible. We might pass over in silence the success
with which Antony reverses what we normally mean by
sympathetic imaginativeness. But the speech is, for its further purpose, a failure; he makes himself, for anyone who
loves him — and who indeed doesn't? — supremely unkillable.
He presents to Eros a ripe sentience, an overpoweringly
sensuous vulnerability. Brutus and Cassius understood the
need for something like impersonality at such a moment;
Brutus has Strato hide his face and Cassius covers his own.
But Antony is, as it were, all too there in person; he has no
hard surfaces to present; he is, as we have so often noted
of him, plump with feeling. Never can a more palpable bosom
have offered itself to the sword. Of course the sword fails of
its task.

If Eros cannot kill him, neither can Antony — with any
promptitude — kill himself. His failure presents a cruel spectacle, not I think because we care only for adroitness and
cleanliness in such affairs, but because his life is now being
protracted beyond what decency can tolerate and compassion can bear. No mere inconsequential irony attaches to
these and the last few remaining events of Antony's life.
Shakespeare might be plucking at our nerves when he has
Antony botch his suicide, but there is nothing arbitrary
about Antony's inability to find anyone who will mercifully
— it's no longer a question of nobility — kill him. The excru-
ciating indignities that attend his last hours are the price he
pays for having made himself too much a man, too much a
thing of emotion: for his followers an object of too piteous
and reverential a love. Our moral sense easily accommodates
the idea that penalties attach to hardness of heart; we are
more reluctant to believe that nature also penalises its opposite. But could anything be more pointed than the preparedness of his guards to offer laments over a half-alive Antony,
but not put an end to his pain?

First Guard.　　　　　　　　　　　　What's the noise?
Antony. I have done my work ill, friends: O make an end
　　　　Of what I have begun.
Second Guard.　　　　　　　　The star is fall'n.
First Guard. And time is at his period.

All.   Alas, and woe!
Antony. Let him that loves me, strike me dead.
First Guard.   Not I.
Second Guard. Nor I.
Third Guard. Nor any one.

                      (Exeunt Guards)

The tributes and the tears that have flowed so freely through the play flow still; but their crazy inappropriateness here, their being the last things Antony now requires, their positive hindrance of what he does want, is given us with the sharp apparentness of something close to farce. Here is devotion indeed! Everyone, it seems, is too beautifully devoted to Antony to help him. 'Let him that loves me, strike me dead' – he might have fared better with an appeal to loyalties less warm and affections less intimate. As it is he could not have fared worse. There is more than just the prudence of the ordinary soldier in the frantic refusal and dispersal of the guards; they shy from Antony as from some untouchable. The murderous instincts that a Macbeth or a Coriolanus calls up might strike us as paying, after all, a greater tribute. They certainly pay a more serviceable one. He who lives by the sword shall die by the sword; he who lives by love enjoys the same justice but dies at the hands of a crueller antagonist.

To mis-marry two phrases of Bradley's, 'there is a horrid aptness' in his description of Antony as 'love's martyr'. But if we feel the indignities of Antony's prolonged finish to be his natural fulfilment, we are not finding satisfaction in a melodramatic morality. Antony's crime is not passion. We do not see him dazed by lust or profaning by carnality. His love for Cleopatra does not rattle the gates of our respectability. It could have seen more wildness and done him less harm. What his story speaks most of is purpose melted in the warm human glow, an unmanning, in the name of melancholy affectionateness, relentless and contagious. Of those in close and constant contact only Cleopatra remains immune. Love is not, in her, at war with her best purposes and her shrewdest practicalities; it is not tepid or accommodating, but neither is it tearful and piteous. Strangely, for many readers, anything that smacks of self-preservation in Cleopatra requires extravagant ingenuities of explaining away, as if love to be love must be desperate and self-consuming. Quick-wittedness and even the smallest dash of cunning seem to spoil it all. Such, I suppose, are Antony's men. But it is Cleopatra's way, it seems to me, that Shakespeare finds delightful and even, in the cheerfullest possible way, inspiring.

3 · SWEATING LABOUR

Except for when she is turning on displays to beggar public belief, and we rely upon the words of interested reporters for our sense of those, the Cleopatra that Shakespeare gives us owes little to Plutarch's. I would not say that when we catch her most intimately we are back in the bright, youthful world of Beatrices and Rosalinds, but those girls are more closely related to her, more her intellectual if not her spiritual cousins, than is Plutarch's Queen of 'flickering enticements':

> she suttelly seemed to languish for the love of Antonius, pyning her body for lacke of meate. Furthermore, she every way so framed her countenaunce, that when Antonius came to see her, she cast her eyes upon him, like a woman ravished for joy. Straight againe when he went from her, she fell a weeping and blubbering, looked rufully of the matter, and still found the meanes that Antonius should often-tymes finde her weeping: and then when he came sodainely upon her, she made as though she dryed her eyes, and turned her face away, as if she were unwilling that he should see her weepe. All these tricks she used. . . .

We know where we are, even if Plutarch's Antony does not, with that lady. Certainly our Cleopatra is not above using tricks, but can we be sure that what we have here is all dedication to performance?

Cleopatra. Where is he?
Charmian.   I did not see him since.
Cleopatra.
　　See where he is, who's with him, what he does:
　　I did not send you. If you find him sad,
　　Say I am dancing; if in mirth, report
　　That I am sudden sick. Quick, and return. (*Exit Alexas.*)
Charmian.
　　　　Madam, methinks if you did love him dearly,
　　　　You do not hold the method, to enforce
　　　　The like from him.
Cleopatra.   What should I do, I do not?
Charmian. In each thing give him way, cross him in nothing.
Cleopatra. Thou teachest like a fool: the way to lose him.
Charmian.   Tempt him not so far. I wish, forebear;
　　　　In time we hate that which we often fear.
　　　　　　Enter Antony.

> But here comes Antony.
Cleopatra.   I am sick and sullen.

The exchange with Charmian reminds us that there are tricks
and tricks, and it is not simply our knowledge that they all
work that prevents our earnestly pondering which work best.
Our eye is upon other things. We are surprised at once, I
think, at the extent to which Cleopatra shows herself as
jittery. We would not have supposed from what we saw of
her in the first scene that she would be liable, in this relation,
to quite so much unease. She announces the wiles that will
control Antony, and even though she does not prevent his
leaving, controlling him does not prove difficult; but she is
not in control of her own states of feeling. Even Charmian's
interjection is not aimed at a relaxed and assured, play-
acting Cleopatra, nor is her dismissal of it easy or urbane.
When Antony does arrive Cleopatra is not true to her scheme.
We must assume, given what Antony has to announce, that
he enters more in sadness than in mirth, but Cleopatra does
not dance at him. 'I am sick and sullen' sounds more like
fact than calculated fancy. But can we tell which is which
as the scene proceeds?

Cleopatra.
> I know by that same eye there's some good news.
> What, says the married woman you may go?
> Would she had never given you leave to come!
> Let her not say 'tis I that keep you here.
> I have no power upon you; hers you are.
Antony. The gods best know —
Cleopatra.   O, never was there queen
> So mightily betray'd! yet at the first
> I saw the treasons planted.
Antony.   Cleopatra, —
Cleopatra.
> Why should I think you can be mine and true
> (Though you in swearing shake the throned gods)
> Who have been false to Fulvia? Riotous madness,
> To be entangled with those mouth-made vows,
> Which break themselves in swearing!
Antony.   Most sweet queen, —
Cleopatra.
> Nay, pray you, seek no colour for your going,
> But bid farewell, and go: when you sued staying,
> Then was the time for words; no going then;
> Eternity was in our lips, and eyes,
> Bliss in our brows' bent; none our parts so poor,

> But was a race of heaven. They are so still,
> Or thou, the greatest soldier of the world,
> Art turn'd the greatest liar.

Reporting upon this scene H. A. Mason finds little to write
in his usually full 'notebook':

> Nothing is clear to me in the following dissembling
> scene between Antony and Cleopatra. The two charac-
> ters themselves do not quite know where they stand. . .
> neither he nor she can ever speak out honestly. Cleo-
> patra looks for a moment as if she were going to drop
> play-acting. . .*

A moment of confessed blankness from Mr Mason can sometimes be worth many another critic's page of unhampered
perspicuity, but an improper scruple seems to be restraining
him here. It is not just that it is as unhelpful faced with this
scene, as with any other in which they both appear, to speak
of 'the two characters' as if they perform equally; nor that
Cleopatra's loquacity provides all the reason we need why
Antony cannot speak out at all, honestly or otherwise. What
most ensures that the reporter's pad stays empty is the
assumption that honesty is one thing and play-acting another.
As a general rule we cannot, I suppose, do without some such
distinction, but there are natures that confound it; and in
this scene in particular it seems to me done for us, and with
poignancy, that Cleopatra's exasperation, with herself as
much as with Antony, shows itself in perplexing alternations
of the assumed and the felt. Certainly those 'feminine arts'
which Johnson found 'too low' are all given an airing, and
they remind us of how much of the ordinary lives side by
side with its opposite in Cleopatra. That in itself accounts for
much of her exasperation: the experience of being an uncommon woman in the toils of what is to appear so often in
this scene as a common passion. There are limits to how uncommon any passion can be, and the threatened disloyalty
of separation is more liable than most things to bring any
lover hard up against those limits. Brought to them as she is,
of course Cleopatra will look more ironically than ever upon
the extravagant protestations that love throws up. It is distinctly Antony's language that she parodies in 'Eternity was
in our lips, our eyes'. She acts it beautifully. But no sooner
has she mocked its exorbitance than she embraces it: 'They
are so still'. To know the grand absurdities of love is not to

*H. A. Mason, *Shakespeare's Tragedies of Love.*

wish to be without them. Well, she might not quite know
where she stands, and indeed she is to go on shifting her
ground for many lines yet. But she has her surenesses, and
thrown back upon them by Antony's accusation that she is
'idleness itself', she speaks without equivocation:

> 'Tis sweating labour,
> To bear such idleness so near the heart
> As Cleopatra this. But sir, forgive me,
> Since my becomings kill me, when they do not
> Eye well to you. Your honour calls you hence,
> Therefore be deaf to my unpitied folly,
> And all the gods go with you! Upon your sword
> Sit laurel victory, and smooth success
> Be strew'd before your feet!

If we like our honesty plain and unadorned we have it here.
Infuriating as some of her twists and turns have been throughout this scene, I see no reason to believe she exaggerates
the amount of sincere effort that has gone into them. There
is a dignified weariness about these words; she speaks more in
resignation than in defiance, brought by Antony's obtuse-
ness to say more, perhaps, of what she feels than she would
have wished. There is a certain stage of coming up against the
brute fact of felt passion that renders protective wiles and
taunting recrimination superfluous. I see no irony in Cleopatra's blessing Antony's journey. She is past that; she gives
in and lets him off.

It is not *this* Cleopatra that we are reminded of when, in
a chapter entitled 'Cleopatra, but not Antony', the hero of
Aaron's Rod refuses in his soul the fatal allure of the all-
adoring, all-consuming, high-priestess of love:

> She would drink the one drop of his innermost heart's
> blood, and he would be carrion. As Cleopatra killed her
> lovers in the morning. Surely they knew that death
> was their just climax. They had approached the climax.
> Accept then.
>
> But his soul stood apart, and could have nothing to
> do with it. If he had *really* been tempted, he would have
> gone on, and she might have had his central heart's
> blood. Yes, and thrown away the carrion. He would
> have been willing.
>
> But fatally, he was not tempted. His soul stood apart
> and decided. At the bottom of his soul he disliked her.

Think you there was, or might be such a Cleopatra? Or is she
in this guise the veriest myth, perpetuated over the ages in

answer to the needs and promptings of men's fantasies—a
fabulous creature born of fervid male longing and cold male
terror? Something of the kind seems to be betrayed in that
characteristically Lawrentian note for such an encounter: the
'Oh no you don't!' of the remote-souled, spindly-masculine
integrity, husbanding its hallowed treasure. What Cleopatra
anyway would breakfast heartily on that? The two Cleo-
patras do not have much in common, but there is a closer
relation between the Antony that Aaron does not want to
be and the Shakespearean Antony that is. For the latter,
when he seeks his consummation in a kiss does also—though
he would never put it to himself like this—seek his annihi-
lation in it; the world of deeds and large activity is arrogantly
defied in the infatuation, but that is only another way of
saying that it is willingly discarded. Which, of course, is not
what Cleopatra—the Cleopatra of our play—had in mind at
all. 'Ah, ha! y'are caught', she might say, as she imagines
hooking Antony with her angle, but it is a live Antony that
she fishes for. Her palate is not tickled by the Antony who
mopes and pines upon her trencher. That that is where Antony
ends up is—if we must talk of faults—more his than hers.

However, if Cleopatra does not mutter triumphant incan-
tations over the demise of her lover's soul and manhood, she
is not an entirely blameless spectator of all that befalls him;
nor does she have no points of contact with the lurid legend
she has inspired. It is for good reason an old story that the
grand male qualities that most excite a passion in women
like Cleopatra, are the least likely to survive it. Cleopatra
makes no bones about the importance to her of Antony's
being the greatest of soldiers and the most liberal of men—
great in his liberality because he has, until the requiting of
the passion takes it from him, most to give. But the lordly
munificence she loves is an effect not a cause of Antony's
successful soldiering. She has herself small interest in the
strategies of warfare, and no stomach for combat. It is the
reputation, the majesty, the after-battle relaxations that she
cares for. It is Caesar, not Cleopatra, who loves the actual
soldier in Antony. And Caesar is surely right, whether or not
we share his preference, in believing that the distinctive
soldier in Antony, and the distinctive lover, cannot live
together. It is entirely to Cleopatra's credit that she has no
desire to keep the lover and—so far as she can understand it
—the soldier apart. Taming Antony has never been her intention. But she is the victim of her own powers—as Actium
decisively demonstrates. There is no reason to disbelieve
her words to Antony on that occasion:

> O my lord, my lord,
> Forgive my fearful sails! I little thought
> You would have follow'd.

They have all the surprise and bewilderment of innocence. She has done the job of catching Antony too well. Such would have been a victory for the Cleopatra who has designs upon the proud aloofness of Aaron Sisson; but for this Cleopatra, who would love no less than the lord of lords, but has no desire to eat or drink him, it might have been a tragedy.

Might have been, but isn't. For as it turns out she refuses to learn a lesson, face a fact, or pay a price. She does not thereby subvert the truth – that is but critics' fancy – but she does flout our expectations and even, if we are stern, our demands. Comedy is often a matter of suffering averted; in the broad comedy of the last act of this play suffering is simply declined.

The proposition that the last act of *Antony and Cleopatra* concerns itself with and even celebrates love transcendent will usually provoke the argument that such is merely the effect of a sleight of hand. Neither position strikes me as adequate, though the latter has more sense in it. Shakespeare does indeed, for Act V, seem to have shifted the grounds of his interest. But he has nothing underhand to gain from it; nothing that we have earlier seen is made, by its esprit, less true. Far from celebrating virtues that have not been dramatically present, the last act, if we are to complain of it at all, rather fails of justice to those of Cleopatra's that were given us with such inwardness in her early exchanges with Antony. If we now marvel at her more, we know her less. It is as if, having seen to it (as the saying is) that no one gets away with anything, and having given us with merciless exactitude Antony's torpid decline, Shakespeare now grants himself the space to enjoy the other possibility – we might think of it as a possibility distinctly feminine. It has much in common with what Henry James finds to wonder at in the life of George Sand:

> nothing is more striking than the inward impunity with which she gave herself to conditions that are usually held to denote or to involve a state of demoralization. This impunity (to speak only of consequences or features that concern us) was not, I admit, complete, but it was sufficiently so to warrant us in saying that no one was ever less demoralized. She presents a case prodigiously discouraging to the usual view – the view that

there is no surrender to 'unconsecrated' passion that we
escape paying for in one way or another. It is frankly
difficult to see where this eminent woman conspicuously paid. She positively got off from paying—and
in a cloud of fluency and dignity, benevolence, competence, intelligence.

Much in common, but not everything. The 'usual view'
that George Sand discourages sounds more inflexibly respectable than any that is turned upon Cleopatra, within
the play or without it. It is not, for example, on account
of its inherent improprieties that we blink at Cleopatra's
final consecration of her passion; nor do we complain that
she spiritualizes what was worldly in it. Indeed, part of
what is surprising about her fluency and dignity to the last
is that they should be put so exclusively to the celebration
of the worldly, remembering too that the same worldliness
has involved her in searching out all possible alternatives to
self-sacrifice before she wholeheartedly embraces it. What
strikes us is not so much that Cleopatra doesn't pay, as that
she doesn't notice: not her extraordinary escape, but her
extraordinary freedom. Unlike any other major character
in Shakespearean tragedy, Cleopatra is allowed, after the
event as it were, to clean up her own story, restore a grandeur
to what was squalid and, despite the presence and the plans
of Caesar, arrange as she would like it her exit and her finish.
Nothing is permitted to prevent Cleopatra's being, to the last,
entirely herself.

But are we then to say that she achieves her freedom only
by means of what James goes on to imagine some readers
charging George Sand with: 'the incapacity to distinguish
between fiction and fact'? We cannot avoid the frequently
quoted exchange with Dolabella:

Cleopatra.
>His legs bestrid the ocean, his rear'd arm
>Crested the world: his voice was propertied
>As all the tuned spheres, and that to friends:
>But when he meant to quail, and shake the orb,
>He was as rattling thunder. For his bounty,
>There was no winter in 't: an autumn 'twas
>That grew the more by reaping: his delights
>Were dolphin-like, they show'd his back above
>The element they lived in: in his livery
>Walk'd crowns and crownets: realms and islands were
>As plates dropp'd from his pocket.

Dolabella.   Cleopatra!

Cleopatra.
Think you there was, or might be such a man
As this I dreamt of?
Dolabella.   Gentle madam, no.
Cleopatra.
You lie up to the hearing of the gods.
But if there be, or ever were one such,
It's past the size of dreaming: nature wants stuff
To vie strange forms with fancy, yet to imagine
An Antony were nature's piece, 'gainst fancy,
Condemning shadows quite.

This scene often proves to be the burial-ground of many good-natured disagreements over *Antony and Cleopatra.* I suppose it is inevitable that Cleopatra's turning philosopher of aesthetics and perception will lead critics with a similar bent to argue that this dream does indeed become—this beautiful poetry *is*—reality. And equally inevitable is the counter-argument—impregnable, were it not so often quite so literal—that such an Antony never was, at least not in this play. But shouldn't Antony, for the good of both sides, be left out of it? Dolabella's infinitely tender words are in answer to a question itself already poignantly rhetorical—looking to boundless futurity as much as to the recent past for a verification it does not expect. It is his resistance, however tender, even to the possibility of such an Antony that sparks off Cleopatra's passionate assertion. And even that drops quickly into a wistful, almost private musing, and rests its knotty conclusion upon a conditional clause. Leave Antony—the Antony we have seen—out of it, and Cleopatra's dream is wonderful. More marvellous is her imagination if this Antony never was; and more poignant that she should have denied him.

The organization of Cleopatra's thoughts in this scene, the careful sifting of her various alternatives throughout the final act, the raising of her spirits when at last she finds her way—or rather when the only way finds her—suggest that she is under no more illusion about the realities that were her past than she is about those that circumscribe her present. She is under no illusion, but in the natural buoyancy of her spirits, knowing neither cynicism nor dejection, she plumps for one. From now until the end of the play we are in a similar position and make, with alacrity, a similar election. Why should we not? Finally to claim that Cleopatra is only fooling herself is as silly as claiming that she isn't.

V

An Impossible Person
Caius Martius Coriolanus

1 · WONDERFUL IMPARTIALITY

'I must read Shakespeare?' inquires Charlotte Brontë's
Robert Moore defensively, as Caroline Helstone thrusts a
volume at him.*
'You must have his spirit before you,' she replies. 'You
must hear his voice with your mind's ear; you must take
some of his soul into yours.'
Robert is apparently acquainted with the 'musts' of
moralistic coercion, for he queries sharply,
'With a view to making me better? Is it to operate like a
sermon?'
The work Robert so darkly suspects of designs upon his
native depravity is *Coriolanus*. And indeed, before and since
1849, the play has had many readers whose expectation that
it will 'operate like a sermon' has very thoroughly ensured
that it does nothing else. Some, like Hazlitt, have thought the
text deplorably chosen and have objected to the preacher's
manner of handling it. Others, like Wyndham Lewis, rejoicing
in a delectable confirmation of their cherished prejudices,
have barely been able to suppress whoops of glee as pulpit-
vengeance is thundered upon 'the demented "aristocrat",
the incarnation of violent snobbery.' Or, like L. C. Knights,
more in sorrow than in anger, they have mourned over the
lost soul Coriolanus who, knowing nothing of 'the ideal of
mutuality in a healthy social organism' (as embodied in
Menenius's fable of the belly), and having no 'adequately
integrated and responsive life', is attended to the gates of
hell, with the critic as his melancholy confessor.
All of which makes Caroline's rejoinder highly pertinent:
'It is to stir you; to give you new sensations. *It is to make
you feel your life strongly.*'
Equally pertinent, too, is her warning: 'And you are not

Shirley, Chapter 6.

going to be French, and sceptical, and sneering? You are not going to think it a sign of wisdom to refuse to admire?'
'I don't know.'
'If you do, Robert, I'll take Shakespeare away.'
Very proper of her, too. There's really no point in arguing with your Robert if, faced with a Coriolanus, he is going to 'think it a sign of wisdom to refuse to admire.' But Caroline needn't have worried. Robert, as he steeps himself in the play, finds he has no such inclination:

> The very first scene in 'Coriolanus' came with smart relish to his intellectual palate, and still as he read he warmed. He delivered the haughty speech of Caius Martius to the starving citizens with unction; he did not say he thought his irrational pride right, but he seemed to feel it so . . . The warlike portions did not rouse him much; he said all that was out of date, or should be; the spirit displayed was barbarous, yet the encounter single-handed between Martius and Tullus Aufidius, he delighted in. As he advanced, he forgot to criticize; it was evident he appreciated the power, the truth of each portion; and, stepping out of the narrow line of private prejudice, began to revel in the large picture of human nature . . .

Caroline needn't have worried about Robert. But Robert needs to worry about Caroline. For if we have once felt that Shakespearean largeness forcing us to 'step out of the narrow line of private prejudice', it becomes important to know what to do with this girl at our elbow (or in our head)—the one who is keenly eyeing our reactions, ardent for proper detestations, and vigilant against improper empathies. For Caroline, it quickly transpires, is no enemy of sermons, provided they are sermons of the right political complexion. She is, in short, an exponent of the 'democratic-hygienic' reading of Martius's character, and she is forever distracting us from the play with her commentary: '*There*'s a vicious point hit already', comes the reproachful murmur. 'You sympathize with that proud patrician who does not sympathize with his fellow men.' Or (should we fail to be scandalised by Coriolanus's scheme of revenge), '*There* I see another glimpse of brotherhood in error.' And one could wish, for Robert, some better guide to what Coleridge called 'the wonderful philosophic impartiality of Shakespeare's politics.'
'Impartiality' may be too passive a word, and 'politics'

(however beneficently extended in scope) too narrow a one for this play – 'sprightly, walking, audible, full of vent' as it is. But Coleridge's prompting is helpful. It is in political impartiality that Shakespeare begins. Granting effortlessly that all acts have a political dimension, and that no man can live in a social vacuum – propositions that are as true as they are uninteresting – his attention focuses promptly upon the staggering variety of ways men have found of *being* political and social. He does this, not in order to evade the political, but in order to confront a prime political datum: for this multivalent, self-cancelling variety is, to political science, what inertia is to physical science – a fundamental property of the matter it deals in, a brute fact which patriots, politicians and reformers alike must eternally contend with.

Which makes it peculiarly irritating to discover, on the first page, that modern editors have conspired to remove one variety of the political from the play altogether. I'm referring to the silent liquidation (at line 54) of the Second Citizen – one of Shakespeare's brilliantly characterised extras. He's there for all to see, in the Folio text (the only text we have) – putting in his 'one word, good Citizens'; unhappy with the demagogic creation of scapegoats ('consider you what services he has done for his country?'); winning some unexpected support amongst these indecisive and uneasy mutineers ('*All.* Nay, but speak not maliciously'); and piquantly contrasted, in his firm moderation, with the vacillating extremism of First Citizen.

I say 'vacillating', because the two could never have been conflated with each other, if it had been noted that that leading revolutionary, First Citizen, begins his stage life by *halting* the march on the Capitol ('Before we proceed any further, hear me speak' – a proposal surprisingly, though, if you think about it, understandably welcome to his followers); gradually talks himself back into courage by resisting Second Citizen's unacceptable version of moderation; is newly galvanised by reassuring sounds from the other side of the city; and then, at the very moment he has got his insurrectionary juggernaut into motion, blows the whistle on it yet again – 'Soft, who comes here?'

Does this seem puzzling? Only if we are thinking in terms of stage-mobs (the picturesquely choreographed kind who cry ' 'Rah! 'rah! rhubarb! rhubarb!' in the background, while a single resounding spokesman declaims their grievance to the audience). But Shakespeare knows how much subtler the dynamics actually are; knows how ordinary folk, driven to extremity, will find their hearts pounding at their own temerity – particularly the ordinary folk who, all unsought, find themselves heading a mob. He knows the panicky sense of exposure that follows any break with lifelong habits of passivity and deference – so that the same misery which has brought the mutineers together is liable to drive them apart again in terrified self-preservation; knows especially the precariousness of the group solidarity without which none of them dares stir a muscle. In this state of dread and desperation it can easily happen to a man that he snatches at any pretext for delaying the moment of final commitment: 'Soft, who comes here?'

It is only a solitary old man who 'comes'. But the ancient habits of subservience in First Citizen are too strong. For this is a patrician! And with one last muttered 'He's one honest enough, would all the rest were so', he melts into the crowd, to be heard no more.

As a result Menenius finds himself searching in vain for the ringleader: 'What work's my countrymen in hand?' he asks mildly. 'Where go you with bats and clubs?' (No one stirs.) 'The matter?' (Still no response.) 'Speak, I pray you.'

The editors apparently feel so keenly for Menenius's bewilderment here, that they have provided him with the ringleader he is unable to detect. Shakespeare's conception is finer. Who, in this faint-hearted assembly, will dare to speak up? First Citizen was eloquent (and sincere) enough when it was a matter of telling his supporters what they most wanted to hear, but he is quite unmanned by the new atmosphere of chastened deference. Who then? The same man who was quirky enough to question the majority view before, who seems to welcome the patrician's arrival as likely to break up the entrenched battle-lines of ignorant confrontation, and who is about to emerge as grasping, better than any, the one unanswerable sanction of oppressed misery (his reply to the benignant query, 'Mine honest neighbours, will you undo yourselves?' is 'We cannot sir, we are undone already'). So finally it is Second Citizen's stolidly matter-of-fact voice that breaks the silence, at once disowning his primacy in the matter, and accepting with a shrug his necessary implication:

> Our business is not unknown to th' Senate. They have
> had inkling this fortnight what we intend to do, which
> now we'll show 'em in deeds.

Then (perhaps at the sight of some tiny fastidious gesture of recoil on Menenius's part?) he adds, 'They say poor suitors have strong breaths. They shall know we have strong arms too.' If there is a touch of garlic about the remark, there

is also a whiff of rising and respectable resentment.
Second Citizen, anyway, has crossed his little Rubicon,
and thereafter he has no choice. He is anything Menenius
cares to make of him. But what is he to do? He can't stand
there, meekly imbibing idiocies about the patricians 'caring
for you like fathers', without a syllable of protest. But as he
speaks, he becomes the hostage of his own eloquence:

> Care for us? True indeed, they ne'er car'd for us yet.
> Suffer us to famish, and their storehouses cramm'd with
> grain: make edicts for usury, to support usurers; repeal
> daily any wholesome Act established against the rich,
> and provide more piercing Statutes daily, to chain up
> and restrain the poor. If the wars eat us not up, they
> will; and there's all the love they bear us.

He can't help it that he is too percipiently mistrustful of
anecdotal inconsequences about Bellies, to forget the
gnawings of his own empty one. Yet it is that very percipience that makes the patrician mark him down as a prime
target for deflation, a trouble-maker.

And thus, with sublime unconsciousness and with acute
irony, Menenius turns this man, potentially his most valuable
ally, into the seditious agitator we have watched him refusing to be. And by the time Menenius has enlisted the
laughter of his fellows, by deriding his unplebeian fluency,
by flaunting a superior patrician good-humour (deliberate,
not rash like his accusers), and finally by belching at him for
a cheap laugh (the Belly's 'smile'), the transformation is complete. Menenius has *made* him 'the great toe of this assembly',
and feels free, consequently, to treat him as 'one o' th'lowest,
basest', or (what is the same thing) 'poorest of this most wise
rebellion'.

There's no more point being angry at Menenius, than there
is in trying to idealise him — though both approaches have
been tried. The same ironic eye which takes in the grotesque
inappositeness of the charge against Second Citizen, also
records the poor brute's comical bewilderment — 'I the great
toe? Why the great toe?' Besides, Menenius, no doubt about
it, has genuine talent as an arbitrator. His genial expediency
is one of those mixed virtues so necessary to political life;
and it stands in the most interesting of relations to that
monolithic version of Principle we are shortly to encounter
in Martius. Our feelings, personal and political, are now com-
plicated to the point where we must notice each small twinge
of contradiction: the fact, for instance, that men hungry for
bread, appealing to a well-fed patrician, are told that they

'receive the *flour* of all,/And leave me but the bran'; must notice that the claim, 'No public benefit which you receive/ But it proceeds, or comes from them to you,/And no way from yourselves', hardly constitutes an answer to the complaint that they are receiving no public benefit at all, except the right to famish, be pinched by usurers, and be drafted to the wars. We notice it all the more sharply because Second Citizen is momentarily flummoxed: 'It was an answer, how apply you this?' Yet for all this, Menenius's genuine benevolence of intent is not in question.

There is something more than 'impartiality in politics' at work here. In his masterfully prescient way, Shakespeare is mobilising the self-defeating energies of political contradiction. With positive zest, he searches them out, compels them into new aggregations, setting up changing fields of force for the entry of each new character. The next of which, of course, is to give a violent wrench to our perspectives:

> What's the matter, you dissentious rogues,
> That rubbing the poor itch of your opinion,
> Make yourselves scabs.

It's a pretty tough-minded (or po-faced) audience that can repress a smile at this point. That sardonic, laconic Coriolanian sense of humour keeps cropping up in this play,* and it has a nasty knack of getting under our conscientious defences. We do not say we 'think it right', but we 'seem to feel it so'. And anyway, it is extremely difficult to disengage, from the overt and withering scorn, a potentiality of contemptuous affection – a difficulty exquisitely rendered in Second Citizen's muttered disgust: 'We have ever *your* good word.' That odd mix of exasperation and inurement, amusement and contempt, is surprisingly void of resentment. Scabs are admittedly loathsome, but we need to take the pitch of the remark from the gruff offhand syllable which is usually excised when the remark is quoted – 'Thanks.'

> – Hail, noble Martius.
> – Thanks.

Any actor who can deliver the subsequent two-and-a-half lines ('What's the matter. . .' etc.) in the hectoring, braying voice of the bully-prefect, should have his Equity card instantly revoked.

---

*Cf. ' "Shall remain" '!/Hear you this Triton of the minnows? Mark you/His absolute "shall"?'; or 'they threw their caps/As they would hang them on the horns o' th' moon'; or 'Bid them wash their faces,/And keep their teeth clean.'

Now I'm not proposing a Coriolanus who is, beneath a rough exterior, a true lover of the people – unless in the strictly comparative sense suggested by the Second Officer, who believes so little in 'love' between great men and the people, that he's prepared to wonder whether Coriolanus mightn't display it. No, it *is* an expedient lie of Menenius's to suggest that 'he loves your people'. But Martius's contempt is not just that of 'a very dog to the commonalty', either. What makes it so difficult to appraise is its impersonality. The scorn is, generically, for anyone whose identity derives from the itch of opinion, or has to be sustained by scratching. However inappositely, he has captured a chronic absurdity about the self-generated grievances of little men. We laugh, and are complicit. And in any case there is a cleanliness about his frank combativeness which is not to be found in Menenius's phoney conciliation. We should remember that it is not Martius but the silver-haired father of the people who first refers to his 'good friends', his 'honest neighbours' as the *rats* of Rome.

But at once, and very pointedly, Shakespeare's eye falls upon the galling contradiction. No sooner have we sensed a possible cleanliness, than the inappositeness, too, begins to glare: for here is Martius, compounding Menenius's blunder by rounding on the very man who has been defending him against mob passions, and jeering, 'He that will give good words to *thee*, will flatter/Beneath abhorring.' What does Second Citizen now make of his earlier magnanimity: 'What he cannot help in his nature, you account a vice in him'? We are not shown, but we may guess. If one of the things Martius 'cannot help in his nature' is kicking people like Second Citizen, then one of the things Second Citizen cannot help in his, is admiring, even while he is being kicked, the man who does the kicking: 'We have ever your good word.'

Certainly this is what makes Martius – personally, politically, tragically, the 'impossible person' Bradley describes: everybody *does* involuntarily admire him. And no less so for perceiving that he is utterly in the wrong.

The citizens whom Martius treats so insultingly when he stands for election, nevertheless have to be 'lesson'd' before they manage to feel the resentment they are amply entitled to. Sicinius will have this as just another exasperating instance of their 'childish friendliness' – a disposition unlikely to promote the rapid establishment of democratic institutions in Rome, with himself at their head. We, I think, are free to detect, as well, a sturdy good sense which knows that the insult has passed right over their heads. Menenius rather redundantly reminds them that 'He has been bred i' th' wars. . .and is ill-school'd/In boulted language.' But they hear the man clearly enough without the reminder. 'Noble deeds', they recognise, require a 'noble acceptance', and that involves putting aside petty resentments. It is very much a part of the dialectic that Coriolanus generates by his mere existence, that what is plainly their political folly should be felt, equally and simultaneously, as their humanity and decency—indeed as a crucial kind of justice. We do not, I think, feel more respect for them when, duly lessoned, they fall to bellowing, 'It shall be so, it shall be so'—though they are, at that moment, showing their political wisdom.

Cominius is favoured with an equally close-up view of Martius's faults (the man accuses him, at one point, of purveying 'praises sauc'd with lies'); yet he meets it all with an indulgent smile, his benevolence undeterred and his warmth unimpaired. There is no hint that he is overcoming justifiable resentment by dint of moral effort. His feeling, plainly, is that these little faults of temper are negligible and it would be inexcusably small-minded to dwell upon them. For Cominius, Coriolanus is a unique case.

Even the Tribunes, in the comically naive conference that ends the first scene, find something to marvel over in Martius's nature:

Sicinius. Was ever man so proud as is this Martius?
Brutus. He has no equal.

And out they trot to hear the dispatch made, anxious to witness 'in what fashion/More than his singularity, he goes/Upon this present action.' The small tribute of their avidity is amusing and revealing. Nobody is immune from the fascination.

Also revealing, is their bungling use of the word 'proud'. (First Citizen managed much more precision when he remarked that Martius was proud 'even to the altitude of his virtue.') We are all familiar with the way charges of *pride* and *arrogance* can be mere reflexes of perplexity in a mind at a loss to account for its own involuntary awe. One of the reasons, surely, for taking an interest in the man at all, is precisely this propensity of his for sticking in the craw of those who offer to assimilate him—'Was ever man so proud?' There has to be some personal distinction there to create the problem. And as he had done with Antony and Cleopatra, Shakespeare takes a keen pleasure in rendering the babble of adulation and censure and speculation, amidst which

Martius lives. A very shrewd comic intelligence is at work, that is to say, in the interest *he* takes in the interest *others* take in his problematical protagonist.

For they are all busy making over this unassimilable lump into digestible gruels of their own concoction. Cominius purveys him, for the Capitoline table, as a thing of blood, an iron juggernaut of war. For Titus he is the earth-shaker, the thunderer. For civilian friends, ecstatically awaiting his arrival from Corioli, he's a kind of perambulating tally-stick of attested military efficacy (the hilarious grisliness of the wound-count tells us more about the counters than the counted). For his mother he can be, at one time, gentle Martius, only son of her womb, apple of her eye; at another, a vast idol of insensate destruction; then a kind of big brother who will be sent to thrash the bully tribunes; and later, a dishonest lout who never in his life showed his dear mother any courtesy. The same man is also a viperous traitor seeking to wind himself into tyrannical power (a truly 'silly' charge, as Bradley observes). Then he is a butcher killing flies, a red-eyed Alexander throned in gold, an engine, a god wanting nothing but eternity and a heaven to throne him in. His nature is too noble for this world. He is a viper that would depopulate the city. Or he may be 'my son Coriolanus', subject, like other mortals, to dyspeptic aberration, but ultimately tractable to his old Uncle Menenius.

Amid all this anarchic pandemonium of partiality and flat misrepresentation there are certainly degrees. Cominius's automaton of war comes close to the monstrosity we actually see abusing and menacing his terrified troops, or emerging half-flayed from Corioli gates; but it tells us nothing of the 'Flower of Warriors', the natural leader who can touch the very quick of valour in common soldiers, so that they shout and wave their swords, take him up in their arms and cast up their caps (Cominius has none of this charisma: he relies sensibly on a comradely rationality—and this also is admirable).

The confusion of warring commentary is, of course, one of the things that *makes* the play 'sprightly, walking, audible, full of vent'. It's a characteristic Shakespearean way of activating our discrimination. For the mere existence of Coriolanus—this 'most valuable Sir'—is as much a challenge to *our* dispassionate intelligence and *our* largeness of spirit, as it was to the Tribunes, to Aufidius, to Volumnia, who failed, or to the Capitoline janitors, to Titus, Cominius, Menenius and Virgilia, who succeeded in rising to the challenge. We may very justly resent being put in the situation of having to 'come up to' a man of whom we repeatedly disapprove, who is defectively intelligent about some of his prime allegiances, and who, at times, seems like some great overgrown child. We may feel, with Robert Moore, that 'all that' – the martial clangour, the warrior-ethic – is 'out of date'; but we will be forced to add, lamely, 'Or *should* be.' We may judge that the flagrant élitism of Coriolanus's avowed principles absolves us from all necessity of respect; and then find ourselves exclaiming, with R. in Brecht's lively dialogue, 'But the crystal clarity of Martius's harangue! What an outsize character! And one who emerges as admirable while behaving in a way that I find beneath contempt!'*

R's frustration is very just. The admiration and the contempt are both far too powerful to be denied; yet they refuse to coalesce into a single sentiment. The energy of feeling is locked in contradiction – a quality Brecht was well-equipped to understand, and greatly relished in the details of the first scene:

B. We'll note that.
R. Why?
B. It gives rise to discomfort.

The step from 'discomfort' to vivid participation ('*B.* That seems to me splendidly realistic. Lovely stuff') is a short one, once we recognise it is discomfort with *reality* we are feeling.

For Shakespeare has not invented the contradiction. Coriolanuses exist, massive boulders of obstructive matter across the smooth path to egalitarian complacency. And acknowledging that, we are pricked into vivid wakefulness. There is something here to be grasped, mastered. And under pressure from these 'new sensations', we feel our life – and especially our intellectual life – strongly.

There lies the objective, the analytical challenge of the play.

What is also asked of us is a subjective knowledge of our own reactions to a man like Martius. For he has proved just as 'impossible' a person in the corridors of criticism as ever he did in the porches of Rome. So, like Aufidius, we need to be able to distinguish an honourable emulation from the 'root of ancient envy' – bindweed of the soul, nasty stuff

* 'Study of the First Scene of Shakespeare's "Coriolanus"', in John Willett (ed.), *Brecht on Theatre*, pp. 252–65.

which, however assiduously it is rooted out, will keep springing up again.

Not but what one feels a good deal for Aufidius. Some kinds of human greatness can be bitter to contemplate—especially in an enemy.

> I think he'll be to Rome
> As is the osprey to the fish, who takes it
> By sovereignty of nature.

And there is always the temptation, confronted with an effortless 'sovereignty of nature', to try to cut it down to size—take the side of the fish against the osprey, and thereby deny the powerful upsurge of admiration implicit in the very metaphor. Aufidius is following a more strenuous path when, at the end of all his attempts to 'place' Martius, to 'understand' and 'explain' him, he turns to his Lieutenant with a sour laugh, and throws in his hand:

> But he has a merit
> To choke it in the utt'rance.

The concession, it is plain, is not a piece of generosity, and it brings Aufidius small joy to make it; but he is horribly to discover that the price of *not* making it, of *not* 'coming up to' Martius in this way, is to fall into that meanness of envy, of which there are many examples in the play, and which is always given us as shabby, defeated, contemptible. The Antiate Lords are right: even when the vaunts of this unholy braggart have passed the bounds of all reasonable patience, still 'the man is noble', and still he must have 'judicious hearing'.

Giving him judicious hearing need not involve explaining anything away in Martius's nature. I have no ambition to set old Nietzschean factions marching to the sound of an antique Roman drum. I hope, simply, to do justice to the size of the Coriolanian 'impossibility', for the size is, I believe, tragic—*Macbeth*-tragic. And not often recognised as such.

2 · NO MORE INTROSPECTION THAN A TIGER

Anyone familiar with Bradley's excellent British Academy lecture will know how effortlessly he avoids the envious sniping which has beset much criticism, and how subtly and circumstantially he handles the vexed question of Coriolanus's 'pride'. He knows there is a 'tangle' here, and he deals conscientiously with it:

Though he is the proudest man in Shakespeare, he seems to be unaware of his pride, and is hurt when his mother mentions it. It does not prevent him from being genuinely modest, for he never dreams that he has attained the ideal he worships; yet the sense of his own greatness is twisted round every strand of this worship. In almost all his words and deeds we are conscious of the tangle. I take a single illustration. He cannot endure to be praised. Even his mother, who has a charter to extol her blood, grieves him when she praises him. As for others,

> I had rather have one scratch my head i' the sun
> When the alarum were struck, than idly sit
> To hear my nothings monster'd.

His answer to the roar of the army hailing him 'Coriolanus' is 'I will go wash.' His wounds are 'scratches with briars.' In Plutarch he shows them to the people without demur; in Shakespeare he would rather lose the consulship. There is a greatness in all this that makes us exult. But who can assign the proportions of the elements that compose this impatience of praise: the feeling (which we are surprised to hear him express) that he, like hundreds more, has simply done what he could; the sense that it is nothing to what might be done; the want of human sympathy (for has not Shelley truly said that fame is love disguised?); the pride which makes him feel that he needs no recognition, that after all he himself could do ten times as much, and that to praise his achievement implies a limit to his power? If anyone could solve 'this problem, Coriolanus certainly could not. To adapt a phrase in the play, he has no more introspection in him than a tiger.

This will serve admirably as an introduction to the scene following the battle (I. ix), where the question of Martius's pride/modesty most acutely arises. But it's a scene which rewards closer attention than Bradley gives it, and if the reader will help me by turning to it, the following notes may suggest in what ways:
(1) Shakespeare, whose stage directions are preserved with unusual fullness in the Folio text, has noted that Martius enters 'with his arm in a scarf'. It's an instruction to the producer, and an invitation to us, to think a little about real battles and real wounds. When we find Martius sporting a sling we can safely conclude, I think, that he is hurt, has

wounds upon him which smart for other reasons than 'to hear themselves remember'd.' That piece of understated irony (another tonality of the Coriolanian sense of humour) is as much factual as it is ironic, and the irony is enriched when Cominius insists on treating the wounds as mere metaphors for a misplaced modesty.

Martius. I have some wounds upon me, and they smart
          To hear themselves remembered.
Cominius.   Should they not,
          Well might they fester 'gainst ingratitude,
          And tent themselves with death.

    Likewise, when Martius proposes washing his face, it is not out of indifference to the roar of the army hailing him 'Coriolanus': he is beginning to feel what it takes Cominius another thirty lines to notice—'The blood upon your visage dries, 'tis time/It should be look'd to.' Martius is deeply gratified and expresses his satisfaction in the terse style natural to him—a style which has the great virtue that, stumbling into no embarrassment, it creates none:

          I will go wash:
          And when my face is fair, you shall perceive
          Whether I blush or no.

The amused glint in the eye belies the grimly downturned mouth, and the two together clear the way for a plain-spoken confession of hearty obligation:

          Howbeit, I thank you.
          I mean to stride your steed, and at all times
          To under-crest your good addition
          To th' fairness of my power.

It is an unmitigated pleasure to confer benefits on a man, if he can take them as handsomely as this—and Cominius clearly feels that pleasure.
    (2) Even the catastrophic lapses of tone—e.g. 'I. . .cannot make my heart consent to take/A bribe, to pay my sword', in response to a piece of freely offered munificence!—are preceded by an overt appeal which might be paraphrased, 'Spare me, friends; you know I'm bad at these things':

          Pray now, no more:
          My mother, who has a charter to extol her blood,
          When she does praise me, grieves me:
          I have done as you have done, that's what I can. . .

The unintrospective tiger has noticed this much about

himself, at least. And isn't the tone of amusement at his own foibles, and indulgence towards those of a parent who has, after all, 'a *charter* to extol' her blood, rather engaging? This is very much the man who, when asked later to 'repent what he has spoke' to the Tribunes, gives a dry laugh: 'For them? I cannot do it to the gods,/Must I then do't to them?' The way he lives with the exigencies of his own nature is not devoid of irony.

(3) There is one wholly understandable reason for flaring up at the sound of the *'long flourish'*. The brass band takes a piece of instinctive carelessness —

> I do refuse it,
> And stand upon my common part with those
> That have beheld the doing —

(so careless, indeed, that it doesn't even care if its contempt for the 'beholders' is manifest), and treats it as if it were a deliberately calculated effect. Someone has given the preconcerted signal for the fanfare, and Martius would like to wring that person's neck. He may be dimly conscious of some bad faith in his modesty, but he knows it isn't bad faith on *that* scale.

So he loses his temper, uglily and foolishly. The comedy of Cominius's urbane attempt at pretending that he hasn't, that he is merely 'too modest', while nonetheless administering a mild rebuke, is really delectable. Under that prompting, Martius's imperilled magnanimity revives, and with some deprecatory wryness at his own expense, he makes amends — conceding the possible existence of the 'blush' with which he nevertheless declines to embarrass others. (A tiger, in short, of some natural, if unreliable, tact.) And Shakespeare adds a final dash of bitters to the mixture with his personal touch (refining on Plutarch) of the forgotten name.

Now there *is* a touch of naivety about the military hero we see in this scene. And I daresay he is not the first military hero to have displayed it. But it is not the naivety of Bradley's 'huge boy', founded upon 'self-ignorance'. Above all, it is not a naivety we can safely patronise — supposing naivety to be ever safely patronisable. Martius's naivety is rather like Martius's pride: not a flaw, not a charge to be brought against him, but a problem about him. There is, after all, a curious continuity in human nature between naivety and integrity. . . as Lawrence points out:

> While a man remains a man, a true human individual, there is at the core of him a certain innocence or naivete

which defies all analysis, and which you cannot bargain
with, you can only deal with it in good faith from your
own corresponding innocence or naivete. This does not
mean that the human being is nothing but naive or innocent. He is Mr Worldly Wiseman also to his own degree.
But in his essential core he is naive. . .

('John Galsworthy', in *Phoenix I*)

Martius is lucky in his friends. Most of them are willing,
and able, to meet him as he asks to be met—in good faith
on the grounds of their own different but corresponding
innocence or naivety. They do not try to bargain with him,
except in jest, as Titus does with the wager of the horse—
the whole relish of which lies in the absurd idea that they
should ever enter into these commercial, horse-trading relations. Or if they are forced to bargain with him, they are
apologetic about it, like Cominius, deprecating the 'part'
he has put his friend to: 'Come, come, we'll prompt you.'

'Friends of noble touch', Martius calls them. And nowhere does the nobility show more strikingly than in their
sense of what is due to the friendship. When Martius's Volscian
Army comes against Rome, Cominius, despite the desperate
situation, finds it quite unthinkable that he should use the
plea of friendship to dissuade him from his chosen course.
If anybody is in the wrong, he seems to feel it is himself:
'Who is't can blame him?' Mercy? 'Who shall ask it?' His
best friends would therein show like enemies. One would
have thought Cominius had little enough to accuse himself
of, in the matter of the banishment, and J. C. F. Littlewood*
has gone so far as to accuse Shakespeare of indulging here in
political sentimentality in order to rehabilitate his discredited
hero—of excusing the inexcusable by falsifying Cominius's
nature. I see neither falsification nor excuse. Cominius's
veneration, and his sense of what is due to the friendship,
go so deep that he is carried into total political obliviousness.
His shame at the blot that has stained Rome, and him with
it, is acute enough to make him grimly and irresponsibly
exult that the wrong is to be avenged. How can he honour-
ably intervene now? It is simply repugnant to him to trade
upon friendship. And the speech in which he recounts his
reception (when he is persuaded so to trade) is full of disgust at such errands, and of a reflexive glorying in the man
who has no need to run them:

*His two articles on the play, in *Cambridge Quarterly*, II (1967) & III (1968),
are a pleasure to disagree with.

> I tell you, he does sit in gold, his eye
> Red as 'twould burn Rome: and his injury
> The gaoler to his pity. I kneel'd before him;
> 'Twas very faintly he said "Rise," dismiss'd me
> Thus with his speechless hand. What he would do
> He sent in writing after me. . . .

Titus Lartius, throughout, pays the same unembarrassed homage – brotherly, unsubservient, full of a sense of the honour he does himself in honouring Martius. We do not have to stand in Titus's relation to the hero, to feel that there is something in all this that must be taken seriously. A man is known by his friends.

Amongst whom, it is a mistake to count Volumnia. The contrast is very striking. Just compare Cominius's proud reticence and self-withholding, with this hungry hoarding of the power affection may confer:

> I prithee now, sweet son, as thou hast said
> My praises made thee first a soldier, so
> To have my praise for this, perform a part
> Thou hast not done before.

Not so much bargaining, this, as veritable horse-trading! If Cominius knows his friend, then Volumnia does not know her son. Indeed, with her overweening sense of the instrumentality of other natures ('I have lived,/To see inherited my very wishes,/And the buildings of my fancy:/Only there's one thing wanting. . .'), she cannot *begin* to understand a nature which rewards its deeds with doing them.

I'm suggesting, in short, that we might treat with caution the usual presumptions about this mother-son relationship, and that we might press Bradley for evidence when he assures us that Coriolanus (on two crucial occasions) 'consents. . . solely because his mother bids him and he cannot resist her chiding.' Naivety entails a vulnerability, granted; but it may also confer an immunity to certain kinds of persuasion.

The first of these crucial occasions (III.ii) provides striking illustration, anyway, of the extent to which Martius, is *not* to be bargained with. For by the time his massive silence has lasted fifty lines, the people who have been applying every available crowbar to his will, are reduced absurdly to discussing him in lowered voices, and in the third person – as if he were some kind of meteoric portent of unpredictable properties, dropped suddenly in their midst:

Menenius. Only fair speech.
Cominius.   I think 'twill serve, if he
          Can thereto frame his spirit.
Volumnia.   He must, and will.

The comedy is not simply at the expense of some 'huge boy'
having a fit of the sulks. It is at the expense equally of those
who are so needlessly hard pressed to guess what is going on
in his mind as he is advised to emulate in humility 'the ripest
mulberry,/That will not hold the handling.' We may grant a
man the right, perhaps, to decline replying to proposals of
the kind Volumnia is putting to him—especially if his
affection for the proposer is strong enough for him not to
enjoy refusing her. And we may grant it the more readily, if
we have noticed all Shakespeare's indications that the crisis is
too grave, by now, for him to have any real choice anyway.
There is nothing hyperbolic about the Senator's picture of
'our good City' cleaving in the midst and perishing: 'All's
in anger' in this 'dangerous present'. Which is, I take it, what
Volumnia wants him to face up to, when she takes up sharply
his favourite phrase of slanging dismissal—'Let them hang'—
with a literal reminder of the probable sequences: 'Ay, and
burn too.'

With every new influx of agitated patricians from the
market-place, it becomes more obvious that his first furious
vindication of personal integrity—delivered in Ercles' vein,
a real speech to tear a cat in—simply cannot stand (if it
wasn't already obvious in the rant itself):

> Let them pull all about mine ears, present me
> Death on the wheel, or at wild horses' heels,
> Or pile ten hills on the Tarpeian Rock,
> That the precipitation might down stretch
> Below the beam of sight; yet will I still
> Be thus to them.

And to clinch the point, Shakespeare creates, for a second,
an inimitably sage 'Noble' who, full of gravity, self-importance, and patrician unction, remarks into his beard: 'You do
the nobler.' Something has gone badly wrong when you get
allies of that kind.

Martius, in the course of this scene, must effect a very
difficult revolution in his own mind. He has to prepare himself, somehow or other, for an ordeal which will, by his
body's action, teach his mind a most inherent baseness.
Critics have scoffed at this way of putting things. But anyone who thinks it over-sensitive, too naively egocentric in

outlook, or imagines that such venial actions can be performed with impunity, might ponder the political career of
Sir Francis Bacon—or even Richard Nixon. No. Martius
knows the thing is both impossible and necessary. And being
exactly the reverse of a Hamlet, he wrestles with the matter
in silence, his few responses revealing little more than irritation at being interrupted—'Let go.' 'Well, what then? what
then?' 'Tush, tush.' 'Why force you this?'

The kind of mind for which Hamlet is the type of all
humanity regards this incommunicativeness of Martius's
with vinegared suspicion. The man *has* to be stupid—stupid
as (it is well known) all men of action are. But Coriolanus's
silences—his moments of steadfastly *not* soliloquising—may
be filled with something just as important as Hamlet's loose-
souled lucubrations. There are other forms of moral intelligence besides the kind that is perpetually proclaiming itself.
Some of them rather attractive. And the moment when
Martius completes his ruminations and breaks silence is very
attractive, in its mixture of exasperation, wryness and
resignation.

He has already been amusing about insinuating nods and
counterfeit bewitchments performed with the aid of one's
hat (shades of Osric?), but now, with a felicity of phrase
he frequently commands, he gets the absurdity of it all to
a tee:

Must I go show them *my unbarb'd sconce*?
Must I with my base tongue give to my noble heart
A lie, that it must bear?

(No answer forthcoming, since they all know he must, and
hope *he* knows it.)

Well? I will do't:
Yet were there but this single plot to lose,
This mould of Martius, they to dust should grind it
And throw't against the wind. To th' market-place:
You have put me now to such a part, which never
I shall discharge to th' life.
Cominius.   Come, come, we'll prompt you.

Magnanimity in a necessary yielding does not need to disguise
what the yielding costs—least of all from those who, like
Cominius, are sympathetically aware of it anyway. If there is
any false note here, it is in the way he wears his 'noble heart'
unhappily near the region of his sleeve—a touch, this, of the
Martius who is 'naive' in a less creditable sense of the word.
And we are likely to wonder whether a man who talks so

innocently of surceasing 'to honour mine own truth' hasn't begun to do so, by so talking.

The sanctions of merely personal 'truth', however, he is progressively putting behind him, and we need not be surprised at these last ghostly twinges from the amputated 'integrity'. What is surprising is to see them being brought on by the very mother who is striving to suppress them. Unlike Cominius, Volumnia hasn't heard the firm resolution behind the sardonic 'Well, I will do't. . .To th' market-place.' Knowing the enormity of her request, she doubts that it has really been acceded to, and she begins to over-persuade, cajole, wheedle — 'I prithee now, sweet son. . .' Her sweet son grunts his already-yielded assent. But she has sown the seed of misgiving. A deed that requires such elaborate fumigation must be noxious. And as he puts to himself what it *is* he must do — be possessed by some harlot's spirit, wear the smiles of knaves, and shed the tears of a schoolboy — his whole nature rises in revolt, and he suffers the relapse Volumnia had been fearing. He will not do't! Deadlock.

Now, as we all know, this is the moment when the warrior-hero collapses under maternal chiding and proves himself the booby we have always suspected him really to be. If we all know it, there is no arguing. But the fact that Volumnia addresses him as a stupid and stubborn schoolboy does not prove he *is* that schoolboy. Mothers have been known to fail to notice that their sons have grown up, and Volumnia is very much the mother to so fail. Similarly, the fact that he steadies himself in his earlier resolution *after* she has spoken does not prove causation. Given her volubility, there are few moments he could choose to announce his decision which would *not* come 'after she has spoken'. No one disputes the potency of the brand of maternal blackmail wielded by Volumnia —

> Thy valiantness was mine, thou suck'dst it from me:
> But owe thy pride thyself.

Strong men have blenched under its potency. But is it potent over this particular son? Isn't it possible, above all, to assent to a deed, while absolutely *dis*senting from the sophistries and casuistries which have been urged in its support?

It all depends whether 'Chide me no more' is spoken in a tone of chastened puerility. . .or of indulgent satire. Martius's tone often does run to satire, indulgent and otherwise: we might recall

> This last old man,
> Whom with a crack'd heart I have sent to Rome,

> Lov'd me, above the measure of a father,
> Nay, godded me indeed.

Nobody knows better than he, that people *will* have their
own special conceptions of him. There is very little he can do
about it. Menenius 'gods' him; his mother 'chides' him. He,
meanwhile, must settle his own conscience.

He does so: there is one last spasm of revulsion and – the
operation complete – Volumnia's son manfully, if not exactly
cheerfully, waves his lost limb:

> Pray be content:
> Mother, I am going to the market-place:
> Chide me no more. I'll mountebank their loves,
> Cog their hearts from them, and come home belov'd
> Of all the trades in Rome. Look, I am going:
> Commend me to my wife. I'll return Consul,
> Or never trust to what my tongue can do
> I' th' way of flattery further.
> *Volumnia.*   Do your will.
> *Exit.*

I know this is not the usual reading of the scene. But then,
the usual readers seem not to have noticed the way Volumnia
is behaving: she won't favour him with so much as a glance
('Look, I am going'), and, mumbling that highly disgruntled
'Do your will', she makes an immediate (and also highly disgruntled?) exit. Mind you, if she has seen the drift of his
rather bitter parody of 'The Soldier's Farewell' ('Commend
me to my wife') – delivered by a hero departing to be humble
as a ripe mulberry before 'woollen vassals' – she might well be
more galled than gratified. 'Do your will! I want no part of
it.' At all events, she doesn't seem to share the commentators' conviction that *she* has done *her* will. Something in
the manner of his consent seems to have stuck in her gorge.

It may be urged that the Martius we see at the beginning of
the scene shows no such manly independence, but is visibly
distressed that his mother does not 'approve him further'.*
But if we restore Volumnia's entry to the place the Folio text
assigns it, her son's musings take on a different colour—for
she is present as he muses. He angrily discusses her apostasy,
while she stands angrily silent; and it is to force her into
speech that he rounds on her finally, with his 'I talk of *you*!'

---

*Coriolanus may have been the victim of a semantic vagary here: the watery
and condescending 'approval' of twentieth-century manuals for parents has only
a fortuitous connexion with Shakespeare's strong and positive word.

> I muse my mother
> Does not approve me further, who was wont
> To call them woollen vassals, things created
> To buy and sell with groats, to show bare heads
> In congregations, to yawn, be still, and wonder
> When one but of my ordinance stood up
> To speak of peace or war. I talk of you.
> Why did you wish me milder?

It's not hard to see what has happened. The Volumnia who arrives at line 6, in no fit state for speech, has been remonstrating with him, wishing him milder, as he strode furiously back from the market-place—and he has simply left her standing. It is against *her* that he affirms his determination to be still 'thus to them'.

Which is not to say, of course, that his damaging reliance upon his mother's estimate of the 'woollen vassals' doesn't stare at one from the lines: it is there in his very astonishment at her apostasy. But there is some difference, between being angry at a parent for deserting a position you had supposed you profoundly shared with her, and being so hurt and puzzled at the withdrawal of parental 'approval' that you whimper in distress. Coriolanus has many faults, but he does not whimper.

In Act III Scene ii, then, we watch Martius confronting an issue which has been foreseeable from the moment he first strode onto the stage. He has reached the point where blind adherence to his 'essential core of naivety' would be very questionable as a version of *integrity*. He is obliged, now, to be 'Mr Worldly Wiseman in his own degree'. He professes no edification, finds no peculiar gratification in serving the common good by lying, cogging and mountebanking. These things remain what they are—'a most inherent baseness'. But extremities have spoken, and reasons and justifications are redundant. How does one address oneself to this kind of predicament? With a flat recognition of necessity, and the minimum of fuss: 'Must I. . .? Well, I will do't. . . Well, I must do't. . . Look, I am going.'

(The level at which this yielding is pitched may provide some guidance to the later yielding, when even fiercer extremities speak. For isn't it a tragic transposition of 'Well, I must do't', and much the same grim spirit of resignation, that we hear in Act V? And isn't the mother who has carried her point just as irremediably excluded, there, from an understanding of her own act?

Oh my mother, mother: Oh!
You have won a happy victory to Rome.
But for your son, believe it, oh believe it,
Most dangerously you have with him prevail'd,
If not most mortal to him. But let it come. . .)

At the end of a packed scene Shakespeare adds a delightful
touch. It may have nothing to do with Volumnia's departure,
but suddenly the man who has been massively recalcitrant to
instruction is benignly at his ease, and it is his mentors who
are all of a flutter—especially Menenius. Martius seems to
find the reversal of roles rather amusing. Continuing his
parody of 'The Soldier's Farewell', he fastens on the adverb
embodying all his friends' comical fears of an irascible
relapse, and he teases them (it is the only word) with it:

Cominius Away. The Tribunes do attend you: arm yourself
To answer mildly: for they are prepar'd
With accusations, as I hear, more strong
Than are upon you yet.
Coriolanus.   The word is, Mildly.

(I don't know what Roman infantrymen did when they gave
the password, but whatever it was, Coriolanus does it here
with mock sternness.) Then he relaxes:

Let them accuse me by invention: I
Will answer in mine honour.
Menenius.   Ay, but mildly.
Coriolanus. Well, mildly be it then. Mildly. *Exeunt.*

He is about to re-enter the world of 'sway' to which, despite his firm conviction that it represents 'their way', not his,
he is perpetually gravitating—drawn partly by the sense
of his own 'desert', partly by the political necessities of the
Roman state, and partly by the 'desire' he would like to deny
in himself. He is terribly vulnerable to that world—as Sicinius
is about to demonstrate. But that vulnerability itself may be
seen as the exactly computed price he pays for retaining 'a
certain innocence or naivety which cannot be bargained
with'. We watch that innocence making a last exit here,
joking with its friends.

In the final scene of Act III, Shakespeare insists that we
settle our allegiances, and makes it impossible for us to do so.
On one level—as a choice between Martius and Sicinius—the

matter is grotesquely obvious. Sicinius understands bargaining so well that he understands nothing else; there is an
obscene blank where *his* integrity should be. Yet this is precisely what makes him a good and efficient politician—one
who serves the cause of social justice with single-minded
devotion, and works to ensure that in time Rome will see
(for more than a brief respite between wars)

> Our tradesmen singing in their shops, and going
> About their functions friendly.

(Whereas Coriolanus attempts to burn Rome to the ground,
and failing to do so, destroys himself.)
    Without the labours of the Tribunes, the people would be
held forever

> In human action and capacity,
> Of no more soul nor fitness for the world
> Than camels in their war, who have their provand
> Only for bearing burthens, and sore blows
> For sinking under them.

It is not only in this persuasive verse that Shakespeare has
given us grounds for finding this state of affairs intolerable.
Furthermore, no small part of the Tribunes' efficacy is their
knack of seeing clearly, and stating trenchantly, what is
wrong with the great antagonist whose virtues they are incapable of understanding:

> if you will pass
> To where you are bound, you must enquire your way,
> Which you are out of, with a gentler spirit. . .

Or again,

> You speak o' th' people, as if you were a god
> To punish; not a man of their infirmity.

Yes, we feel the justice of the rebuke. Also we know the
rebuker has no shred of a right to it; that his concern for the
people is hollow as a worm-eaten nut; and that Martius may
speak of the people as he pleases, for he is *not* a man of their
infirmity. We cannot make the choice. The terms remain
incompatible.
    In the banishment scene, Sicinius achieves his culminating
loathsomeness: lying and knowing he lies, governing the
ventages of Coriolanus's soaring insolence with his finger and
thumb, to play any tune he pleases. And he is abetted at
every furious turn by his victim, who is providing him with
more pretexts and justifications than he has breath to employ.

Is it a noble nature, we ask, that is easier to be played on
than a pipe? A nature 'too noble for this world', perhaps —
but Menenius's attempt to 'god' Coriolanus can be construed
in two ways, is more treacherously equivocal than he perceives. Yet isn't it also in the very nature of nobility to detest
manipulators so heartily that it scorns to anticipate their
stratagems? We are balanced on that knife-edge of judgement
— the one the two Officers so sanely epitomised for us:

> For Coriolanus neither to care whether they love or hate
> him manifests the true knowledge he has in their dis-
> position, and out of his noble carelessness lets them
> plainly see't.
> *2 Officer.*
> If he did not care whether he had their love or no, he
> wav'd indifferently 'twixt doing them neither good nor
> harm: but he seeks their hate with greater devotion than
> they can render it him. . .Now to seem to affect the
> malice and displeasure of the people is as bad as that
> which he dislikes—to flatter them for their love.

What is it that Martius manifests in front of the mob? 'Noble
carelessness'? Or a deliberate affecting of 'malice and dis-
pleasure'? It is the same old, inextricable tangle.

Yet I believe few people have watched or read this play
through without feeling a tremendous surge and lift of exul-
tation when Martius finally shakes off all the dirty encum-
brances of political jobbery, and recognises the mob for
exactly what, at that moment, it is being—a 'common cry of
curs'. The super-ego may urge what it likes, but one does not,
in the course of that speech of passionate denunciation,
pause to scan the crowd, to see whether average decency of
the Second Citizen's kind is being unfairly arraigned. One
knows in a peripheral kind of way that it is. But that is really
beside the point. There are moments when, notwithstanding
the perils that attend generalisation, a generalisation is justified. And this is one of them.

Bradley is right: 'There is a greatness in all this that makes
us exult.' And not only can we feel the greatness without prejudice to our political humanity; it is a prime fact, for any
meaningful political humanity, to *know* that we can. The
most steely and durable of abstract principles will always
have its melting-point. And the moment when Coriolanus
utters the impossible words, words which on any view of
man's social nature are ludicrous and absurd—'I banish you'
— is also the moment when we most intensely 'exult'. It *had*
to be said. The whole preceding action has created the

necessity. The fusion-temperature of principle has been reached.

Which does not prevent principle solidifying again. This is, I think, what begins to happen a moment later, when Coriolanus throws out something that may be the precondition, that sounds like the unconscious enabling assumption which lies behind his whole undoubted triumph —

> There is a world elsewhere.

And we retort, half in contempt, half in awe, *'Where?'*

3 · A WORLD ELSEWHERE

By the time Act III is complete, we have discovered — if we're ever going to — the intense pleasure there can be in knowing there are to be no answers, only piercing questions. The Coriolanian impossibility has declared itself for the giant thing we have dreaded *and* hoped it would prove. Act IV opens under the shadow of a correspondingly large, *'Now* what?'

To judge from some of the accounts of Acts IV and V that one reads, the mountainous question delivers itself of a mouse of an answer. Coriolanus is to be discerned astonishedly discovering that a man *cannot* stand as if he were 'author of himself, and knew no other kin', and that it is *not* 'virtuous to be obstinate'. Which makes him a very edifying simpleton: not even the simple Othello was so stupendously blind to the obvious as such a Coriolanus would be. In fact nearly all the phrases invoked to support this view of him are taken from a speech where he puts the obvious to himself as just that, and measures its unanswerable force against his impossible predicament. But in order to understand that predicament we need to examine his route to it.

Suppose the Martius we see taking a serene farewell at the gates of Rome, rejoicing in the clarity of feeling that goes with the simplification of his situation, has really given no thought to his future. Perhaps deliberately. What has happened has happened, and by and large he is glad it has happened. Beyond that he does not go.

> 'Tis fond to wail inevitable strokes,
> As 'tis to laugh at 'em.

All he knows, instinctively and instantaneously, is that Cominius's offer to accompany him is quite out of the question. This pilgrimage is no one's affair but his. It's one of those moments that follow a serious rupture with one's habits of life, when one wants to be alone with the stirring consequences. The world is all before one, where to choose, and if Providence is not one's guide, then something better is—an exhilarated sense that one may start again and do better. It's a scene that must take place *at the gates* of the city one is leaving, and before the 'world elsewhere' has acquired any pressing reality. Martius is very winningly human in the way he feels that exhilaration, in the ease with which he puts behind him all resentment but the wryly humorous ('the beast/With many heads butts me away'), and in the heightened way he perceives the worth of these 'friends of noble touch' he is about to leave. If this is delusion, it is a common and graceful one, and not at all dishonourable to human nature.

And suppose, too, that the thought which occurs immediately to us—that there is only one spot in the world elsewhere, and one man on that spot, to whom he *can* go—has not occurred to him. Suppose him never to have realised how profoundly he relied upon the existence of one noble antagonist in an ignoble world, a lion one could be *proud* to hunt. Suppose him to have thought he was merely putting a strong feeling into an amusingly exaggerated shape, when he remarked,

> Were half to half the world by th'ears, and he
> Upon my part, I'd revolt to make
> Only my wars with him.

(It was, after all, inconceivable enough then, that Aufidius ever should be upon his party.)

The exile begins.

And it is utterly different from the exile envisaged while he was surrounded by the warm regrets of his friends. There is cold and hunger; ostracism and isolation. It is a pariah's life. He is quickly reduced to 'mean apparel' (Shakespeare's stage-direction), so that even menials titter at the claim that he is a 'Gentleman'. 'A marv'llous poor one', they retort, thinking themselves very witty. When he finds himself in a kitchen, 'The feast smells well' and he could wish he appeared more like a guest. He finds he is living, for the most part, 'Under the canopy. . .I'th' city of kites and crows', and sets a new value, consequently, upon roofs: 'Let me but stand, I will not hurt your hearth.' He has to learn to be unwontedly polite to the citizenry: 'Save you sir. . .Direct me, if it be your will. . .Which is his house, beseech you?. . . Thank you sir, farewell.' The enforced change of manner bears to him only the sour flavour of humiliation. How are the mighty fallen!

Meanwhile the world wags on. The man who was to be loved when he was lacked is largely forgotten, or if remembered, remembered as a chapter in past history. The instantaneous respect he is accustomed to commanding, seems to have vanished with his name and identity (and will only return with it – 'Nay, I knew by his face that there was something in him. He had, sir, a kind of face, me thought. . .I cannot tell how to term it'). The Volscian wars grind into a new phase; spies exchange information; generals meet and banquet. And he knows nothing of it. The friends who were to hear from him still, while he remained above the ground, hear nothing. They don't even know where he is. It's not surprising, for they were to hear never of him ought but what was like him formerly, and *that* letter cannot be written. When he enters a Volscian stronghold – a place he has only ever imagined as groaning under his wars – he experiences a ghastly pang of unreality, so little does he recognise the self he brings through the city gates. His life has become one long, purposeless vagrancy, and it is very bitter to him.

It is not in his nature to complain, only to act, reward his deeds with doing them, be their servant in his way. But whose servant? What act? Slowly it comes to him – the inevitable enormity, the one act left, the one destination. It is suicidally dangerous? As if that mattered to one who also is 'longer to live most weary!' In this living death, actual death can hardly appal. And so he finds himself outside Aufidius's house, then in the kitchen – the only place where he can gain admission – and likely to be thrown out of there. It is the lowest ebb of his fortunes, and he doesn't care if they end here.

I don't believe there is much supposition about all this. I've just put together the things Shakespeare tells us. And once they're together, is there anything so very enigmatic or inexplicable or unsatisfactory about the things Martius puts to himself as he stands, momentarily becalmed, outside Aufidius's house?

> Oh World, thy slippery turns! Friends now fast sworn,
> Whose double bosoms seem to wear one heart,
> Whose hours, whose bed, whose meal and exercise
> Are still together, who twin (as 'twere) in love
> Unseparable, shall within this hour,
> On a dissension of a doit, break out
> To bitterest enmity: so fellest foes,

Whose passions, and whose plots have broke their sleep
To take the one the other, by some chance,
Some trick not worth an egg, shall grow dear friends
And interjoin their issues. So with me:
My birthplace hate I, and my love's upon
This enemy town. I'll enter. If he slay me
He does fair justice: if he give me way,
I'll do his country service.

It is not a Macbeth soliloquy – for the very good reason
that Martius lives with his conscience in ways a great deal
more implicit than Macbeth does. But it is thoroughly of a
piece with his two other soliloquies (those in II.iii and V.iii),
and provoked by much the same feelings – that he has got
himself into an insufferably false situation for which he is
entirely responsible, and it is too late to do anything about
it. The damage is done, and ' 'Tis fond to wail inevitable
strokes'. Caught masquerading idiotically in the gown of
humility, the note had been

I am half through,
The one part suffer'd, the other will I do.

In all three soliloquies there is the same jagged dialectical
movement from one impossible alternative to another, the
same tight-lipped disgust at himself, and the same final
shrug of acceptance – though his third and last 'shrug of
acceptance' (in V.iii) has an astonishing depth and resonance
in its savage self-parody, its travesty of the falsity he has
embraced:

Let the Volsces
Plough Rome, and harrow Italy, I'll never
Be such a gosling to obey instinct; but stand
As if a man were author of himself, and knew no other kin.

The man who stands outside Aufidius's house, in any case,
is not unimpressive. His native terseness always grows upon
him when he is driven to conducting moral reviews. And
there is precious little profit to be derived from *this* review,
small reason to dwell at length on the self-betrayal which has
grown from pitifully trivial causes – 'Some trick not worth
an egg'. He is now, unless redeemed by Aufidius's 'fair justice', an irrecoverable traitor. Why go on about it? Best know
it and have done. 'So with me. . .' For Martius, I suspect, the
whole occasion is just another illustration of an unquestioned
axiom: only when things have gone drastically awry is introspection necessary at all. He therefore performs it grudgingly.

I hope, by now, it is unnecessary to insist that this is neither a silly nor a shallow view; nor does it make him some kind of moral infant. There are plenty of moral infants who are highly adept at the internal inquisitions Martius despises, and I have not noticed that their adeptness preserves them from error. To each according to his native genius. Given Martius's native genius, he knows as much about himself as he profitably can, and if he comes to disaster it is less out of 'self-ignorance'—which would make a homiletic tale—than out of a fundamental contradiction in the constitution of things, to which he is subject, and to which he will not bow—and that makes a tragedy.

It is part of that fundamental constitution of things that solitude must now be his lot. I know he is capable of happily dramatising it to himself as the fate of the lonely dragon. But that was 'at the gates'. Once through them, there is no dramatising. A radically social nature, which loves and is loved by its friends, takes its revenge. There is a deep and growing reserve, a refusal of all names, a withdrawal upon the self which is eventually to produce the most massive silence in all drama. His only response to Aufidius's long tumbling exultant speech of welcome is, 'You bless me, Gods.' Cominius he dismisses 'with his speechless hand'. To Menenius, it is 'Away.' What words he offers are windlassed out of him. What would be the use of words? 'My affairs/Are servanted to others', and what I think of those affairs, is my affair.

We may not think it 'honourable for a nobleman/Still to remember wrongs' (if 'wrongs' *are* what he is remembering: for, despite his talk of 'My rages and revenges', we see little sign of vindictive heat, and much sign of a judicial austerity which even Cominius finds awesomely impersonal). No, it is not honourable. Very little can be, now. But neither would it be honourable, for one who has freely servanted his affairs to others, to imperil their whole enterprise by indulging in private repinings. One must, however uneasily, respect the newly scrupulous Coriolanus, deaf to every 'private whisper', who checks at each point that his integrity to the Volscians is sans crack or flaw. This is a man who has learned very thoroughly to submit private will to public benefit—which is what we thought we wanted him to learn—and it is making a Moloch of him.

This is one of the play's great structural ironies.

Another and more terrible irony is forming itself around the person of Aufidius.

When we first meet him, Aufidius is a man 'sham'd' in 'condemned seconds', and disposed, as one is in moments of humiliation, to think very ill of himself. He is furious, furious, furious – with everyone. . .except Martius. For right at the outset we are to hear the strange plangent note of judicial impartiality towards his great antagonist. *His* (Aufidius's) emulation may be without honour, *his* valour poisoned, and *his* uncontrolled fury foaming over all 'embarquements', but he never deludes himself that Martius suffers any stain from this:

> Five times, Martius,
> I have fought with thee; so often hast thou beat me:
> And would'st do so, I think, should we encounter
> As often as we eat. By th'elements,
> If e'er again I meet him beard to beard,
> He's mine, or I am his.

The note of frank wonder is only less of a tribute than the uncontrolled fury itself – part of the fury, indeed, comes from Aufidius's knowledge that it *is* a tribute. So, in rage, he exaggerates his own infamy:

> Where I find him, were it
> At home, upon my brother's guard, even there
> Against the hospitable canon, would I
> Wash my fierce hand in's heart.

It has been a bad day for Aufidius, but he is not that man. Not yet. He is very nearly the great spirit who is the exact antithesis of it. When he actually meets Martius 'at home', there's not the remotest need to invoke 'the hospitable canon': his feelings take one great bound of generosity, and all his potential magnanimity finds magnificent release. Potching, wrath and craft are left far behind, as he discovers the liberating truth that he has fought this man because he loved him:

> Let me twine
> Mine arms about that body, where against
> My grained ash an hundred times hath broke
> And scarr'd the moon with splinters; here I clip
> The anvil of my sword, and do contest
> As hotly and as nobly with thy love
> As ever in ambitious strength I did
> Contend against thy valour. Know thou first
> I lov'd the maid I married; never man
> Sigh'd truer breath; but that I see thee here,
> Thou noble thing, more dances my rapt heart

Than when I first my wedded mistress saw
Bestride my threshold. Why, thou Mars, I tell thee
We have a power on foot, and I had purpose
Once more to hew thy target from thy brawn,
Or lose mine arm for't. Thou hast beat me out
Twelve several times, and I have nightly since
Dreamt of encounters 'twixt thyself and me –
We have been down together in my sleep,
Unbuckling helms, fisting each other's throat –
And wak'd half dead with nothing. . .
. . . A thousand welcomes!
And more a friend than e'er an enemy;
Yet, Martius, that was much. Your hand;
    most welcome.

This scene has had some grudging readers. Bradley's mournful conviction that Aufidius was 'a man of straw', a character 'wanted merely for the plot', remained unshaken by it. And Wyndham Lewis could hear in it only 'the same frantic and luscious sensuality of strife' that we get in *Troilus and Cressida*. Luscious? I don't expect to escape the imputation of terrible nameless psychic perversions, but I must say the mobilisation of the mental health squads strikes me as rather comical. People have a way of triumphantly detecting the continuity between erotic and martial feelings here, as if it were something an insidious Shakespeare were trying to conceal from them. It is the oddest kind of concealment. And doesn't one have to be rather an anaemic reader to hear, in all the leap of sinew and rapture of approbation, nothing but a threat to one's cherished sanities? Of course it dances Tullus's rapt heart to see before him that noble thing, the most absolute Sir of both his dreaming and his waking worlds! And it is percipient of him to recognise that no more important person has ever bestrid his threshold – however genuinely he may have loved the maid he married (and that lady, if she's sensible, need find no odium in the comparison). Tullus glories in the content of those bizarre dreams of his, because he glories in the passions of strife and mastery which they enact. And I do not hear Shakespeare the therapist tut-tutting from behind the couch.

This meeting is a fulcrum for the play as a whole. At the end of Act III there was room for being morosely sceptical about this 'world elsewhere'. Now, for one heart-stopping moment, we are to wonder whether Martius's utterly indefensible faith isn't going to prove justified in the event. If it does, the gods do indeed bless him, for he has no right to expect it. Somewhere on the periphery of our field of vision

we may glimpse Rome, his Rome, smoking in heaps of ruin,
but the exhilarated upthrust of hope against hope is too
powerful to give us much time to contemplate that. Truly, he
has been misplaced, miscast, misapplied in Rome; perhaps
here he may find his proper sphere. If it is at all possible, it
would be a meagreness of spirit to want to deny him the
possibility.

For all its momentaneous potency, however, this is very
much a hope against hope; and it takes only one line from
Aufidius, on his next entry, to put an end to it:

> Do they still fly to th'Roman?

This, lamentably, is what we always knew. The old sanctions
have resumed their interrupted sway. He is not 'Martius,
Martius', 'worthy Martius', 'thou Mars', any longer; he is
'th' Roman'. The alien, the enemy he always was. The respite
was illusory. And Aufidius, sickeningly, is already far enough
gone in envy, to betray it to a subordinate.

The chronic sense of justice which is the scourge of his intelligence still plagues Aufidius; but its note is now glummer,
bleaker:

> He bears himself more proudlier,
> Even to my person, than I thought he would
> When first I did embrace him. Yet his nature
> In that's no changeling, and I must excuse
> What cannot be amended.

>   . . .although it seems—
> And so he thinks, and is no less apparent
> To th'vulgar eye—that he bears all things fairly,
> And shows good husbandry for the Volscian state,
> Fights dragon-like, and does achieve as soon
> As draw his sword: yet. . .

His very indictments turn helplessly into encomiums:

>   . . .or whether nature,
> Not to be other than one thing, not moving
> From th'casque to th'cushion, but commanding peace
> Even with the same austerity and garb
> As he controll'd the war; but one of these
> (As he hath spices of them all)—not all,
> For I dare so far free him—made him fear'd,
> So hated, and so banish'd: but he has a merit
> To choke it in the utt'rance. . .

Aufidius's involuntary rectitude has put him on the rack.

He has cast himself for the subtle devil whose subtlety will outsmart the bold Coriolanus he admires to idolatry. But he fails to put the properly high, diabolic value upon subtlety. Finds it, instead, despicable.

He may stoke the fires of his own injury and make others believe he is 'a man by his own alms impoison'd, and with his charity slain', but at the very moment he is rehearsing the conspirators in their charges, he betrays his utter disbelief in his cause: 'That I would have spoke of.' (Whether it's to the point, or I believe it, is no matter – I'd have it spoke of.)

> And my pretext to strike at him, admits
> A good construction.

Pretext? Admits? Construction? In the quick of his being he is humiliated by the thing he must do.

Given the manifest way Coriolanus *has* 'sold the blood and labour' of their 'great action', Aufidius's difficulty may seem puzzling. But like so many others, he's unable to *feel* the outrage he's entitled to. He is obliged to fabricate it. He has to whet his contempt for those 'few drops of women's rheum which are/As cheap as lies', with a ferocity that reveals the peril he stands in, of being *genuinely* 'mov'd withal'. Martius always has this subversive, and quite unconscious, capacity to move Aufidius on levels of his nature which he can't control. And the commentators who have chosen to be pert and sceptical about his remorse –

> my rage is gone,
> And I am struck with sorrow –

have not been listening to this man, or to the gnawing torment his susceptibility has been consistently producing in him. Aufidius, having done his 'striking', is himself 'struck' – struck while he is still standing, in what was supposed to have been triumph, on the corpse of his honour, all the self-engendered rage slipped like sand through a sieve, and only the sorrow left.

It is a tableau, but one with a chilling retrospect, as we look back down the road he has travelled from that moment of exultant recognition when he had embraced, in Martius, a larger, freer, nobler world, and was filled with a sense of boundless potentiality. They had been, then, each other's 'world elsewhere'. Mistakes could be buried. Potching and craft could be forgotten. It *could* be thus. . .Alas for human hopefulness! Upon some dissension of a doit, some trick not worth an egg – the crude envy of a neglected chieftain, for instance (a sentiment Aufidius can't even respect in himself)

– the world was to take another slippery turn.

If we ask what it is that breaks the integrity of this so very nearly noble man, there is a kind of answer discernible in an early throwaway remark of his:

> bring me word thither
> How the world goes: that to the pace of it
> I may spur on my journey.

Unexceptionable enough, you might say. Who is not obliged to spur his journey to the world's pace? Everyone is Mr Worldly Wiseman in his own degree. But Aufidius's natural degree has been infinitesimally – that is to say, cynically – distended (we know this because he knows it), and the naïve honourable part of his soul correspondingly lamed. To such a man, the sight of Martius's honourableness cannot be for long anything but gall. It is too tormentingly close to what he himself might be. Mercifully, it need not torment him long: for the Coriolanus who boldly seeks service with the Vols-cians has put his mercy and his honour at difference in him, and however little *he* may know it, Aufidius knows it like the subtle devil he has chosen to be. Martius's Roman friends imagine that the sack of Rome will be a triumph and grati-fication of revenge to him. Martius's Volscian enemy knows better:

> When, Caius, Rome is thine,
> Thou art poor'st of all; then shortly art thou mine.

Aufidius's long wait makes for some of the most powerful effects in Act V. His murderous pertinacity and immobility hold all the menace of a dedicated predation. And there is the additional fascination, that the victim knows he is being watched, accepts it as only natural, and is grimly self-possessed. I don't think it is reading too much into the den-sity of their exchanges to detect, in Tullus, a devastated sense that the last shred of justification has been stripped from him by his victim's long cool gaze of knowledge. Martius is searching for the peer in honour who had spontaneously embraced him – though he knows he is no longer to be found; and Aufidius's speech is that of a man who will do anything rather than meet those eyes:

Coriolanus.   This man, Aufidius,
        Was my belov'd in Rome: yet thou behold'st!
Aufidius.   You keep a constant temper.

.   .   .   .

Coriolanus.   My partner in this action,

> You must report to th'Volscian lords, how plainly
> I have borne this business.
> *Aufidius.*   Only their ends you have respected,
> Stopp'd your ears against the general suit of Rome:
> Never admitted a private whisper, no, not with such
>   friends
> That thought them sure of you.
> *Coriolanus.*   This last old man,
> Whom with a crack'd heart I have sent to Rome,
> Lov'd me, above the measure of a father,
> Nay, godded me indeed. Their latest refuge
> Was to send him.

Coriolanus, rather poignantly, would like to have the costliness of his rectitude noted. But that only makes Aufidius more stiffly official. He concedes the 'constant temper' with an ill-concealed impatience for the moment when it will be overstrained enough to snap.

That moment comes almost at once. The suppliant women enter the Volscian camp. And Martius insists, with the now familiar scrupulosity, that his enemy shall be both witness and judge of his conduct:

> Aufidius, and you Volsces mark, for we'll
> Hear nought from Rome in private. Your request?

Does he want an audience because he expects to perform well before it? He might equally want it so that he won't appear to have been covering up for the catastrophic dereliction he now knows is imminent. Or he may wish simply to keep before himself the true acuteness of his dilemma. He is at least unashamed to expose its nature fully to all parties.

But in the event, it is not the whispered comments of a human audience that discomfit him. At the moment of his catastrophic dereliction a more appalling sound comes to his ears—the derisive laughter of the gods at 'this unnatural scene', reverberations of cosmic irony at the expense of the 'happy victory'. They may laugh. The nemesis was so infinitely foreseeable, so inevitable, so just. . .and so unnatural. The unnaturalness begins in the spectacle of mother kneeling to son for blessing, but it loses itself in vistas well-nigh endless.

But let it come.

And with a gesture that leaves no questions what 'it' is, he turns in one last piteous appeal to 'its' instigator and fulfiller:

> Aufidius, though I cannot make true wars,
> I'll frame convenient peace. Now good Aufidius,

> Were you in my stead, would you have heard
> A mother less? or granted less, Aufidius?
> *Aufidius.* I was mov'd withal.
> *Coriolanus.*   I dare be sworn you were:
> And sir, it is no little thing to make
> Mine eyes to sweat compassion. But (good sir)
> What peace you'll make, advise me: for my part,
> I'll not to Rome, I'll back with you; and, pray you,
> Stand to me in this cause.

Any pretence of immunity is gone. Since he can no longer 'make true wars', only 'frame convenient peace' — for Coriolanus a confession of bankruptcy — charity can be the only ground of his appeal. He is pitifully derelict, a broken man — but one with all the courage of his vulnerability. That courage is the more impressive for the fact that he is incapable of exploiting it, apparently unconscious of its pathos. He is simply deeply moved — 'Oh Mother! Wife!'

Neither mother nor wife shows anything but glad gratitude. I don't think we are invited to believe that either of them has the faintest inkling of the disaster that has overtaken their beloved Caius Martius. That disaster, nevertheless, and the contradiction at the heart of things which makes the disaster inevitable, fills our whole view until the wholly foreseen catastrophe completes the action.

4 · TO PLEASE HIS MOTHER. . .

It is, however, arguable enough to have been frequently argued, that the real contradiction is not to be found 'at the heart of things' at all, but in Martius's very personal psychology, and in the military pathology of his upbringing. Why else should Shakespeare give us the tale of the mammocked butterfly? Why else devote so much space to the Roman matron, his mother, who 'is the perfect embodiment of what has been called "the taboo on tenderness"' and whose comment on the mammocking ('One on's father's moods') is, L. C. Knights tells us, 'worth several pages of analysis'? Professor Knights withholds the analysis; but Wyndham Lewis is not so reticent: 'It would appear that Shakespeare means at this point to show us the true Coriolanus, a cruel and stupid child.'

Is it naive to point out that it is Martius Junior who is guilty of the insecticide, not Martius Senior? The child may be father to the man, but I doubt that legal responsibility was what Wordsworth had in mind. And speaking of Wordsworth...

> A very hunter did I rush
> Upon the prey;—with leaps and springs
> I followed on from brake and bush...('To a Butterfly')

Wordsworth was fortunate not to take a tumble and get childishly enraged at the proximate cause—an accident that can overtake the most even-tempered of toddlers. But even if he had, it would not have constituted proof of cruel stupidity. As parents, we may be occasionally distressed by the infant passion for experiment, and the infant vagueness about cruelty, but as adults we hesitate to call in the psychotherapist every day of the week.

There is, in other words, a different comment to be made on young Martius's rebarbative behaviour—and his mother makes it: 'A crack, madam.' Or, as Littlewood nicely translates: 'A little devil'.* Virgilia's motherly good sense strikes me as more to the point than the therapeutic zeal of the critics.

The normal man, as a percipient Freudian once remarked, has yet to be found—and when found, cured. And if we give ourselves up to the hectic pursuit of normalcy we are going to miss a great deal in this play: not only this quintessential touch of Virgilia's sanity, but some piercing and delectable comedy as well. For what is reprehensible in little Martius, as behaviour, becomes hilarious in Volumnia and Valeria, as approbation. When Shakespeare has dedicated such a superb ear to the mimicry of the Valerian lady-visitor, it would be churlish not to relish it:

> A my word, the father's son! I'll swear 'tis a very pretty boy. A my troth, I look'd upon him a Wednesday half an hour together: has such a confirm'd contenance. I saw him run after a gilded butterfly, and when he caught it, he let it go again, and after it again, and over and over he comes, and up again: catch'd it again: or whether his fall enrag'd him, or how 'twas, he did so set his teeth, and tear it. Oh, I warrant how he mammock'd it!

Volumnia. One on's father's moods.
Valeria. Indeed la, 'tis a noble child.

That inimitable voice, still to be heard tinkling over Spode

---

*OED quotes Heywood: 'It is a rogue, a wag...a notable dissembling lad, a Cracke.'

and cake-stands, offers no very authentic insight into the child mind. It is just a piquant example of the 'better mirth' which Virgilia is accused of being likely to 'disease'. When she declines the charming invitation to 'turn her solemness out a door' in such company (and we've already noted her as so little addicted to the Valerian 'mirth', that she wants to withdraw the moment the lady is announced), it may tell against someone, but is that someone necessarily Virgilia?

Certainly Shakespeare put the episode there for a purpose: it tells us something (not everything) about a Roman up-bringing; it shows that in Rome you don't have to be a dragonish Volumnia to share, in the most charmingly vapid way, the martial assumptions about what is proper to the son of a distinguished soldier; duly translated it may tell us some-thing about the sturdy little 'crack' who is later, by a child-ishly sturdy remark ('A shall not tread on me. . .'), very nearly to flaw his father's resolution; and it tells us some-thing rather surprising about the woman Martius has married — someone who is neither a replica of his mother, nor, in her quiet intransigence, exactly her opposite either. In short, it opens many gateways to speculation, and the richness of its possible implications and applications is, I suggest, the reason for its inclusion.

But there seems to be, in the ethos of post-Freudian en-lightenment, a terrible gravitation from the self-evident proposition that Coriolanus is given us as very much his mother's son, to the not-at-all-evident proposition that he is given us as *no more than* his mother's son. First Citizen, in other words (the man who wants to kill Martius in order to have corn at his own price), is our hero's most penetrating critic:

> though soft conscienc'd men can be content to say it was for his country, he did it to please his mother. . .

Surely it is possible to register this as a piece of shrewdness that will have to be weighed along with other shrewdnesses, without believing that Shakespeare is slipping into our palm a key to unlock the mysteries of Coriolanus's nature.

In any case, if this 'truth' about Martius is available to a man who does not know him, a man who simultaneously wants to kill him, and is afraid to address him, it needs cautious handling. Isn't there a strong hint that First Citizen is only able to enunciate it at all, because it is what everyone enjoys saying when they 'sit by th' fire, and presume to know what's done i' the Capitol'? The mythos of the great man necessarily comprehends an institutionalised weakness or

two ('He drinks, you know.' 'Really?' 'Heavily!' 'Tsk! tsk!'),
upon which the helplessly dominated dwell gratefully.
Shakespeare has simply introduced an interesting consider-
ation from a suspect quarter. Yes, of course! Volumnia is more important in her son's
world than most mothers contrive to be. Why not? She is un-
deniably impressive: ˙the very fervency of diagnostic disintegration that critics submit her to, confesses as much. And
how can a Martius *not* respect that rarity in his world, someone who mocks at death with as big a heart as he? someone
who does not fear his dangerous stoutness? someone who is,
in anger, if not exactly 'Juno-like', then certainly more impressive than your average mortal (the mere sight of her at
the end of a street has Brutus and Sicinius falling over each
other in their panic to decamp)? These claims which Volumnia makes for herself have never attracted serious confuta-
tion. The only question is what Shakespeare asks us to make
of these qualities.

So, before we assume a simple hostile stance – see all as
pathological 'taboo on tenderness' (and doesn't *courage* always impose some such taboo?) – we might ponder the
element of surprising selflessness in Volumnia's avidity of
possession. Because, in this fearsome woman, Shakespeare
has delineated a possessiveness which grounds itself upon a
vast respect for the other (male) nature. It's exaggerated, sure
enough. But readers familiar with other varieties of possessiveness may find it in themselves to feel something refreshing,
liberating, about Volumnia's very intensity. It is partly an
intensity of respect.

> When yet he was but tender-bodied, and the only son
> of my womb; when youth with comeliness pluck'd all
> gaze his way; when for a day of kings' entreaties, a
> mother should not sell him an hour from her beholding;
> I, considering how honour would become such a person,
> that it was no better than picture-like to hang by th'
> wall, if renown made it not stir, was pleas'd to let him
> seek danger, where he was like to find fame: to a cruel
> war I sent him, from whence he return'd, his brows
> bound with oak. I tell thee daughter, I sprang not more
> in joy at first hearing he was a man-child, than now in
> first seeing he had proved himself a man.

Virgilia's quiet inquiry is pertinent: 'But had he died in the
business madam, how then?' – more pertinent than Volumnia's reply to it; but if we believe it's important to a growing
lad to 'prove himself a man', then Volumnia has performed

one part of a parent's function with great conscientiousness. And who is going to argue that she didn't read the needs of this particular growing lad with some exactitude? There is no sign that Martius, under some different regimen, would have made a good constitutional lawyer, or run a farm contentedly in the Sabine hills. She has served his native pride and potency with percipient dedication. Which is uncommon in a parent. What she falls victim to is that terrible, familiar temptation — to re-annexe, in the name of one's sacrifices, the personality the sacrifices were supposed to be freeing. That can happen to any parent. It is only to be profoundly deplored if the re-annexation is successful. But is it?

One of the prize witnesses produced by what one can only call 'the Prosecution', is Virgilia — a figure of great pathos, neglected by her mother-besotted husband, exciting compassion by her very uncomplainingness, brain-washed and brow-beaten by the matriarch who is the real wife, and with whom she is obliged (Plutarch says, and Shakespeare seems to assume) to share her marital home. Far be it from me to ignore the blind infatuation of the mother-in-law, and the sad plight of the daughter-in-law whose natural reticence makes her a prey to perpetual rigours of exhortation, and licences of misconstruction. There is a sharp eye cast upon the tensions and emulations endemic to this, the most chronic ground of comedy. But it is a radically *comic* eye, and I do find myself doubting that Virgilia's quiet self-possession has ever been seriously breached. Doubting, above all, that the good understanding between wife and husband is vulnerable to the pressures Volumnia brings to bear on it. In this connexion, the episode of Coriolanus's triumphal entry (II.i.153-94), though brief, is pertinent.*

There are puzzles in the sequence, but all the lines can be made to work without recourse to emendation. And something interesting then begins to emerge about Martius's relations with these two women:

Onto an already populated stage (five principals, plus a token crowd) comes the procession, with *'Captains and Soldiers and a Herald'*. Proclamation, fanfares and a general shout. The crush is so great that Martius has to have his mother pointed out to him — presumably as she thrusts forward, without being able to reach him. He extricates himself, meets her, and kneels for the absolutely normal Elizabethan

---

*Once again we need the Folio text (where 1.171 is given to Cominius, not Coriolanus, and we are spared editorial guesses as to which remarks are addressed to whom).

(if not Roman) parental blessing. She lifts him to his feet, and looks with glowing eyes into his face:

> Nay, my good soldier, up:
> My gentle Martius, worthy Caius,
> And by deed-achieving honour newly nam'd—
> What is it? "Coriolanus" I must call thee?
> But oh, thy wife!

Now, why does Volumnia break off, before she has had a response to her burning rhetorical question? Why does the tone (comically intense enough for the widowed mother of the school-captain at a prize-giving) plunge dizzily towards bathos, with 'But oh, thy wife!'? It could be conscientious, though unwilling self-correction. But then, how long would it take Virgilia's husband to note, and appreciate, her patient expectancy which is so characteristically mute? 'My gracious silence, hail.' Hasn't he been looking past his mother, at his wife—noting both her silence and her tears?

Many readers, however, have found something grotesque and inept in his way of meeting those tears:

> Would'st thou have laugh'd, had I come coffin'd home,
> That weep'st to see me triumph? Ah my dear,
> Such eyes the widows in Corioli wear,
> And mothers that lack sons.

This is, again, a matter of tone. Without discounting the element of warrior-callousness, one can make out other things that co-exist with it. We know Virgilia has been keeping lonely vigil in her own house, refusing, even at the cost of some unpleasantness, to cross the threshold 'till my Lord return from the wars.' The perpetual strain of anxiety has made her impatient of extraneous company, and quiveringly sensitive to the mere mention of blood. She has been sighing as she sewed—much to Volumnia's irritation. If we know this, might not her husband? And might he not address himself to the grounds of her anxiety with a characteristically tough-minded, but not untender, reminder that what she feared might happen, and could have happened, has not happened—or not to him?

However it is, Martius now disappears from the dialogue for several minutes, even though Menenius addresses him twice, first directly ('thee'), then obliquely ('You are three. . .'), and even though his conversation with his mother has been left very much up in the air (which would explain, incidentally, why she might not know 'where to turn'— 1.172). The simple stageable explanation for his disappearance

is that he is pre-occupied with the person to whom he spoke
last — Virgilia, who either replies inaudibly, or wordlessly (as
she is to do in Act V, with an eloquence which dazzles her
husband: 'Oh, a kiss. . .').
Cominius, meanwhile, is coping jocularly with Menenius's
ecstasy ('And live you yet?'). But he has not mistaken its
real object — the old man's 'son' Coriolanus — nor failed to
notice the effect upon the old man of this inadvertent
neglect. So with his usual tactful aplomb he, as it were,
plucks the hero's sleeve, soliciting attention for Menenius's
sententiousness ('We call a nettle but a nettle;/And the faults
of fools but folly') with a loud 'Ever right!' And Martius,
with an audible start, takes the hint:

> Menenius, ever, ever.

Hands are grasped, many hands, and as the procession is
re-grouped, with some marshalling shouts from the Herald,
Volumnia presses forward again. She must have the consummation of her interrupted intimacy. There must be confirmation, from her son, that in all this tumult of publicity,
there exists, unimpaired and inviolate, their eternal secret
commonwealth of two:

> I have liv'd
> To see inherited my very wishes,
> And the buildings of my fancy:
> Only there's one thing wanting,
> Which (I doubt not) but our Rome
> Will cast upon thee.

Her son's response is not freezing exactly. It is gentle, re-
spectful, even tender. But it is nevertheless an unqualified
refusal of the emotional complicity she is so burningly
offering:

> Know, good Mother,
> I had rather be their servant in my way,
> Than sway with them in theirs.

It is the remark of a man who has given his own nature and
limitations a fair deal of intelligent scrutiny. Hence the firm-
ness. He is no stranger to her fantasy-addictions. But there is
'my way', and there is 'their way'. And 'your way', know,
good mother, is too much theirs. The huge 'vessel under sail'
of the battle-scenes, before whose stem men bowed like
compliant weeds, also knows its harbour and is preparing to
drop anchor there.
In a sense Coriolanus would have made no tragedy, had he

been able to hold to this anchorage. But Shakespeare here
rules out the interpretation that he falters in his sane self-
knowledge 'solely because his mother bids him'. Though she
is plainly part of the problem, we know that, under her most
intimate pressure, he can be calmly inflexible.

The faltering we *do* witness, shortly afterwards in the
Capitol, is a more complex matter, in its perceptible depths
of moral discomfort, than over-persuasion by a dominant
parent. Martius, sadly, wants the consulship *for himself*. To
our embarrassment (not to mention Cominius's and Menenius's) we find ourselves watching a Coriolanus perplexed in
the extreme. A man who first '*stands*' (before he has been
called for?), then sits; is no sooner needed than he '*rises, and
offers to go away*;' is requested to sit, and finally exits
abruptly, grotesquely complaining of having his 'nothings
monster'd'. The sense of being complicit in some huge
falsity which he does not understand could hardly declare
itself more artlessly or profoundly. It is an unquiet conscience he carries with him out of the Senate-house.

The whole to-do is, in a sense, needless: 'All's well, and
might have been much better, if he could have temporiz'd.'
But he cannot. Cannot inquire his way with a gentler spirit.
Simply cannot. It is the one impossibility. And the price of
asking a favour 'kindly' is the one price he is incapable of
paying. He ought therefore to abjure the honours which only
that price will buy. Instead, he blunders into standing for the
consulship and spends another Act-and-a-half fighting clear
of the self-imposed falsity – only to discover that he must
pay for his desertion of the grounds of his own nature, by
banishment, isolation, death.

There is a play to be written, in which this catastrophe is
directly traceable to the terrible distortion of a potentially
noble nature by a fervently misguided parent. It's a pity that
Arthur Miller, that sentimental family man of noble intentions, didn't write it, and then there would have been no
danger of confusing it with the play Shakespeare *did* write.

5 · GREAT NATURE CRIES

All comment naturally converges, like Martius's wars, on the
scene outside the gates of Rome – Act V Scene iii. Since this
is the point where Shakespeare feels there is least need to
modify his Plutarch, we may guess it was the germinating
seed of the whole drama. Reading this part of the *Life*, perhaps, was what convinced him that the subject was for him.

He pays his debt of respect and gratitude by unembarrassed
borrowing.

But consideration of the debt to Plutarch brings us
promptly up against significant changes. For instance, Plutarch's Coriolanus 'held his peace a pretty while, and answered
not a word' in the *middle* of his mother's speech; and at the
end, when 'her selfe, his wife and children, fell downe upon
their knees before him',

> *Martius* seeing that, could refraine no longer, but went
> straight and lift her up, crying out: Oh mother, what
> have you done to me? And holding her hard by the right
> hand, oh mother, said he, you have wonne a happy vic-
> torie for your countrie, but mortall and unhappy for
> your sonne: for I see my selfe vanquished by you alone.

That last sentence — pitched in a more sentimental tonality,
and spoken by a more sentimental Coriolanus (one plainly
incapable of 'refraining' for long) — Shakespeare replaces by
the essential tones and gestures of *his* Coriolanus. Not 'I see
my selfe vanquished by you alone': instead, 'But let it
come.' Not 'what have you done *to me*?' but 'What have
you done?'

It is striking the way Shakespeare's Roman never off-
loads moral responsibility. He not only doesn't do it, it
seems never to have occurred to him that he might: if it had,
there might have been some after-taste of pathos in Act V
Scene iii — the pathos of the sadly misunderstood but nobly
enduring hero. No such matter. 'But let it come' — a sentiment not even as self-conscious as stoicism, but tense with
all the vibrancy of Martius's naive, honourable soul. He has
never before seemed so grand, so doomed — for he has now
paid the full price of that problematical naivety of his, and
its integrity is unimpaired. In the world of human consequences 'this man has marr'd his fortunes' a second time,
beyond all hope of recovery; and there is much else that is
marred too. But Shakespeare has driven the antinomy to this
extremity partly so that we shall know how little (*and* how
much) we care for the 'world of human consequences'. The
only quantification of the 'little' and the 'much' is that
which the whole play accumulates upon this minutely
evaluated sequence; and I don't intend to undo Shakespeare's
work by putting a figure on it.

It makes a vast difference, nevertheless, to our personal
computation of the sum, if we believe that Martius attends
to the voice of 'Great Nature' primarily because his mother
bids him. That is to reduce a moral crisis in which his whole

nature should be on trial, to a pitiful contest of wills: the fate of a whole city has come to hinge, farcically, upon the suggestibility and docility of an overgrown schoolboy. It is no more 'tragic' than a play centering upon the moral consciousness of Idi Amin could hope to be. I can only conclude that those who offer to describe the scene to us in such terms regard the play as a flop from this point onwards.

The Plutarch version is at least better than that—though rendered rather squashy by sentiment about 'natural affection'. *His* Coriolanus determines at first 'to persist in his obstinate and inflexible rancker.'

> But overcome in the end with natural affection, and being altogether altered to see them: his heart would not serve him to tarie their coming to his chaire, but coming downe in hast, he went to meete them, and first he kissed his mother, and imbraced her a prety while, then his wife and little children. And nature so wrought with him, that the teares fell from his eyes, and he could not keepe himself from making much of them, but yeelded to the affection of his bloud, as if he had bene violently caried with the furie of a most swift running streame.

Touching, perhaps, but not very gripping. The incipient over-ripeness has been emulated by many critics of this scene, as if they thought it would be a virtue in Shakespeare if he felt things in this way; but the indulgent prose awakens one to the austerity of deep feeling in Shakespeare's handling. His Coriolanus doesn't alternate like a yo-yo between 'inflexible rancker' and 'natural affection'. He knows what is coming the moment he hears the 'shout within': Menenius is *not* to be their 'latest refuge', and he *is* to be tempted to infringe his vow 'In the same time 'tis made'. So be it. As the women make their slow and diffident advance across the stage, he notes each detail, probing his reactions, putting things to himself:

> My wife comes foremost, then the honour'd mould
> Wherein this trunk was fram'd, and in her hand
> The grandchild to her blood. But out, affection!
> All bond and privilege of nature break!
> Let it be virtuous to be obstinate.
> What is that curtsy worth? Or those dove's eyes,
> Which can make gods forsworn? I melt, and am not
> Of stronger earth than others. . .

The inner debate continues; but, unlike Plutarch's hero, he

is not 'overcome with natural affection' so that 'his heart
would not serve him to tarie their coming to his chaire'.
Not seen 'coming downe in hast'. The procession halts,
kneels, waits. And still he makes no move. As far as they
can tell, it is the same man who dismissed Cominius, and
'there is no more mercy in him, than there is milk in a male-
tiger', as Menenius has it.

But Menenius does not know his friend as Virgilia knows
her husband. She sees that the eye is truly changed, not so
much 'Red as 'twould burn Rome', as red with something
else. And while even Volumnia bows in submission, she
comes boldly forward, moving at the very moment that
Coriolanus's demeanour might have warned her back:

> Let the Volsces
> Plough Rome, and harrow Italy, I'll never
> Be such a gosling to obey instinct; but stand
> As if a man were author of himself, and knew no
>   other kin.

Virgilia. My Lord and Husband.
Coriolanus. These eyes are not the same I wore in Rome.
Virgilia. The sorrow that delivers us thus chang'd,
>   Makes you think so.
Coriolanus.
> Like a dull actor now, I have forgot my part,
> And I am out, even to a full disgrace. Best of my flesh,
> Forgive my tyranny: but do not say,
> For that forgive our Romans. O, a kiss
> Long as my exile, sweet as my revenge!
> Now by the jealous queen of heaven, that kiss
> I carried from thee, dear; and my true lip
> Hath virgin'd it e'er since.

Martius neither resists, nor pretends to resist. It is all over,
the moment she lays explicit claim to her knowledge of him
— he may *think* these eyes are not the same, but she knows
better. And the kiss seals her conquest, by abandoning all
thought of conquest but that which follows, of necessity,
from her *being* the best of his flesh. Lips that argued could
be denied; but those that kiss are unanswerable. And Shakespeare is uninsistently definite that it is a long, utterly surprising, utterly dazzling kiss—long as his exile, sweet as his
revenge. He has understood, in other words, that he must
choose between the two sweetnesses—has perhaps already
chosen.

The odd hieratic-rhetorical formality of his remaining
words to her—one of those odd tricks that sorrow shoots out

of the mind?—has many meanings. There is danger for him in revealing any feeling under the watchful eye of Aufidius; there is a natural rebellion against the constraint, and a constraint inherent in the very feelings themselves—all of which might well conspire to create an artificiality of tone. Yet even through the artificiality, one hears a moving decency and cleanliness of emotion. Need we be surprised to learn that Martius sets great store by a scrupulous fidelity, and thinks his wife might be glad to know that the lip she has just kissed is 'true'? ('True' refers, I take it, to something more than conscientious abstention from camp-followers.)

There is, in any case, constraint and constraint, and the sequence provides several varieties. Young Martius makes him a little volubly tongue-tied at first —

> The god of soldiers,
> With the consent of supreme Jove, inform
> Thy thoughts with nobleness. . .

—though he is quick to see where he went wrong, and rephrases with much grace: 'That's my brave Boy.' He had experienced the same difficulty before he could arrive, *via* chaste icicles, at the right tone towards 'dear Valeria'.

But there is a different order of constraint in his dealings with his mother. He is so conscious of potential neglect, that he flagrantly *mis*calls his quiet conversation with Virgilia, 'prating'. Volumnia's kneeling throws him into a hyperbolic flurry that sounds profoundly uneasy. This is certainly the behaviour of a son who is going to find it desperately hard to defy his mother—supposing he intends to. But might it not also be the behaviour of a son who will find it equally hard to yield to her, knowing his compliance will be misunderstood, misconstrued, and possibly perverted? Is he going to have the rare humanity which can yield nonetheless, taking silently upon itself the whole burden of misconstruction, and thus, silently, neutralising it?

He cannot rely, with Volumnia, on Virgilia's largeness of soul which refuses to exploit affection—refuses in proportion as it knows the affection is utterly to be relied upon. On the contrary, he only has to hear her ominous word 'suitors' to be dismally conscious that the bartering and bargaining has begun. There is nothing for it but to call the Volscian lords around him and resume his official chair of state. That is the footing on which she insists she shall stand with him. So be it. 'Your request?'

Only one thing, in the course of the next ninety lines, wrings a word from him—and it is not one of the all-too-

numerous logical thumbscrews his mother applies. It is
nothing she says. It is a piece of poignant childishness from
the boy. That can make him groan aloud; whereas Volumnia's admittedly powerful argumentation produces only a
deeper progressive silence ('Speak to me, son. . .Why do'st
not speak?'), in which she becomes more and more conscious
that he is letting her 'prate'. She tries supplying him with
the arguments in rebuttal which he is *not* offering, and she
rebuts the rebuttals. Whereupon 'He turns away.' She kneels,
and he will not even look at her ('Nay, behold's'). It is only
when she is finally 'husht', and all the clamour of manipu-
lation and possession has finally confessed its futility by
dying away, that he acknowledges the other efficacy she was
unconscious of possessing, and *'Holds her by the hand silent.'*
It is utterly dignified behaviour, from a man who, whatever
else he may have sucked from Volumnia, *owes his pride him-*
self—and is the finer human being for it.

It is another of the play's great structural ironies that this
finer human being is, quite certainly now, a ruined and
doomed human being. He 'cannot make true wars'. There is
no place for him in life. The total dereliction, which Shakespeare was only able to orchestrate in gorgeous pomp for his
doomed Othello, has here got into the very line and sinew
of the music. Play it on any instrument, and it is great.
Othello still decked himself in the plumes of the troop he
claimed to be farewelling. Coriolanus's valediction is steely
and sparse with the useless emotion it is controlling. It is
speech that hurts. And that kind of speech moves us on a far
deeper level than speech that consoles.

A necessary acquiescence to the voice of 'Great Nature' is
not less, but more momentous, if the mother to whom one
kneels in spirit is a woman whom one knows for one's betrayer. Emotionally, personally, morally, Volumnia *is* the
betrayer, as only those who trade in human feelings can be.
He knows that, and knowing how, refused, she will persist
in seeing herself as some pathetically disregarded 'poor hen
fond of no second brood', he also sees he is doomed to know
it alone. He bows, therefore, not to 'his mother whom he
wants to please', but to *the Mother in her,* who speaks in
spite of her, in the unimpeachable accents of 'Great Nature'.
And he does so in lucid despair of her ever understanding.
That he also, in some crucial sense of the word, 'loves' her,
is just another element in the 'unnatural scene' that pro-
vokes the laughter of the ironic Gods.

But let it come. It is his affair alone. To the women, the
occasion is simply one for unrestrained joy and celebration,

and he doesn't try to darken their delight or to stop the sun dancing for them. How are they to understand his tears as Aufidius does—who perceives their inevitable consequence? He feels about for some tactful, consoling ordinariness, and finds it: 'But we will drink together'. It is one of life's minor heroisms to be capable of that, at such a moment.

There follows one of the most chilling transitions in literature. From the triumphant uproar in the Roman streets (in which Coriolanus is more deeply forgotten than ever before, and the 'patroness, the life of Rome', in the person of Volumnia, is celebrated with every festive noise known to urban man) we cut to the whispered perfidy of Aufidius and his faction. 'It' has come. The once-noble Tullus rehearses his grievances in a voice that wheedles and whines with all the petty rancour of neglected merit—and is fawned on for his self-degradation. No more 'world elsewhere' for Martius: *this* is his world.

Protest is muffled in the dumbness of inevitability. If 'I banish you' *had* to be spoken, by the same necessity, so must 'Kill, kill, kill, kill, kill him.' If you choose to be a lonely dragon, you also choose the dragon's lonely death. Except that Martius did not choose. He merely was what he had to be—proud even to the altitude of his virtue. And we have always known that virtue to be self-annihilating. It matters little now, what we hear from him: 'never of me aught/But what is like me formerly' was what he promised we should hear; and that will be quite sufficient for Aufidius's purposes. We have never been so sharply aware of the deadly ambiguity in this nobility of his.

In the event, he *is* 'like himself'. Painfully ignorant of his duty to learn from experience, he does the instinctive 'noble' thing, and is engulfed. Does that invalidate the 'virtue'? Just so much, and so little as Macbeth's degrading death, true to *his* nature, invalidates his virtue. The Shakespearean tragic universe offers no guaranteed connexion between integrity and survival-value. Humanity may stand in perennial need of certain personal qualities which it is nevertheless totally unable to accommodate. We cannot say, with any conviction, that Rome was wrong to banish him: but Rome *was* wrong to banish him. Also Rome *had* to banish him. The existence of a Coriolanus entails these contradictions. If it is so, it is better to know it than to construct theoretical utopias from the bricks of obstinacy.

And it is better, too, not to pretend that 'the integrity which should become a state' can easily dispense with his kind of integrity. When he dies, something essential to Rome dies with him — and it is not just a warrior to fight her wars for her. For his impossible élitist politics ground themselves upon 'real necessities'; and I doubt that anyone contemplating the history of democracy will find the necessities much less real than he claims:

> Where gentry, title, wisdom
> Cannot conclude, but by the yea and no
> Of general ignorance, it must omit
> Real necessities, and give way the while
> To unstable slightness. Purpose so barr'd, it follows
> Nothing is done to purpose. . . .

It is a perception and a truth which democracy ought to be able to contain. Democracy is after all committed to containing all truths a citizen may hold, on the grounds that he holds them. All truths, that is, except the anti-democratic ones. These, and their propounders, cannot be tolerated, must be (justly) banished. And 'general ignorance' is mobilised to chant 'It shall be so.' We approve the verdict, deplore its execution. Perhaps we don't even approve the verdict, just admit its necessity. We may be tempted, in this predicament, to round on Coriolanus and berate him for being so impossibly *not* a man of our infirmity. But that is futile; for that is precisely his virtue for us.

There is no solution but the destructive one. There one may contemplate a steely kind of fitness in things, which only irony can comprehend. And Shakespeare provides that comprehensive irony.

Martius seeks his world elsewhere, in defiance of human infirmity, and finds it is the same world he banished. Rome or Antium — where's the difference? The same infinitely malleable populace, splitting the air with welcome one minute, and howling for vengeance the next; the same scheming politicians playing upon crude susceptibilities; the same 'good but most unwise patricians', caught short by the rapidity of events; and the same Caius Martius entering alone the mortal gate of the city — but that he has now no 'lawful sword' and his shunless destiny has caught up with him. It is Rome all over again. In many ways a better Rome and ·a wiser Martius. With this cold proviso, however, that these are not his beloved and loathed Romans — they are aliens, strangers, a people for whom he does not exist. The vanity of human wishes!

> His Fall was destin'd to a barren Strand,
> A petty Fortress, and a dubious Hand.

The climate is iron-hard and bleak with a Johnsonian irony. The march may begin in military state, but it rapidly degenerates into a shambling rout. He is stripped progressively, of the dues of faithful service ('Traitor'), of the rights of conquest recorded in his name (now a 'Robbery'), of his martial attributes, and his manhood ('Boy'). The moment of his life when he has been most the moral adult is travestied as puerility. And horribly, grotesquely, excusably, he falls to boasting—though even here we can hear the voice of the man who wants death, quickly, and nothing but death:

> Cut me to pieces, Volsces, men and lads,
> Stain all your edges on me. Boy! False hound,
> If you have writ your annals true, 'tis there,
> That like an eagle in a dove-cote, I
> Flutter'd your Volscians in Corioli.
> Alone I did it, Boy!

It is the last bitter irony that the man who, taken up in the arms of his jubilant troops, was heard crying ecstatically, 'Oh me alone, make you a sword of me!' should be crying thus, as other troops (surely the same, in some important sense) stab and trample him to death. He has chosen instrumentality and, as instrument, he is now discarded. Was this what he wanted all along?

> The instantaneous cessation of enormous energy (which is like nothing else in Shakespeare) [writes Bradley] strikes us with awe, but not with pity. . .Roman and Volscian will have peace now, and in his native city patrician and plebeian will move along the way he barred. And they are in life, and he is not. But life has suddenly shrunk and dwindled, and become a home for pygmies and not for him.

Coriolanus, Bradley concludes, 'cannot leave the same impression as the supreme tragedies', dealing, as it does, only with 'simple human feelings', and having little place for 'the mystery of nature'. The judgment carries its own refutation.

I would suggest—gratefully and respectfully, for he has shown me more about this play than anyone else I've read—that with a very slight jog administered to his favoured perspectives and priorities, Bradley might have been explaining why the play *was* in fact a supreme tragedy—supreme in its unmysterious humanity. For the icy hardness of the closing moments is not inhumanity. It is Shakespeare withholding the impertinence of elegy, and the irrelevance of pity, from a man who has never needed either.

NOTE

Any reader surprised by the text of Shakespeare encountered in these essays is referred (in the case of *Macbeth, Antony and Cleopatra* and *Coriolanus*) to the Folio for verification. The textual difficulties of *Hamlet* are too familiar to call for either apology or discussion here.